Kwabena: An African Boy's Journey of Faith

Kwabena:
An African Boy's Journey of Faith

Dr. David Mensah

Essence
PUBLISHING
Belleville, Ontario, Canada

Kwabena: An African Boy's Journey of Faith

ISBN: 1-894169-03-4

First Printing, March 1998
Second Printing, June 1998
Third Printing, July 2000

Essence Publishing is a Christian Book Publisher dedicated to furthering the work of Christ through the written word. For more information, contact: 44 Moira Street West, Belleville, ON, Canada K8P 1S3.
Phone: 1-800-238-6376 • Fax: (613) 962-3055.
Email: info@essencegroup.com
Internet: www.essencegroup.com

Printed in Canada
by

Essence
PUBLISHING

To my brother Abraham, who went home too soon.

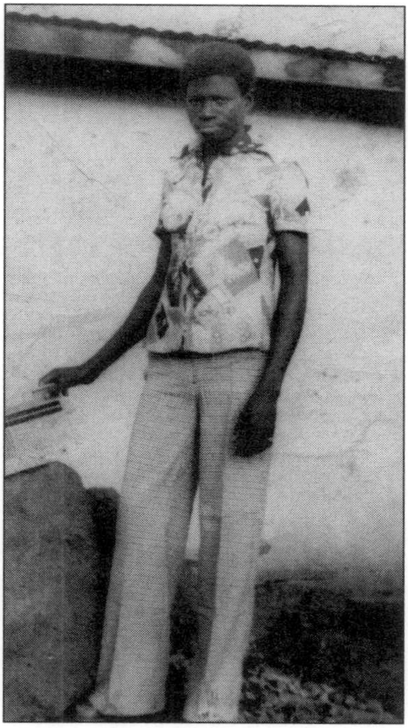

Table of Contents

ACKNOWLEDGEMENTS

In 1979, when I first met Mr. Gene Paisley and his wife Laura Paisley, little did I know that they would become such good parents and friends in Christ. They have worked hard and located the publisher of this book. Gary and Elenor Paisley have been true friends who have supported me in many ways. Grant and Emily Paisley gave me good advice that prevented me from throwing away a very important gift. I am very grateful to the Paisley family, who have loved me so much and have made me forget some of the hardships described in this book.

Dr. Douglas Webster and his wife Ginny Webster, as well as Mrs. Webster, Senior, did the preliminary editing and proofreading of the manuscript and encouraged me to publish the book. I am grateful to the Websters for their kindness and the bond of friendship that exists between us.

John Schram, Canadian High Commissioner to Ghana, and Alena Schram made vital suggestions for the final draft. They also kept encouraging me to get it published. Without their encouragement the manuscript might still be tucked away in a drawer, gathering dust. Thank you very much, Mr. and Mrs. Schram.

Dr. Dittmar Mundel, of Camrose University, Alberta, spent several very hot days in my office in Ghana and typed almost half of the manuscript. I am grateful, Dittmar, for your effort.

My wife, Brenda, and three daughters, Elizabeth, Deborah and Carole, have made me forget the difficult days in my past as there is much laughter and family support in our home.

For the peace and grace shown to me by the Lord Jesus, I will continue to proclaim His name and will sing His praise with the multitudes in heaven after this life.

FOREWORD

I met David Mensah nearly twenty years ago on a hot August day in Toronto. It was rumoured on campus that a new African student, who had arrived from Ghana to study at Ontario Bible College, was afraid to come out of his room. I knocked on his dormitory door and met a brother in Christ whom I would grow to deeply love and respect. The immensity of this man's identity, however, was concealed by the shy demeanour of a half-starved African boy who looked like a bewildered refugee locked in a prison. Little did I know then what an extraordinary person I was meeting.

This book is his story, told in his own African voice, revealing the depth and power of the gospel of Jesus Christ. He invites you into a world of harsh tribal life in northern Ghana, with its dark superstitions and brutal hardships. Terrorized by his uncle and tutored in the occult, David's life appears to hang by a thread. But God breaks in on this wild African boy, who is strangely affected by a Muslim holy man who speaks of one name, "Jesus."

From scrounging for food in the rotting garbage of Tamale to completing a PhD at St. Michael's College in Toronto, David Mensah takes you on a journey of faith that will remind you of Abraham in the wilderness and Joseph in Pharaoh's court. David is a modern example of the heroes of the faith described in the eleventh chapter of Hebrews. Who could have imagined that the lonely African student I met that day would return to Ghana with his beautiful wife and three daughters to carry on a holistic gospel ministry to his native tribe? Who would have thought that this emaciated, homesick African brother would be used of God to fill the stomachs and souls of his fellow Africans? This is a story that needs to be told, for it is part of God's great salvation history story. I invite you to meet David Mensah.

Douglas Webster, author of several books including
Christian Living in a Pagan Culture and Spiritual Direction

Part One:
The Beginning

1

The Deg Tribe

I WAS BORN IN NEPUI, A SMALL VILLAGE IN Northern Ghana. My father's name is Kwame Sohn and my mother is called Abena Fulamuso. Our tribe (the Deg tribe) emerged as the result of a fierce fight over the head of a dog.

The Sissala, or Grushi, tribe in the Upper Region of Ghana observed an annual rite in which a dog was killed to appease dead ancestors. The meat of the sacrificed dog was shared among the elders of the tribe, who were responsible for conducting the ceremony. But the dog's head was reserved for the tribe's priest, because dogs in that region are usually very tiny and their heads are considered delicacies. This particular year, as the day was getting late and the proceedings coming to an end, it was brought to the chief elder's attention that the dog's head was still sitting on the idol (the medium through which sacrifices are made to appease the gods or ancestors). For some reason, the chief elder ignored tradition and ordered that the head should be shared among all of the elders. That quick decision brought horrible consequences!

One of the elders divided the dog's head and gave a portion to every man in the group. They were about to enjoy their special treat, when one of the elders complained that the elder responsible for the division had kept a very large chunk for himself. A demand arose for a resharing of the dog's head. The accused elder objected, claiming that his share of the delicacy included a payment for his labour in dividing the meat.

"This is greed," shouted one of the elders. "Bring back the meat!"

When the accused elder realized that other elders were very serious about getting the meat from him, he quickly crammed several chunks of it into his mouth and swallowed them. His actions enraged the rest of the group. He was punched, kicked and beaten by the other elders, who hoped they could induce the return of the meat. But no – his stomach was strong and he was not about to let out this delicacy.

News of the incident quickly spread to the rest of the village, called Jefisi, and a tribal war erupted. Many people were slaughtered; others fled into the jungle to save their lives.

Among the lucky ones who escaped were my first ancestors – Juge, his younger brother, Gbange, and their wives. They travelled about two hundred miles in the jungle, eating only wild fruit, until they came to a place where the land was good for farming. The senior brother decided to stay there. He built a little hut and settled. Today, this village is called Jugboi, which means the home or town of Juge.

Gbange moved on for a distance of three miles, to the Black Volta River, which now borders the Northern Region of Ghana and the Brong Ahafo Region. He settled there and built a hut. Today, his village is called Bamboi, the modern version of Gbangeboi, which means the home of Gbange.

These two ancestors and their wives multiplied to make the present indigenous Deg tribe known as Dega (Deg-land).

As the Deg increased, they found neighbours across the Black Volta, the Brongs. The tribes traded with one another. As the tribes bartered together, the Sissala, or Grushi, language, which Juge and Gbange and their wives spoke, underwent some changes. Many Brong words infiltrated, causing a distortion of the original language. Today, only a few words of Sissala have remained.

This trading with the Brongs also caused the Deg tribe to develop into three language zones. Those who were close to the Brongs became known as Nyanboi Tena. The part of Deg that was furthest away from the Brongs began to call themselves Dega (meaning the true Deg). The intermediate group, the meat in the sandwich, so to speak, became known as Mangom. To this day, each of these language zones periodically claims superiority over the others.

Early in their history the Dega built a tribal war village, which they named Manchala. It was in this important village that my father, Kwame Sohn, was born. It was considered prestigious to be related to anyone from Manchala. In fact, both of my parents came from important villages. Jugboi, where my mother was born, became the war village of the Mangom.

Although several characteristics of the Dega tribe have changed over time, many customs have remained. They love festivals, intense idol worship, witchcraft and tribal dancing. It is a very happy tribe, although idol worship has ruined many homes due to the excessive sacrifices that have decimated the already limited supply of cattle, goats, sheep, dogs and fowls.

My father lived in Manchala, where he learned a great deal of witchcraft. He was the second child of his parents. My great-grandfather's home, my father told me, was a frightening place. As he described it, "All the ugly existed there." It was known as the *Brafuo-dem* or the "home of assassins." According to my father, my great-grandfather was a trained killer, employing both the sword and witchcraft. In times of tribal war, he was second to none in destroying human life. He also carried out secret missions to territories of tribal enemies. His friends called him Brafuo Bin Brafuo (assassin without equal).

When a tribal chief died, it was my great grandfather's duty to make sure that the chief did not travel the celestial road alone. Several human heads must accompany him. The number of heads depended on the chief's age. If the chief was young, perhaps in his fifties, he would need only a few companions since he was still strong. But should the chief be in his eighties, he must have several people to accompany him on his celestial journey. He would need some young men to carry him in case he became tired of walking. His wives usually were the first to be beheaded. I am told that the senior wife usually considered it a privilege to go with her husband. Usually the younger wives would flee to their relatives, as soon as they were sure the man was going to die. Their timing had to be just right, however, for if the chief recovered and the wives had fled, their lives were in danger.

Nepui

The state of my father's house was so treacherous and ugly that he longed to move away from his family when he was fully grown – a practice that is not very common in our tribe, even today. His opportunity came after the death of his father. He was able to leave home and cross the Black Volta to Nepui. He had a senior sister and two younger brothers whom he left behind to learn the Brafuo business.

His senior sister became a rain caller and fortune teller. I have seen her dance in fire several times. One of his brothers learned the trade of witchcraft – and learned it well. His friends gave him the name *Pansabinsi* for holding on to tradition. For my uncle, tradition meant keeping every minute detail of idol worship and witchcraft. As a small boy, I often heard my father comment that my uncle's adherence to and knowledge about witchcraft had changed his physical appearance so much that he looked like the devil himself!

When my father arrived at Nepui, he worked hard and soon established a farm for himself. Nepui happened to be only three miles away from Jugboi, my mother's village. My father's farm was between Nepui and Jugboi. He soon became quite successful, growing *pia* (African yams), *dua* (cassava) and corn, among other crops. During harvest season, he was able to sell yams. He started selling yams to women from Jugboi, who would often come to the farm and buy directly from him and then retail them later. It was through this commerce that a relationship developed between my father and mother. It was interesting to hear them discuss their own versions of how their romance began.

According to my father, all the women who came to buy yams from him were viewed simply as customers, even though from time to time he hoped that some day he could marry a beautiful woman. He confessed that the first time he saw my mother with her ***kangba*** (yam carrying basket) he stared at her so intently that the yam he was holding fell and broke into pieces. Abena was exceptionally beautiful. My father admitted that he admired her very much, but insisted that he always treated her as he did the other customers. There were no special favours.

My mother's story is different. According to her, my father made several kind gestures to her whenever she went to buy yams. For instance, after she had made her purchase, my father would give her two or three extra yams to take to her mother. My mother claimed that the end of the hide-and-seek courtship occurred one day when she had just loaded her ***kangba*** full of yams. My father asked if she needed help to lift the luggage to her head. She replied that help would be appreciated. My father lifted the basket for her and then, in a very courtly gesture, held her hand as she crossed an area made slippery by a recent rain storm.

But whenever this story was told in our household, my father would contest the account, claiming that my mother grabbed his hand as she crossed the wet area. In any event, following this controversial incident, my mother's interest in going to that farm changed from yams to true love. She could not wait to sell off her yams so that she could join the next group going to the farm. As a child, whenever I wanted to tease my parents, I would simply say, "Now tell the truth, who first took the other's hand?"

Their marriage was a rare case of a Mangom woman marrying a Longoro, or Deg, man. My father said his love for my mother was so strong that he was able to convince his relatives to cut out most of the tribal red tape and protocol in arranging their marriage.

Yaw Kara

After their marriage, the young couple decided to stay at Nepui. It wasn't long after their marriage that my brother Yaw Kara arrived. I understand that Yaw Kara was an adorable baby, and a real delight to the new parents. His name Kara was my grandfather's name. My father intended that when Yaw Kara was eight years old he would be sent to Manchala to learn the traditions of our home.

This type of learning is one way our culture is preserved. There are still many older Ghanaians who believe that teaching the young orally in stories and songs is the most effective way of educating. I doubted this assumption until recently, when it suddenly dawned on me that not many people in western society know much about their great-grandparents. I recall my grandmother telling stories about my great-grandfathers – five generations back. She could not read or write but she knew almost everything about our history. I would listen to her in amazement. One time I asked her how she memorized all of this, and she simply said, "You don't memorize, you just get to know if you have good ears. Yes, you need good ears!"

It seems that my mother and father made a miscalculation and I appeared on the scene too soon. My brother Yaw was very small when I arrived. My mother said people used to call us twins because she was breast feeding both of us at the same time. I was a big boy and drank more than my share of the milk. My good appetite deprived my brother from gaining weight, and soon his health deteriorated.

It was said that there wasn't any disease or epidemic that passed by without Yaw's personal knowledge. Be it measles, upset stomach, nose bleeds, chicken pox – you name it and he had it! My mother and father did all they could to keep their first-born son alive. Because of the numerous sicknesses that set him back, it wasn't long before I outgrew him. I even began walking before he did. I was rough, tough and bullied him.

As we grew, I acted as a senior brother, fighting his fights and warding off others who tried to take advantage of him. But secretly I cheated him. My father had maintained tradition and decreed that whenever anything was to be divided between his children, Yaw, being the oldest, would choose first. But it is also part of Deg culture that the youngest child is responsible at mealtime for dividing up the meat for all the children. Add to that the additional tradition that children eat in a separate place from their parents, and the stage was set for the deception I played on Yaw. During the sharing of the meat, I remember always dividing the meat into three portions. My brother would often ask who the third piece of meat belonged to. I told him it was reserved for *Chamachoklo* (the unidentified). By the time I was about five years old, I was so shrewd that I was able to make Yaw accept that we had an unidentified person in the house, and that I was his or her representative in all our dealings – especially matters relating to meat and food.

Yaw was a kind, gentle boy. He loved me and would do anything for me. He never wanted to fight with me, probably for two reasons: first, because he dearly loved me, and second, because he figured he would not win a fight with me anyway, so why bother!

After keeping *Chamachoklo*'s meat or food for a while, I would sneak around and before Yaw realized it, the item was gone. I cheated him for most of our childhood years.

Well, "Be sure your sin will find you out." One day my father took my brother and I with him as he worked the farm. When he inspected his traps, he discovered that one of them held a yam rat. These are huge rodents that destroy yams. With their paws they will burrow through a yam mound and cause havoc. Farmers hate the activities of these rats. The rats are very clever and can destroy several tubers of yams before they are caught.

It takes great skill to trap them, because they keep pulling all kinds of surprises on the farmers. For instance, a farmer will put a trap on a yam that has been freshly eaten, hoping the rats will return to it. Somehow, these wily pests can sense when a trap has been set. But, as soon as the trap has been removed, the rats reappear. A single female rat can keep a farmer going in circles for as long as three months before getting caught or changing farms. Yam rats are usually so greedy that they eventually get caught. The male rats are relatively easy to trap. The good news is that when a rat is trapped, it becomes a complementary item to the whole farming enterprise. The Deg people love the meat of these rats. They are not overly tasty, but in Ghana, meat is meat, especially in hard times – when flying insects in the north had better fly very high!

On this day, my father singed the rat and cut off the tail for Yaw and I to roast over the open fire and eat. I, of course, quickly took charge and roasted the meat. After that, I divided the food and, as usual, included *Chamachoklo*'s portion. By this time, Yaw had stopped questioning about when *Chamachoklo* would come for his or her share. But my luck had run out. Without my knowledge, our father had been watching the proceedings as I divided up the rat's tail. After I had devoured *Chamachoklo*'s share, my father called my brother Yaw and enquired about the third piece of meat, as if he hadn't clued in to my scheme.

"Don't you know?" said Yaw with a serious face. "The third portion is for *Chamachoklo*."

"When is *Chamachoklo* coming for the meat?" demanded my father.

"I don't know, but Kwabena will know," replied my brother innocently.

My father summoned me to his presence and demanded that the third portion of the rat tail should be given to him so that he could take it to *Chamachoklo.* There I was, standing with my head lowered, watching and twisting my toes as if they could conjure back the rat tail from my stomach.

"Since when has Kwabena been reserving things for Chamachoklo?" my father asked Yaw.

"All the time," he answered.

Did I ever get it that day! I think my dad destroyed two whips on me. However, the beating did not hurt me as much as Yaw's eyes. After I had finished crying, he came and stood by me with a confused mixture of feelings. He was sobbing with me because this was the first time my father had used a whip on one of us. Yaw knew I was in pain, as there were a few cuts on my back. But at the same time, his eyes were like search lights whenever I raised my head and looked at his face. He seemed to be asking, "Were you really cheating me all the time in the name of *Chamachoklo*?" After that day, my father kept a vigilant eye on me whenever I had the opportunity to divide something, and Yaw became very cautious about trusting his younger brother.

This incident over the rat tail brought several changes between Yaw and me. Since no portions were reserved for Chamachoklo any more, I decided that Yaw could defend himself when it came to fights with other boys. The more Yaw defended himself, the stronger and wiser he got. It wasn't long before he was challenging me. My mother and father told us they had never seen two children fight like the two of us. Sometimes our fights lasted several hours. As time went on, the situation became more ugly, as our parents took sides in our fights. Yaw obviously was my father's favourite, and I could always count on my mother to support me.

Yaw and I had a blanket that served as our sleeping mat. It was spread out on the floor in our room. Every night we battled over territory on that blanket. I happened to be lying against the wall and that was quite an advantage. I would raise my feet against the wall for leverage and then give a sudden push, knocking Yaw across the rest of the blanket, onto the bare cold floor.

Yaw employed several methods to avenge himself. I remember that when my mother's soup was very peppery, he would wait until my parents were not watching and then flick several drops of that hot soup into my eyes. He did this over and over again – and got away with it. It still confounds me that Yaw was never caught in all the times he cleaned my eyes with Mom's soup! Yaw was cunning and careful, whereas I was ruthless and, after the *Chamachoklo* debacle, too impatient for scheming.

I am not surprised that Yaw has ended up being a hunter in the Deg tribe. You have to be a good marksman and sly in order to stay in the hunting business in that part of Ghana. The animals have been hunted so much that most species are becoming extinct. The survivors are so wise that it takes several months for a hunter to even see them. Yet, Yaw's hunting expeditions are usually very successful.

NYAARA KANDIA

With all the fights and schemes, my early years were full of fun. It was fun from morning until night. Above all, it was such a tremendous blessing to have parents who truly loved their children. Those years passed too quickly. We used to dance the tribal dances with the girls and play *Koromoro,* a type of hide and seek game. We were naked and so were the girls. As young as we were, there was no doubt that the girls enjoyed studying us as much as we did them.

One of the games I liked most of all was the *Sikpakuune* game. The boys would line up facing the girls. The girls would be singing in their delicate voices. Then suddenly, one of the girls would break away from the group and announce in song to the other girls that she was in love and about to embark on a quest to find her true love. She would then proceed toward the boys to look them over. Sometimes, a girl would decide to wait and take a look at the boys who might come later on. In that case, she would indicate through song that she was so pretty that none of the available guys were good enough for her. While warbling a sorrowful lament, she would walk back to the other girls and tell them that her journey was a failure. If the girl was in a less finicky mood and willing to settle for one of the available candidates, she would walk down the line of boys like a general inspecting the troops. Following this inspection, she would place an arm around the neck of the lucky guy and walk him back to the other girls, who would scream and shout in jubilation, congratulating their friend on her excellent choice. Then, all the girls would give the chosen boy a hug. Matters concluded with the girl who had started the proceedings walking her "boyfriend" back to the line of boys.

As trivial as this game might sound, it did encourage good behavior from the boys. If you were a bad boy at home, and your deeds leaked out, the chances of being selected were very slim. My mother and father used to show pleasure on their faces whenever Yaw and I rushed home and told them that we both had been selected. On the other hand, it was always sad to be passed over.

Sikpakuune was just one of many pleasures that accompanied a bright moon. As soon as the moon came up, my father would gaze on it from his easy chair and say his favourite phrase, *Nyaara Kandia*, meaning the poor people's lantern. Indeed, the moon is the light of the poor. She brings joy, games and tribal dancing.

The grown up women will play *Mangbe.* This is a game in which the women form a semi-circle, singing and clapping. As the clapping is going on, one of the women will break away, walk a few feet away, then turn and, with a terrific run, toss herself into the arms of the other women, who will throw her high into the air. It is a game in which the females demonstrate to the men how strong, exuberant and capable they are.

The men usually show their strength and talents in the *Kpaana* or *Songo* dance. This is a unique dance, guided by a tom-tom player or, as he is often called, the talking drummer. A talking drummer must not only be a good musician, he must know the family history of all the men in the tribe. The dance begins with a large number of men dancing in a circle around the drummer. Suddenly the drummer summons two of the dancers to come in front of him. This order is communicated through the drum. When they arrive, the talking drummer will pound a rhythm that celebrates the life and achievements of the two men in front of him. Then he moves on to their family histories, mentioning prominent personalities who died long ago. Sometimes the drummer and the dancers will get so involved in the telling of the past that they will begin to weep. "The dead must never be forgotten," the drums will declare.

After this phase, the talking drummer will instruct the two men to demonstrate how good they are at dancing. When this challenge is given, the two men turn to face one another, each man leaning slightly to one side. Practically every part of their bodies will begin to shake in a very graceful manner. It is a delight to see. When the men dance in a way that, no matter how unemotional you are, you will find yourself shaking and swaying with them. Should either dancer's performance lack something, the drummer will let him know it. For instance, if he detects that a dancer's neck is not twisting as it should, he will tell the dancer that the children and women would like to see a little more work on his neck.

Moon days are very valuable to the Deg tribe. They make us feel rich. As poor as the Deg people are, there is one thing they are rich in – joy. The Deg certainly know how to enjoy life! It is a jubilant tribe, filled with people who love to laugh. My father would often tell us, "Laughter is medicine for the soul."

Everything is seen and done in the context of the community. When a cow or goat dies, it is shared. During the occasional festivals, the jubilation of the people is astonishing.

The only time you will see my people sad is when there is a loss of life. When there is a death in the Deg tribe, all the work and activities of the village come to a halt. People will sit as if they did not have any bones in them. The wailing and sorrow exhibited during these times is intense.

For the first six hours after a death has been announced, everyone observes a fast, except for infants. After that, children four years and under are allowed to eat porridge. Although the fasting ends after twenty-four hours, adults are prohibited from eating anything that contains pepper until the body is buried. Porridge and water are considered a "pepper free" diet. Sometimes a body lies in state for three days before it is buried.

When the day of celebrating the funeral comes, *Kpaana* and *Songo* are danced. However, *Kpaana* is now reserved for the funerals of those who are over sixty years old. The situation turns into merry making, even though the immediate family of the deceased is usually very solemn. Following the burial, people may resume their hunting and farming.

On the day after the funeral, the elders of the village gather to inquire about the cause of death. They usually do this by wrapping the deceased person's clothes onto planks, then lifting them onto two people's heads. The two men carrying these planks with the deceased person's clothes, are quickly seized by a spirit that puts them in a trance. At this stage, an elder *Gbogbi* (which literally means rope) comes with a little stick in his hand, tapping the planks. By this act, the *Gbogbi* is inquiring as to why the individual died.

It is amazing how accurate these people are in determining the cause of death. Supposing a man was involved in theft, and, as a result, the family god killed him. As soon as the *Gbogbi* inquires, the planks will move the two carriers to the person against whom the crime was committed. Throughout my childhood at Nepui, I cannot recall an instance in which the cause of death could not be determined.

This method is also used to locate dead bodies. If a hunter does not return from the jungle and it is feared that he has died, the hunter's clothes are placed on planks that are lifted onto the heads of two men. The *Gbogbi* performs his task and the planks will move the two men are moved to where the dead body is located. Such spiritual powers in the Deg tribe are not taken lightly. They are frighteningly authentic.

Because my father had seen so much of this at his home in Manchala, he tended to show a general disinterest in hardcore witchcraft. He had a family god that protected us against spiritual forces that might want to harm us. His involvement in witchcraft was minimal in comparison to others in our village. His friends used to tell him that he was running a risk of living a short life because he kept himself so open. He never considered himself to be "open." After all, Manchala was there, all he would need to do a crisis was to inform his relatives in Manchala. He knew that, though he was not living in Manchala, he was still a Brafuo's son. He often told us our family history and boasted occasionally that, in times of war or severe spiritual warfare, many of his friends who regarded him as a vulnerable man would be surprised.

Witchcraft or not, Yaw and I were never afraid in the Nepui village. It was a haven for us. My father's farm prospered. At the end of the season, many people came to buy yams, pepper, garden eggs, okra and spices. My mother was a hard-working woman. She was in charge of the vegetable plantation. Apart from the crops we harvested each year, we had goats and sheep.

My father was the only man in the village who raised pigeons. They were considered a delicacy. People came from far and near to purchase them. My father gave many as gifts, especially when they were needed to perform certain rituals. The sad thing was that, as a family, we rarely had the chance to eat pigeon meat. My father loved to eat pigeon – though not as much as my mother. In her opinion, pigeon meat was superior to any bird. And in my opinion, there was no one who could cook pigeons like my mother.

As delicacies, pigeons were reserved for important occasions, such as entertaining a guest. As soon as a visitor would arrive, my mother would often be the first to shout, "*boronoma topirii*" meaning, "pigeon day." Although we had many pigeons, my father always acted in restraint, never allowing us to kill more than four at a time.

As much as we enjoyed eating the birds, they were truly our friends. I can still see them flying gracefully, circling our *Som* tree. Some of the birds knew us. They would fly very close to my face or Yaw's whenever we were in the village and they happened to be there. We fed them in our family courtyard. They were beautiful birds with beautiful colours. Seeing them in the air, circling the village, was so gratifying. I have often wondered how we could have been so emotionally attached to the birds and, at the same time, enjoyed their meat so thoroughly. But then, every animal in the village was cherished by its owners, yet when it died there was always a feast.

Meat was a scarce commodity in our tribe. The people usually ate quite a bit of fish, since they were relatively easy to catch. Usually the whole town would cut a huge amount of *bel,* a herb that farmers interplant with the cassava plant. They would gather the *bel* in heaps beside the stream they intended to fish in. Then they would use long, heavy poles to beat the herbs into a finer form, then dump them into the stream. Then everyone ran downstream to wait for fish. When mixed with water *bel* would irritate fish so that they moved to the surface and became quite disoriented. The people moved in quickly and tried to catch them. They had to move fast. The herbs usually lost their punch in less than an hour.

Apart from fish, other meat is hard to come by. It was from fear of running out of meat that my dad was never liberal with his pigeons.

The sad thing about the Deg people is that their animals are reserved for sacrifices to the idols, or kept as bonds to be cashed in times of financial difficulties. Animals are not killed purposely for food. So when an animal dies as a result of disease, it is not buried but eaten. The philosophy of the tribe is that any dead meat, no matter how contaminated, will be fine for human consumption if you cook it well. So we children used to pray for the *Jalkpu wiila* to come quickly. *Jalkpu wiila* is a chicken disease that attacks during the dry season. During this period, several fowls die before the season is over. As I think about it now, it seems even the grown-ups looked forward to this season. They could eat chicken with a good conscience and blame the disease for having to do it. Those were happy times.

The women, in particular, enjoy such times. They do all the cooking and are often bored with the bland soups they are compelled to make each day, simply because the men refuse to kill any animals. Beyond this, it seems to me that the women love to eat meat more than the men do. The men often complain that the women refuse to eat with them. If they ate with them, the women would lose their privileges. They know how to reserve portions of meat in their cooking pots until the men have all gone out, and then they, "do their own thing." To preserve this privilege for women, men are not allowed to look into a soup-cooking pot. The women cherish this custom and are not about to give it up.

The men and women function together well. The tribe has many codes of behaviour that protect both sexes. Generally, it is a homogeneous society, in which the common enemy tends to be poverty. By poverty, I mean the lack of essential things like water and food. Physically and emotionally, it is a rich society. It is a society in which divorce is minimal. Suicide, drug abuse, and most of the vices found in the western hemisphere today are absent. Things like pornography and homosexuality do not even have a name in my dialect. In all my growing years, I heard of only one case of rape.

A look at how the Deg tribe deals with a rapist leaves little doubt as to why that crime is so uncommon. A rapist is called before the elders. He is stripped naked and boys and girls escort him from the centre of the village to wherever the act was committed. The boys and girls will be hooting and giggling at what is to come. The curious ones run ahead to get a good view.

Once the culprit gets to the spot where the crime was committed, one of the elders, who followed the children, will tell him to kneel down. As soon as the culprit kneels, the children cast a dozen eggs at him, soaking him miserably. Then the rapist is escorted back to the centre of the village, still naked, with the slimy eggs running down his body. He must remain in public view in this humiliating state for several minutes, during which time anyone who wishes to do so may taunt and ridicule him. This phase of the punishment ends when a gourd filled with water is broken over the rapist, soaking him further. He is then free to return to his home and dress. After this ritual, the elders convene a meeting to determine how much the culprit must pay to the woman or girl he raped.

But the most devastating punishment is yet to come. A man found guilty of rape will never be able to marry, as no woman in the tribe respects him. This sort of severe treatment has almost eliminated rape from Deg society and has curbed the rise of many of the ugly practices that are eating into the cultures of the so-called civilized world.

I am thankful to the Deg culture for the many good principles it instilled in me during my childhood. We seemed so free in those days. Our parents had only a few things to worry about. Perhaps that is why they laughed so much. The laughter was not half-hearted. It was free and true, like the pigeons in the air.

But there was one terrible form of bondage – the excessive sacrifices that were performed each year to the idols. The idols demanded most of the goats and sheep. Our idols had an insatiable appetite for blood. They required sacrifices from everyone – even the very poor and sick. They protected us, but at a very high cost. The greed of the idols trapped many people in poverty, sucking up their meagre resources.

Sometimes the demands of the idols, interpreted to us by the soothsayer, were very strange, and the appropriate sacrifices hard to find. For example, some particular idol would demand a sheep or goat that had only three legs from birth or a chicken with one eye. It took several weeks or even months before such obscure creatures could be located. For this reason, deformed animals are well cared for in the tribe. Of course, such animals are also very expensive to buy. But a man will do all he can to buy such an animal, once his idol has made the request. Sometimes, when there is no money, several cows or sheep are exchanged for a single deformed animal.

Once, while still a very young boy, I asked my father why people had to use deformed animals for sacrifices. He brushed off the question. But a few years later, when I could be trusted with delicate information, he explained that such unusual sacrifices are demanded after a particular idol has helped a person to defeat an enemy. For instance, a witch may be keeping a woman barren. An idol will help that woman's family identify and locate the witch. After it has found the witch, the idol will demand several unusual sacrifices – animals with bizarre deformities. Once the sacrifices are made, the idol will destroy the witch's spell and the woman will be able to bear children.

"Occasionally," my father said, "A man will ask an idol to eliminate a persistent enemy who wars against his house." After the sacrifices are performed, the enemy is punished or killed. Often the enemy will be struck by lightning in broad daylight without any clouds in the sky. Whenever thunder was heard on a sunny day, it jolted the people in my village. They knew that an idol had brought death to someone, or possibly killed his child or destroyed his house.

The idols did perform many positive functions for our tribe. They served as a police force, identifying criminals and inflicting harsh penalties. People had to behave well or face the consequences. As a result, theft and other crimes were rare. The idols also provided health care. They helped women during times of complicated childbirth. They instructed our fathers on what particular herb to use and what sacrifices they should perform to ward off certain epidemics. Whatever the subject, the information that came from the idols was usually correct.

Some people in the village attempted to manipulate the idols to get them to do their bidding. This never worked. The idols would exploit these people in order to increase the number of sacrifices they received. Often, a man and his enemy would be appealing to the same idol. Not surprisingly, the man who was making the most sacrifices would win. Of course, an idol never informs a man that his enemy is also consulting him. In my opinion, the idols keep such secrets in order to escalate their "prices." Therefore, it was difficult to trust the general or public idols, who commercialized their activities. Most people in the village payed primary attention to their family idols.

The family idols are very faithful and keep keen watch over their particular families. Our family idol was called *Chamanwiah.* The main *Chamanwiah* was at Manchala, my father's town, but, somehow, it is possible to carry part of an idol's protective powers to different destinations through designated sacrifices. The part of *Chamanwiah* or his spirit that stayed with us was very faithful, according to my father. He or she was able to protect us. When a case was beyond his or her capacity, the spirit instructed my father to go to Manchala to the main *Chamanwiah.* When my father received such orders, he would immediately make the thirty-mile walk to Manchala and return the next day feeling better equipped to face the problems that were coming from the spiritual world.

As the years went by, my father's general attitude towards *Chamanwiah,* and idol worship in general, went through several changes. He eventually reached a point where he wanted to be free from idol worship, but by then he had enough knowledge of the dark side of life and its forces that he couldn't afford not to protect his family from them. One day he told my brother and me that he wished there were no idols and that everybody would just love the *Nyundua Korowii* (The God Who Is Up). He said that even *Chamanwiah* respected *Nyundua Korowii* and that he had no equal among all the gods in our land.

"Why don't we make him our idol then?" Yaw asked.

"No, we can't; he is far away and it is only through Chamanwiah that we can get some of his blessings. The thing that pains me is that *Nyundua Korowii* never demands anything from these gods, yet they demand goats, chickens, sheep, money and even cows from us. It is robbery!" My father then quickly apologized to our household *Chamanwiah* for his critical remarks. *Chamanwiah* demanded a white fowl that day from my father for letting his mind wander into a dangerous realm of thinking.

From that day on, both Yaw and I realized that Dad would rather live a life free from sacrifices, and from keeping the many secret codes to avoid offending *Chamanwiah* and the public gods. His attitude was also known to our mother and to two of his intimate friends. It was one of these friends who warned Dad that he was at risk of living a short life if he did not intensify his affinity to the gods. My father lusted after freedom in his heart. At the same time, the reality of a world infested with spiritual powers made him hang on to Chamanwiah and other idols.

Part Two:
The Wandering Years

2

On the Way to Manchala

WHEN MY BROTHER AND I WERE STILL very young, Dad told us that in a few years, Yaw would go to Manchala to begin learning the Brafuo work, the work of village assassin. When Yaw reached the age of about six (neither Yaw or I are certain about the year we were born because our birth dates are not recorded and times and dates do not play a big role in our culture), he was at the stage when Brafuo training usually starts. For some reason, my grandfather, whose duty it was to conduct the training, passed this responsibility on to his brother, Kukur-buo ("lifter of rocks" – though I have no idea whether he really did lift rocks). Because of my father's ambivalent attitude toward idol worship, he resolved not to send Yaw to train as a Brafuo. But *Chamanwiah* was never going to give up pestering Dad.

One day we had just returned from the farm with a yam-eating rat, and mother was peeling yams for *fufu* (pounded yams). The day looked quite promising. *Fufu* and rat meat is quite a treat. There is a saying that the yam rat specifically reserves a certain portion of its juice for when it is cooked with *fufu* because of its obsessive love for the yam. So, there we were with a fat rat nicely cleaned and singed. We greeted mother with special smiles, as we often did when we had a secret to tell her.

She had just finished putting the yams on the fire to cook, when a friend brought in a man who had come to the village looking for our house. Yaw and I did not know him, nor did Mom. As soon as Dad emerged from his room and saw the man, we knew something was wrong. Our father was not happy. Nevertheless, for our sake, he quickly collected himself and acted as if everything was fine. After my mother gave the visitor a drink of water, he and my father retreated into my father's room for a private meeting. This is often the custom when a visitor is carrying important information.

While the two men were talking, we bombarded Mom with questions as to what the visitor could want – questions to which she obviously had no answers. We could tell she was very uneasy. Dad had never taken her to his home town of Manchala to meet his relatives. My mom was afraid these relatives might become angry and use their witchcraft against our household. She had recognized by his accent that the man came from Manchala. What could he want?

Finally, my dad and his visitor emerged. Dad quickly went to Mother and told her that the visitor was not carrying any bad news. He tried to act happy and to make it a pleasant evening. But Mom knew her husband too well to be fooled. She knew that whatever information the man had brought had dealt Dad a terrible blow. She controlled herself and got the food prepared and served. The visitor ate with Dad, and we ate by Mom. Yaw and I enjoyed the food very much and so did the visitor. The two who did not eat well were Abena Fulamuso and Kwame Sohn, our parents.

After the meal, Mom filled a bucket with warm water and gave it to our visitor for a bath. As soon as the man had gone to the bath house (made of woven millet stocks), she drew her chair close to Dad to get the true story.

"Chamanwiah has sent him," Dad said.

"For what?" Mother retorted rather loudly.

"*Sooh ebora* (settle down)," Dad replied in a very kind way. *"Chamanwiah,* in collaboration with other gods in Manchala, has demanded that Kukur-buo should make sure that the Brafuo tradition is kept after his death."

"So what does that mean?" my mother asked.

"Well, the truth is that it is my turn to go to Manchala to maintain the tradition, or send one of the children to be trained."

None of these suggestions, of course, was agreeable to Mother.

"You are not going and none of my children is going either!" Mother said, as her eyes filled with tears. Previously Dad had told her the details of Manchala and the reason he left there. The thought of going to the village and, even worse, of her husband's becoming the head of the Brafuo was not easy to accept. The thought of one of her two children going to train in Brafuo was equally unpalatable. My dad felt the same. He did not want to go back; nor did he want Yaw or I to go.

It was quite an evening for us. Mom and Dad sat with the visitor and chatted into the night. We were all up quite early the next morning for breakfast. After the meal, Dad saw the visitor off. He took his bag and walked with him until the man was out of the village.

The visitor had encouraged my father to act quickly and respond to the request of *Chamanwiah.* The dangers that would befall our house, should he decide to completely refuse the request, were obvious to Dad. He would either lose his life or lose his children. He agonized with this problem for days. My mother became very lean within three days of the visitor's departure. After several heart-rending discussions, they finally decided that it was better to send Yaw or me to Manchala than for my dad to go himself.

"The wisdom in doing this," my father said, "is that if I, Kwame Sohn, should take up this job in Manchala, it will mean that we will all be going there. This implies that they have got not only me, but the children as well."

If my father's children had been girls, they would not have been expected to learn the Brafuo tradition. But because my dad was the first son of his parents, and his first two children were sons, my brother and I were prime candidates for this dark calling. If our whole family were to move to Manchala for Dad to become Brafuo, he would eventually teach both Yaw and me, so that we could inherit the position after his death. If, on the other hand, Yaw or I went, the family would only be losing one member to the Brafuo tradition. And if Yaw or I should have only girls as children, the cycle of inheriting the Brafuo work would be broken. This possibility had a bit of appeal to my dad, though my mother did not like any of the options.

After serious discussions, Mom and Dad decided that I, Kwabena, should go to Manchala to become a Brafuo. They summoned Yaw and me and, in a very solemn manner, announced their decision. Well! Yaw started to bawl and I started to jump and shout for joy. What my parents did not know was that while they were agonizing over what to do, both of their sons were hoping to be the one chosen to become a Brafuo. I kept telling Yaw that I would be selected. We had been arguing about this since the visitor left. To us, it was all a great adventure. Of course, we didn't have the slightest idea what we were desiring.

Mom and Dad were very surprised to discover our reactions. Mom wiped her tears, turned to Dad and said, "What were we worried about?" At least, for the moment, they felt a little better. Our crying and dancing broke the tension and released the emotional strain my parents were under.

Their decision to choose me was based on the fact that, even though Yaw had taken his position as a senior son in the family, he was still skinny and frail from the many sicknesses he had contracted through the years. He was very quiet and soft-spoken. In many ways he was like Mom. Yaw's eyes would fill with tears when he heard of someone falling and breaking a leg or arm. He had such a tender character.

I, on the other hand, was more adventurous and quite rough. I fought almost every child in my age group in Nepui, and sometimes even children much older than I. Many times my mother would sit me down and pull thorns from my feet, thorns I got from wandering through the jungle in bare feet. There were always several cuts on my legs, some healing and some new ones. Mom used to call me "the friend of flies" because the flies were attracted by my cuts.

I also loved to cause mischief. In the corner of our house Dad kept a barrel that Mother used as a water reservoir. Any time this barrel was empty, it was my favourite toy. I would run with terrific speed and as I got close to the barrel I would grab the sides with both hands, tossing my head inside the barrel, with my legs waving in the air. I would stay in that dangerous position for several minutes before pushing myself out again. Mom used to tell Dad to stop me from playing this game. But Dad's philosophy was that dangerous games teach children quickly. So, he was not overly worried once he explained the consequences of the game to me.

Dad's philosophy proved right. One Friday afternoon Mom and Dad were sitting outside relaxing when I started to play my game to defy them and to scare my mom. I approached the barrel with my usual speed. This time my hands missed the end of the barrel and my nose hit it instead. Worse still, I landed inside the barrel head first. My legs were waving, but this time they were waving for help. I panicked, which made things even worse. Then I started to taste blood coming from my severely cut nose.

I started to yell, calling to Dad that I was dying. I knew he was just sitting there and perhaps saying, "So be it!" The thought of him not realizing that I was bleeding and suffocating frightened me terribly. Thank goodness for mother's heart. She was not about to let me learn whatever lesson there was to learn from being stuck upside down in a barrel. It was time to get me out. She rushed to my aid but was unable to pull me out by herself.

"Your son is dying," she yelled to Dad. He helped to yank me out. I knew he would scold me once I was on my feet. So, I got in the first words. "You see!" I pointed to the blood on my face, implying that he was responsible for making me bleed because he did not come to my aid quickly enough. Dad wasn't deterred by my blood-covered face. After all, I was already yapping. To enhance my understanding of who was to blame for this mishap, Dad provided two quick strokes to my behind with a whip. I still remember this episode whenever I look into the mirror and see the little scar on my nose.

Rather than making me afraid, the lesson of the barrel taught me new boldness. There was a hill behind our neighbour's house. Whenever the barrel was empty, Yaw and I would roll it half way up the neighbour's hill. Once we were there, one of us would get inside and roll for a few feet until it was stopped by a log we had cut to be our brake. It was fun.

One day, the daring Kwabena took the barrel to the top of the hill and told Yaw to stop him with a log halfway down the slope. Oh boy! My speed scared Yaw so much that he threw away the log to save his life. Inside the barrel, I felt that this surely would be the end of my life. Indeed, the barrel continued to gather speed and rolled until it was stopped by a shed at the roadside where the women often displayed their vegetables for sale on Fridays. I had rolled past our neighbour's house and was on my way to the truck road. After I got out, I realized that my bladder had misbehaved due to panic. I was more frightened by this barrel adventure than when I got my nose cut. Yaw came to comfort me, but I was so upset I could not stop crying. I told Yaw that Mom would give me a licking for urinating in the water barrel.

I kept carrying on like this until Yaw got fed up and did something he had never done before. He spoke to me in a harsh, commanding voice. "Shut up! And be thankful that you didn't do the other thing in the barrel. The way you were screaming inside, I thought you were doing them both." His authoritative manner cooled me off. We rolled the barrel to the house and set it in its place. I thought the whole ordeal was over. After supper, Yaw said, "Mom, remember to wash the barrel before pouring water into it." Well, that immediately made Mom very suspicious.

"I know that you boys always play with this barrel, so I wash it before pouring water into it. Why then did you need to remind me?" She was rather persistent about this and I knew that Yaw's *okro-mouth* (tattle-tale) had gotten me into trouble. I was looking at him with challenging eyes, twisting my lips and doing all I could to scare him off from telling Mom the truth. He tried to lie to Mom, but he couldn't fool Abena Fulamuso. She was sharp and her eyes fished out information from us when she needed it.

As much as we feared Dad's spanking, we tended to fear Mom's more. Dad used whips, but she used her bare palms, which had become thick with callouses from daily pounding grain in a mortar. They felt like metal brushes on our bare skin. Her hands were quite clumsy when they came down on you. We were thankful that normally she remained calm. Even when she lost her temper, she preferred not to spank us. But should she detect either of us lying, she quickly put those palms to use. They seemed to hit ruthlessly and very painfully. She hit with all her energy, and should you resist falling to the ground on the first hit, you had dug your own grave! Whenever Mom was terribly angry with us we learned to simply lie on the ground and shut up. Somehow, our lying down before her seemed to reduce her anger.

With Mom, it seemed that the older we got, the harder her hits became. I remember one day when she confronted me because I had lied to our neighbour. As she was interrogating me, I decided not to pay attention to her and was making a move to get away. Her palm caught me between my left ear and the lower jaw. You could see her finger marks on my cheek. When Yaw saw me an hour later, he examined my face and without asking any questions simply said, "Boy, she hits hard!" We both broke down and cried. We were puzzled. How can she love us so much and yet hit so hard? I am sure today that those palms saved us from many a trouble.

On the day of the barrel incident the first swat on Yaw's behind made him say quickly that a disaster caused me to relieve myself in the barrel. That satisfied Mom, but Dad took over. He asked about the details of the second barrel incident. After that he gave both of us a good licking. What a day!

I varied my mischievous activities. I went from one thing to the other, usually dragging Yaw along with me. I could count on him for support to plunge into new discoveries. He wasn't about to abandon his junior brother. For me, mischief added to the fun of life. My parents came to agree that I could not be stopped totally from causing mischief and playing dangerous games. They, therefore, resolved to help me minimize the dangerous and reckless activities.

It was this character of mine that shaped their decision to keep their gentle son Yaw at home and to send me to Manchala to train to become a Brafuo.

The day I was to leave for Manchala was one I will never forget. It was as if death had struck our home. My mother simply broke down and her tears could not be stopped. The thought that she would not see her five- or six-year-old son again until he was a grown man, and a trained killer at that, was too hard for her to bear. My dad was not an emotional man. But, on that day, his eyes were red and he spoke very tenderly. Mom made her last porridge for me before we were to walk from Nepui to Manchala to the mysterious house of the Brafuos, now held together by Kukur-buo, the Lifter of Rocks. I ate my calabash of porridge but Dad could manage only a few spoonfuls. He asked Mom to get my things ready. Mom's packing took forever.

"Hurry up, Abena! The sun is growing," my dad said. Finally, she handed me my clothes, bundled in a handkerchief. She also gave us some *fuura,* which she had bought from our neighbour the day before. Dad was to mash the millet flour and give me the *fuura* to drink if I became hungry and thirsty on the thirty-mile journey.

I was looking forward to this adventure until I realized that I was going to miss my brother. That moment came when my dad finally said in an affectionate voice, "Kwabena, *ya kaa"* (let us go now). He tried not to break down in front of us.

"Come on," he said again, heading toward the road. I took my little bag and ran to join him. By this time, Yaw had started to cry. Mom was crying indoors, because she couldn't watch me go. I was crying too, but I went back to tell Yaw that everything would be alright and I would send him gifts from time to time.

"I've got to go," I said. He waved me a goodbye and I finally ran to catch up with Dad, who had gone ahead. I ran past him with a little bit of joy and told him that I was glad we were finally going. I started to talk and trotted back and forth on the road, picking stones and throwing them at the trees. Suddenly, I looked at Dad and realized he was fighting his tears. Finally, he got control of his emotions, and told me he had been contemplating whether our whole family should go to Manchala instead of just me.

He took my hand and we started to talk. He told me that even though I was sometimes mischievous, he really loved his children. He told me also that I should try and be a good boy in Manchala and that he would try to visit me from time to time, as often as he could. He tried to encourage me by saying that I would soon find new friends in Manchala.

We had walked only two miles when we spotted a truck loaded with cattle on its way from Upper Region of Ghana to Kumasi, in the Ashanti Region. Dad started to flag it down as it approached.

"Maybe they'll give us a ride to Mantuka," he said. Mantuka was half way. From there to Manchala there was only a bush path. Several years would often elapse before a vehicle travelled on that path. So we would have to walk that portion of the journey. I had never ridden in a car or truck. This was an undreamed-of opportunity. Lo and behold, the driver responded to my father's signal, and came to a stop a few feet away. Dad gave the driver a few coins and he told us to climb up. Dad passed me up on the ladder at the side of the truck and someone grabbed me and hauled me in.

The truck was full of Zebu cattle, with their huge humps on their backs like camels. There was just a little space behind the cattle where about fifteen people were cramped together. Only a few boards separated the Zebus from the human passengers. The seats in the truck were made of boards. The cows, on the other hand, were standing freely. They had been in this truck for several days, travelling on this rough road. The human cargo was red with dust. As soon as Dad and I were seated, the big engine roared to life again. The sound of the engine sent chills into my stomach.

"That is *Abion igin,*" Dad said proudly. "They make much sound, don't they?" he said to one of the men.

"There are very few things Dad does not know," I said to myself. I was proud of him. I looked at him and we both smiled. He himself hadn't ridden in a motor vehicle for many years, so this was a treat for both of us. I looked behind and told Dad that the trees were moving. The people in the truck roared with laughter. I said I was glad that he chose me instead of Yaw to go to Manchala.

"Good," he said. He knew I was enjoying my ride in spite of the many potholes that were tossing the truck up and down. Our people call these trucks "bone shakers," and they are perfectly right. They do shake your bones when you are inside them.

We had gone for a few miles when an episode developed between me and one of the men in the truck. Underneath the board we were sitting on was a large hole. Some of the floorboards had come off, making it easy to see the tires of the truck. From time to time, the man pushed my left foot through the hole until one of the tires was slightly touching my rubber shoes. My dad had made a pair each for Yaw and me from a discarded tire he found. We used them for hunting mice in the bush. I had put on my pair for the journey from Nepui to Manchala that morning.

The man carried out this secret activity without my dad noticing. He began to keep my foot on the tire longer and longer. At first, I was enjoying the episode, but then my rubber shoe started to get smelly and hot. Suddenly, I yelled. Dad quickly reached out to me and asked what was wrong. I showed him my shoe, which was still warm and very smelly. I related the whole story to Dad quickly, because of the puzzled look on his face as to why my shoes were almost about to burn.

He was so upset with the man that he took him by his hair and started pounding him. But the man was not as weak as my dad may have supposed. He got up and managed to roll Dad off his seat. The rest of the passengers started to yell at the two fighting men. Then the Zebu cattle decided to join in and began a miniature stampede. For a moment, it looked as if the old truck was going to fly apart. The cattle were rampaging about in such a frenzied state that the driver had difficulty keeping his truck on the gravel road. It swerved from one side to the other.

The Zebus broke the boards that separated them from the human passengers and suddenly everyone was in danger of being trampled. It was quite a scene! The driver finally managed to bring the big Albion to a stop and quickly climbed the ladder. The cows were still having a good time and the rest of us were doing all we could to avoid being stepped upon by those giant animals. As the driver saw the zoo-like situation, he yelled with such a voice that not only the people, but the Zebus as well listened to him.

"Now tell me, wats mata?" he asked, with beads of perspiration all over his forehead. His voice at first was low but started to increase in volume and in seriousness as he kept asking, "Wats de mata? Wats de mata?" By this time, the animals had begun to settle down and Dad and his fighting partner were calming down. The driver sent everyone down so that the cows could once again be penned in. He did all the work, along with his partner, who had been sitting with the passengers.

I think that while the two men were attending to the Zebus, the partner related the whole incident to the driver, because as soon as the job was completed, the driver jumped down and asked in broken English, "Who na call Kwame Sohn?" My father quickly stepped forward and indicated it was him. Then the driver began speaking in Twi.

"You just entered this truck and look at the chaos you have caused." He wouldn't even listen to Dad's explanation as Dad took my rubber shoe to show him how the man had mistreated me. The driver made a quick decision: Dad's opponent had boarded the vehicle first and was going on a longer journey. Economically it was wise to keep the first customer, who was paying more for the longer trip.

"Kwame Sohn, here is your money. Take your son and get off my truck." My dad, who could understand him, tried to change the driver's mind because the sun was getting very hot. No, the driver wouldn't agree. Someone in the truck threw my modest piece of luggage from the truck as if to tell the driver he had made a wise decision. The driver jumped into his truck, started the big engine again, and in no time, put dust between us and him.

I was so upset that I started to cry as we stared after the truck, hoping the driver might change his mind. No such luck. Dad took my hand and started squeezing it gently, telling me not to worry. I could tell he was very upset himself. He was so disappointed that he changed his mind about going to Manchala.

"We should return home and abandon this journey for now," he said.

"Why?" I asked. "We can still walk and get to Manchala before midnight." But no, he had made up his mind. Well, I really started to cry then, causing the jungle trees to reverberate with echoes. I followed Dad grudgingly and we started walking back to the house after he had calmed me down.

How thankful I am today as I think of this incident in the truck. Had it not happened, I might have developed into a Brafuo or become a practitioner of a highly specialized form of witchcraft. Today, as I think of the incident, I realize how little things can make a whole lot of difference in a person's life.

As disappointed as I was on our way home, the sight of Yaw running to meet us rejuvenated my spirit. It was as if we had gone on a long journey and were coming home. I could tell by looking at Yaw that he had felt lost while I was away. His lips were very dry, and his face showed that he had done a lot of crying. As soon as we entered the house, Mom brought Dad a drink of water and asked why we had come back so soon. She was thinking that perhaps Dad had changed his mind and that the whole family was about to go to Manchala. Dad related the whole story to her while I did my part with Yaw. I was more interested in letting him know how it was to ride in a truck.

"The trees move too when you are in a truck," I told him. Of course, as far as Mom was concerned, Dad had made the perfect decision.

"It was good you didn't continue the journey after all, *Chamanwiah* will know that you made an effort to come." She quickly got busy to prepare for our evening meal. There was a sense of peacefulness in the house that evening. Both Mom and Dad were able to eat very well. They both agreed to postpone the Manchala trip indefinitely until proper arrangements were made. After all, they now had an excuse.

3

Relative Calm in Nepui

DAD'S FARMING CONTINUED TO PROSPER. He bought more goats and sheep. We did not worry much about the pigeons. They multiplied as long as we fed them millet, which they enjoyed very much. People came from far away to buy the birds. Dad became quite successful and even bought a bicycle. It was one of the first bicycles in the village. He ordered it from a "Lagostian Merchant" – as they called all traders from Nigeria. It was a Raleigh bicycle, and we were respected wherever we went, because of this bicycle.

Even Mom took pride in the bike. One day my brother and I overheard her talking with a friend and mentioning how happy she was that "Dad now has four legs." Anyone who had a bicycle was nicknamed a four-legged person. It was a status that was not easy to achieve. Yaw and I polished the bicycle and oiled it every day. The smell of newness added to our desire to touch the bike and to ask all kinds of questions about it. And, oh, how we loved the sound of the bicycle's horn! Dad never rode the bike to the farm for fear it might get caught on a piece of wood or that a puddle would make it dirty. He rode the bicycle only when he was bathed and groomed.

What a joy those days were! Many people loved Dad, though many others hated him for the comfort of life that he and his family enjoyed. Mom was hard-working. She would wake up early and get all her pounding done. She kept herself very tidy and always made sure that we bathed before going out to play *sikpakuune.* She managed the vegetables on the farm and sometimes outdid Dad in the money she brought in at harvest time. Everything went very well with us.

Because of the mistake my parents made in the spacing between Yaw and I, they almost over-spaced the third addition to the family. I was at least six years old, before Yaw Kumah was born. All of us loved him very much. Yaw and I got most of the things we wanted from our parents through him. He grew fast and soon the three of us became a team in everything we did.

It was a mistake to pick a fight with any of us. The boys in the village of Nepui learned this quickly. We defended one another, no matter whether our brother was at fault or not. Once one of us was engaged in a fight, it became our fight. Most of the people at Nepui complained about us and how we beat up other boys without giving them a chance. Occasionally Dad would have a serious exchange of words, especially when other parents complained that most of the fights among the Nepui youth were caused by us. Dad often scolded us but encouraged us to continue to work as a team in whatever we did. Whenever he felt that we had done something very serious, he would apologize on our behalf.

My dad was a gentle man, very kind and compassionate. He shared his yams and many of the farm products with the needy, especially widows and widowers. Our house was never empty of our parents' friends. During the season when corn or groundnuts were shelled, many men and women gathered in our house to help Mom and Dad. Such occasions were quite educational for the youth. The elderly people told wonderful stories. I remember many occasions when some of those tales brought tears to our eyes. Most of the stories had lessons to be learned. Nepui was a wonderful place to grow up.

The domestic animals roamed as freely as the people. The goats, in particular, behaved as if they owned the village. Doors had to be properly shut or they would enter any room and eat whatever they found. Some of those goats could be pretty sneaky. When a house was empty, they would wait outside until a child entered to drink water or to pick up something and then they would rush in – some times half a dozen of them.

Wild animals were not so delightful. Occasionally, a snake would wander into a room, sending the people into pandemonium. Most Africans fear snakes with a passion. Sometimes the spitting cobras would come around and swallow the eggs our hens laid. The cobras are so fast that it takes a lot of skill and patience to catch them.

Chickens seemed to have many predators. First, there were the fetish priests, who used them for sacrifices. Then there were the special occasions, such as the puberty rites, that required the sacrifice of chickens. Yaw once observed that not a day passed in our village without a sacrifice being conducted. Most of them involved the killing of chickens.

Beyond the human predators, most of the snakes in our village were egg or chicken eaters. But the chicken's most dangerous enemy was the hawk. Many varieties of hawks fed their young with chicks. Their favourite hunting time was about three or four o'clock in the afternoon. They circled the village like bombers zeroing in on a target. Occasionally some of them got caught. At every house, old telegraph wires were set up for the women to dry their clothes on. Sometimes a hawk would dive into those wires and end up in a soup pot.

I will never forget the nightmarish encounter I had with a hawk because of a grasscutter. An African grasscutter looks much like a North American groundhog or woodchuck. Grasscutter meat is another great delicacy among the Deg tribe. Even the delicious yam rat rates very low when compared to a *dagu,* a male grasscutter. Every man hopes to get at least one *dagu* each year. The hunting season for grasscutters is between February and the end of May. During this period, the men of the village surround a particular area and set fire to the grass. The fire chases out the grasscutters and any other animal that happens to be there. Grasscutters cannot run long distances. They get tired after a few yards and are then easily captured. People from the southern part of Ghana often visit our village during this season to buy grasscutters. Some of our men make money from selling grasscutters until the new grass grows up, when grasscutters can no longer be hunted.

I had almost finished a delicious meal of one of these grasscutters when Yaw and I decided to go out and meet our friends. Dad never liked for us to eat meat outside the house, so I hid the head of a grasscutter in my clothes before going out the door. Once outside, I ate all the meat and skin that covered the skull, exposing the bone. A hawk must have mistaken the white skull I was holding for a chick. Without warning, he dove to snatch the object from my hand, but, for some reason, he ended up burying his claws into my fingers. Ouch! I started yelling and running toward the house. Several people started running toward me, shouting encouragement to hang on to the huge hawk. They thought I was holding the bird, not realizing that I was looking for a way of parting with it. It was a most bizarre incident, as the hawk also was convinced that it was I who was holding on to him. He flapped his wings and pecked at my hand. Finally Dad came out and killed the bird. By this time, my hand was bleeding.

Dad was famous for his medicinal insights. He knew many leaves, barks of trees, and roots that could be used to treat numerous illnesses. Within a few minutes after killing the hawk, he was out in the bush and back with fresh leaves. Mother pounded them in her mortar to get their juice out. They mixed a little water with the juice and squeezed it onto my bleeding hand. The tincture gave me pain as one gets from a sharp knife – but it did the job. My hand stopped bleeding within seconds. Dad seized the opportunity to lecture us again concerning his point that we must always finish our food completely before going out.

"I'm sure you will never forget this lesson," he said, knowing very well that we were capable of forgetting anything.

The Dagarti tribe that came and settled among the Deg in Nepui brought guinea fowl with them. I have often wondered why these birds are called guinea fowl instead of "music fowl." The singing of these guinea fowl added another touch to the serenity of our little village. There is nothing like hearing a trio of guinea fowl under the bushy mango and nim trees. But don't think that we loved and respected these birds only because of the music they made; that would be a great mistake.

The Dagartis, when they arrived, boasted that their birds were more delicious than any living fowl on the surface of the earth. Guinea fowl have a sharp taste quite distinct from chicken and they quickly became a favourite with the Deg. However, no matter how much the birds multiplied, they remained very expensive. We craved their meat, but for some reason the idols did not change their appetites from chicken blood to the blood of these new birds. If they had, many would have been sacrificed, which would have made it easy for us to feast on them. Too bad it didn't happen.

In addition to the arrival of the Dagarti tribe, many merchants from Lagos, Nigeria came to settle at our village. In fact, two of them used to spread their mats to display their wares at the back of our house, which faced a major road. They sold clothes, sugar, pins, spoons, and anything you could think of. They would often sit by their wares from six a.m. until five p.m. when they would gather all their unsold items into boxes for another day.

It used to be quite a scene whenever there was a surprise afternoon shower. Merchants who sold clothes would dash back and forth trying to gather the clothes before they got wet. They never trusted other people to help them during such emergencies for fear that someone might take advantage of the confusion and snatch parts of their inventory. They were hard-working merchants. They would ride their bicycles for miles in order to sell their goods. Many times they exchanged their items for yams, which they took to the south and sold there for cash.

While I was growing up, money was not a strong influence in our village. People bartered for goods. The system allowed everyone in the village to do business freely with the Nigerians, since all the locals grew yams. Some, like my dad, had large farms, but there were those with smaller farms. One always had to judge how many yams the family would need to live on until the next harvest. So only a certain amount of yams could be traded for non-edible commodities. Food and water were the only things that people really worried about. As long as there is food to eat and water to drink, cook and bath with, the Deg is happy.

4

The Fire and Our Move to Bendessa

SUDDENLY THE SAFE HAVEN OF our home and the serenity of Nepui village was destroyed. The tragedy started one day when all the men in the village, as well as a few women, decided to dam one of the biggest streams in the area to hunt for fish. The bel leaves could not be used at this time because it was dry season and the leaves moved too slowly on the stream.

Capturing fish during the dry season required a much different approach. The Deg would create a pool of water by building two dams across a stream that contained a bountiful number of fish. The dams were usually mud walls. The pool was then emptied to ankle level by means of buckets and calabashes. It took several hours, sometimes even a whole day, to accomplish this task and many hands were required. This method of catching fish was, by necessity, a community undertaking.

In this particular case, the stream to be dammed was big. A large number of workers were needed. It was to be the last such fishing in the dry season. Preparations started on a Monday. People prepared enough food to last them from Tuesday through Thursday. On Tuesday morning the men went to the proposed dam site, prepared to spend the next two nights there. By the time the older men and women arrived on Thursday morning, the walls across the stream were completed. The draining started as soon as the second batch of people arrived. The number of fish killed that day was phenomenal. Everyone in the village had enough fish to live on for a few weeks.

While most of Nepui was at the stream about six miles away, a mysterious bush fire started on the northern side of the village, the direction of the fishing site. The fire began to move toward Nepui. I had just recovered from a severe headache, so I was weak and unable to participate in the communal fishing. Mom had stayed home to care for me. At first, we felt that someone should go and inform the men about the fire and the way it was moving toward our village. But most of the people who were left at Nepui were elderly and frail. There was also the danger that anyone who entered the bush could be trapped by the fire. The wind was constantly changing direction, making any decision very difficult. The fire came close to the village and then appeared to be veering away. But then, the wind shifted again and within minutes we were confronted by the high flames.

I will never forget my mother's bravery that day. She quickly surmised that the *puul-dua* (the dump) would be a safe place because the fire had passed over it, leaving only a few burning items. She ran to the dump and extinguished the small fires, making it a safe base for her operations. She grounded me there with strict instructions not to move. After making sure that I was safe, she dashed into our neighbour's house and transported all their important possessions to the *puul-dua*. Then she went to our own house.

She had just rescued our belongings when she noticed an elderly, disoriented man moving very slowly from his home across the road. Within a moment, my mother was at that man's side. She brought him to the *puul-dua*, then rounded up several very young children and other elderly people and guided them to the dump. Finally, she could do no more. The fire had spread through the entire village. Her hair was singed and her lips were dry and caked with ashes. She was very upset because she had not been able to find our cat. We stood there helplessly and watched the fire engulf our home. Both Mom and I simply broke down and cried. What a tragic sight it was. Not a single house in the entire Nepui village was left untouched by the fire.

When the fishing crew returned, there was loud wailing and intense grief. No person died in the fire, but many animals perished and the village suffered terrible destruction. In fact, the fire had disfigured our village so much that many people had trouble locating the remains of their homes. The *puul-dua* became my family's home for several days. Many people from Teselima, Jugboi and Jama villages came to help rebuild Nepui. There were lots of fish to eat, but no place to sleep. The stench from the dead animals and the smell of human excrement added to the misery. The public toilet places were all burned to the ground, so the people decided to empty themselves anywhere on the outskirts of the village. It was a miserable situation as the wind kept circulating the combined odour of dead animals and human waste.

The most moving scene for our family was the return of the pigeons. During the fire, they managed to escape and flew away. They were gone for three days. Suddenly, they were back, hovering over the rubble of our home. They had no place to land and rest their little wings. As they glided across the sky, we motioned at them from the dump and whistled at them as we used to do. They circled over us and finally landed in our midst.

The pigeons were happy to see us. They cooed with joy. Dad called them rascals and demanded to know where they had been hiding for the last three days – as if birds could talk. It was a very emotional moment, bringing laughter and tears.

The village was rebuilt, but living there was never the same. A part of the character of Nepui was destroyed by the flames. The worst of it for our family was when we heard it rumoured that the fire had been started through Dad's negligence. My father had built a fire to roast yams before leaving to join the fishing team. The gossips contended that Dad had been careless about extinguishing the fire before he departed. They claimed that after he left, the wind carried glowing embers of his fire to the dry grass. Dad vehemently denied the accusations and said he was sure that he had completely doused the fire.

"Whoever claims that they saw my fire still glowing, why didn't that person put it out?" he often asked. No one ever came to confront Dad openly about this fire, but Yaw and I heard the rumour from our friends, and so did Mom. It was a trying period for our family, especially for Dad. He found it very difficult to ride his bicycle around freely as he loved to do. He was also not visiting his friends as frequently as he used to. And, sadly, most of his friends believed the rumours and stopped visiting us. Many people blamed Dad for bringing untold poverty to the village, since their blankets, pillows, calabashes, and animals were all gone.

Emotionally, Dad was a very strong man and it was this gift that saved him from a total breakdown. However, the situation did affect him mentally. He started blaming himself for Nepui's tragedy. He claimed that his delaying tactics in sending me to Manchala to become a Brafuo had angered *Chamanwiah* and that *Chamanwiah* had finally decided to take action. My mother suggested that it was very unwise to complicate matters by bringing *Chamanwiah* into the case. But, in my opinion, Dad was right. During this anguished period in his life, my father developed a severe eye problem and was constantly dizzy. He had to walk with a stick or hold on to walls. The diviner in the village came to our house one evening and confirmed Dad's suspicions. He told Dad that *Chamanwiah* was very upset with him for not responding to his call. *Chamanwiah* had caused all Dad's problems, he said, and was eventually going to make him blind.

Dad was very upset with *Chamanwiah* for continually pestering him and for being forever wicked toward him just because he refused to become an assassin for *Chamanwiah*. Dad went through a lot during this period. It was in this time that he started to frequent the house of Yaw Wesseh. Yaw Wesseh often called himself "the free man." He had no idol and respected no fetish priest or diviner. His survival as a "free man" was something that attracted Dad. It was also said, in those days, that Yaw Wesseh prayed special prayers but not to idols. There were all kinds of rumours about this man. He was considered dangerous for our people. However, it always amazed Dad that he performed no sacrifices to idols and yet the witches had not yet succeeded in killing or crippling him as they often did to those who refused to serve them.

To our surprise, Dad told us one day that he had a new name, Mosisi (I think for Moses). He said he was tired of worshipping idols and that he was going to live like Yaw Wesseh. That really scared Mom. Mom's father, at Jugboi, was one of the feared fetish priests. Mom told my grandfather what Dad had done. She came back with several warnings from grandpa to Dad that he should not be "foolish like Yaw Wesseh" and that he was risking our lives. It was not clear at that time what exactly Yaw Wesseh practiced. However, it was clear that he believed only in *Korowii Jian* (the big God). He became Dad's close friend and he was able to influence Mom as well. Mom and Dad both lost interest in the "hard-core" witchcraft. However, it was obvious that Dad still carried a fear that *Chamanwiah* could strike him at any time.

To solve this problem once and for all, he decided that we should move from Nepui to a destination unknown to *Chamanwiah.* He didn't tell anybody about this plan except Mom. The two of them agreed to move to a little village called Bendessa in the Brong Ahafo Region of Ghana, completely avoiding the entire Deg land. They sold most of our things, including the bicycle, and gave most of the birds to friends. They sold all the yams, including the seedlings. They now had a little money and could leave Nepui.

My two brothers and I were initially glad for this move, but when the final day of our departure arrived, none of us wanted to leave our old village. It was our life. All our friends were here and we didn't want to leave them. We wept and wept, but Mom was always good in such times. She managed to convince us that the move was good for all of us. Dad, she said, had suffered emotionally since the rumours about the village fire started. Besides, by escaping to Bendessa, there was the possibility that we would all be free of *Chamanwiah.* It sounded good as Mom continued to tell us about the move. She still did not know Bendessa – nor did Dad. I am not sure how they even came to know that such an obscure village existed. But anyway, we moved. We went on foot, carrying all our remaining possessions to Bendessa.

After five days on the road, we finally arrived at our new village. It consisted of twenty to twenty-five huts. The path leading to Bendessa winds its way through the jungle. Nothing made it obvious that we were close to this village until suddenly we were in an open place and there stood the huts. In fact, Dad was so surprised that he went to verify the name of the village from a woman who had just brought in her firewood.

"This village is called Bendessa," she said with a broad smile on her face.

I looked at Yaw and we said simultaneously, "This is Bendessa?!"

"What did you boys say?" Dad asked.

"We said nothing," I replied defiantly.

He sensed right away that we were not thrilled to see the new village. But we were all tired and it was not a good time for him to be stern with us. The woman asked Dad where we were from and where we were going.

"We are from Nepui and we are coming here," he said.

"You mean to settle?"

"Yes."

She laughed and laughed till her whole body shook. "What under the heavens could attract you and your family to Bendessa?" She started to laugh loudly again.

Dad was getting quite peeved by the woman's laughter, but Mom quickly joined her and then said to Dad, "I think this woman is going to be my friend; she is very lively."

"She is lively indeed," Dad responded still frowning.

And Mom was right. Mame Adjoa became her closest friend while we were in Bendessa. Mame Adjoa seemed to be able to laugh off her problems. She and her husband were very poor but very kind. They hosted us for a few days after our arrival.

Dad did not waste any time. He quickly got our hut built, and within a few days it was roofed and we moved into our new home of the next few years. The hut consisted of a big bedroom and a sitting place where Mom did her pounding when it was raining. She also cooked there and we ate and rested there.

The people of Bendessa were generally very friendly. They made us feel welcome. They brought us bananas, pineapples, oranges, and even cocoa pods. Dad talked with the chief and he was given an area to farm, since land is neither bought nor sold in this area, as in many parts of Ghana. Dad was able to buy seedlings with his money from Nepui. The land could be cultivated rapidly and soon our farm had banana trees, oranges, plantains, and many other fruit trees as well as cocoa, yams, cassava, and corn. Mom and Dad worked very hard.

We soon got used to Bendessa and started to enjoy it. The entire village was surrounded by fruit trees. When the oranges and bananas were ripe for harvest, it was a spectacular scene. The beautiful colours of oranges and yellow bananas were a treat to the eyes. During that season everyone in the village was allowed to pick any fruit they wanted without the owner's permission as long as you did not sell it. It was a real community.

There was communal fishing in Bendessa, but quite different than we were used to at Nepui. There always was fish, lobster, crab and occasionally antelope meat in the village.

But there were other things in Bendessa that were less pleasant. The cobra, python, black mamba and a host of snakes battled with the people day and night. People stopped keeping certain domestic animals like cats. The African python had cleaned the village of its cats. Even the goats and dogs were constantly disappearing. Smaller children were never left alone outside the huts.

The first time I saw a python, I almost wet my pants out of fright. They are huge things that move along like miniature trains. A day didn't pass when someone didn't report "the worst yet" snake news. Dad was not very afraid of snakes, but that was not the case with the rest of his family. We hated them with a passion. But we managed, like everybody else, to survive and carry on farming in the midst of these ugly reptiles.

The people of Bendessa knew many herbs that cured snake-bite. In fact, in all the years we lived in that area, we never heard of a person dying as a result of snake-bite. There was a snake the natives of Bendessa called Nanka. Most of the people ate Nanka and even occasionally hunted Nankas in the forest. Nankas were delicacies. Whenever one was killed, the meat was divided among several families. But our family decided not to add any more delicacies to our list of yam rats and grasscutters. Besides, bringing meat of a Nanka home would have caused my mom to have an instant heart attack!

There were also big reptiles like the monitor lizard and huge snails that weighed over a pound. In short, Bendessa was a village of reptiles. The canopy of the jungle kept the land beneath it moist all the time for e crops. The soil was very rich. A very sound ecological environment for reptiles, crops, and people.

The irony of living in Bendessa was that even though there was an abundance of food produced every year, the people did not market these crops. They were so far into the jungle that anything meant for sale had to be carried for several miles. Occasionally the women got together and transported some of the food stuffs to places like Kintampo, Wenchi and Techiman. It took several days to carry out such plans. They brought back salt and kerosene to the village. Salt and kerosene were important commodities because they were not locally produced. Apart from these two commodities, Bendessa could survive without any external help.

Usually by two p.m. the men were back from their farms or from inspecting their fishing nets and traps. Once they were home, they sat around to empty several gourds of *yabra*. This is a drink tapped from the wild coconut palm trees. The alcohol content is quite low. It takes several calabashes before a person becomes intoxicated. But when people became intoxicated by this deceptive brew they were almost uncontrollable. They spoke nonsense and carried out the odd fight.

Yabra is as indispensable in Bendessa as soft drinks are in North America. The men of Bendessa described the virtues of *Yabra* in the most glorious pictures. Some said that it gave them new blood; others said it contained most of the vitamins needed for human health. Other fanatics claimed that anyone who consistently drank *yabra* was inoculated against any snake venom.

I will never forget an incident that occurred in Bendessa regarding a *yabra* addict and a tapper. One of the tappers of the village complained that someone was stealing his drink at the source. The thief went quite early and inspected some of the tapper's gourds that were still attached to the palm trees. He brought them down and drank his fill. Then he climbed up the palm tree and attached the gourds to their original spots, as if nothing had happened. The experienced tapper soon realized what must be happening and located the one tree from which the thief seemed to drink on a consistent basis.

Early one morning the tapper went to the tree, took down the gourd, urinated and emptied his waste into it. Then he added a lot of *yabra* and mixed everything thoroughly. He hung the gourd back in its original place and hid nearby. Soon the thief arrived and climbed the tree and brought down the gourd. He drank his fill. Again, he carefully reinstalled the gourd. But before he got away, the *yabra* tapper surprised him.

"I never knew that my waste could be that complimentary to yabra," he said. The thief, in shock at being found out, gathered a little courage and asked the tapper what he meant by "my waste."

"I mean exactly what I said. The *yabra* you drank is a combination of my urine, waste and some *yabra."*

The thief was so angry about this horrible trick that he beat up the tapper. The case came to the village chief, so we all had the privilege of hearing the story. The thief, of course, lost the case. The chief asked the tapper to indicate what he wanted from the thief as compensation for the many gourds of palm wine that had been stolen over time. The old tapper stood up calmly, cleared his throat, and replied, "*Nana* (a title the Brongs give their chiefs), I do not need any more compensation than what I have received already. As long as this thief here lives whenever he sees me, he will remember that he drank my waste. That is worth more than any punishment we can give him."

All the people at the chief's house roared with laughter. The case ended that way, but within six months the thief had moved away from Bendessa because people, especially the children, made fun of him wherever he went. The thief was not the only one to suffer. The villagers became leery of that tapper's yabra. Some joked that he had never washed the gourd well after the infamous incident. Eventually, the tapper lost his business and had to turn to farming maize.

In spite of Bendessa being so small, it was a village full of action. There were fist fights, which Yaw and I enjoyed watching. The quarrels and all domestic disputes ended at the chief's house. The women in Bendessa were strong people. For the first time, I realized that women could beat men in fights. At Nepui all domestic fights ended with the women being beaten by their husbands. But that wasn't always the case in Bendessa.

Mom and Dad payed little attention to these quarrels and concentrated on their farming. They worked hard and so did their children. Dad made sure that his sons participated in most of the hard work. I am glad he did, because it kept us out of trouble. We were in Bendessa for two years and, despite all our work, the farm did not prosper. So Dad decided that we must move again. Mom liked the idea because of the farm's constant failure and because of the snakes.

My brothers and I did not care either way. Our traumatic move from Nepui seemed to have steeled our hearts about moving. After supper one night, the decision to move was finalized. Mom and Dad decided on the fourteenth of the next month as our moving day.

But Abena Fulamuso and Kwame Sohn were frustrated and unhappy that things did not turn out well for our family in Bendessa. They were also worried that having to move too often would affect their children. Mom, as always, had a way of diffusing tense situations. One morning Mom told us that it was good that we were moving, because one more year in Bendessa would have completed the development of her muscles. Then she would have been able to fight like the Bendessa women and that would have left Dad in a very perilous situation. Dad grinned and we all laughed.

They decided that we should move to Chiaano, a village about five miles away. Dad had developed friendships with some of the men there while still in Bendessa. His friends had spoken to the chief of Chiaano about some land for Dad, once they heard we were leaving Bendessa. A family had recently moved away from Chiaano, leaving their hut vacant. Dad's friends cleaned it up for us. They were such kind people. They also came to Bendessa with their wives and children to help us carry our seedlings from Bendessa to Chiaano. They made our move very easy for us.

When the day to move finally came, it was hard for Mom to leave because she had developed a strong friendship with Mame Adjoa. They hugged and hugged one another, with many tears rolling down their cheeks. Finally Mame Adjoa said, "Don't worry Abena, I will be visiting you in Chiaano regularly. We can still keep our friendship."

We waved goodbye to her and our other friends and headed towards Chiaano. Then, to our surprise, most of the men in the village followed us. We stopped and they caught up with us. When they arrived, we noticed that they had brought various kinds of seedlings – yams, cassava sticks, bananas, etc. – as a gift for us. They accompanied us on the whole five-mile journey. This was their way of expressing their love for us for having stayed in their village for a couple of years.

It was a moving scene when we waved goodbye to our Bendessa friends once we arrived in Chiaano together.

5

Hard Times

THE VEGETATION AT CHIAANO was the same as that of Bendessa – very tall trees with climbing vines all tangled together. The only animals that travelled through the jungle with little difficulty were snakes, monkeys, and the *opesse*, a porcupine-like animal. *Yabra* was tapped here as well and used as a social drink. Even year-old babies were given *yabra*. The people of Chiaano believed that *yabra* purified one's blood. Our family did not find it too difficult to adjust to Chiaano. The people were extremely friendly.

They were experts in catching crabs. Crabs were their major source of protein. At Chiaano we sometimes ate crab meat for breakfast, lunch and supper. The crabs were huge and their meat was very juicy and tasty. There is a spring in Chiaano called Kenye. It is shallow but never runs dry. It was on the banks of the Kenye that the people did their crab catching. The crabs had holes about two to two and a half feet deep along the water. Catching them was easy. Once you were sure that the hole was a crab hole, you thrust your hand into it carefully and quickly. Your hand had to go in very fast to surprise the crab before it could attack you with its giant claws.

There was another reason why one had to thrust one's hands in very quickly and carefully. The abandoned crab holes were often occupied by some sort of water snakes. One bite from one of these water snakes could lead to several days of severe headaches and loss of appetite. Mom was quite enthusiastic about catching crabs until she had a confrontation with one of the water snakes. She was so frightened she almost fainted. After this episode, we all quit crab-hunting and simply traded other things for them.

We soon developed new friends and Chiaano became home. At the beginning of our stay, it seemed that we were finally going to make it. Our yams were doing quite well. Then came two years of rain. The jungle seemed to have an enormous capacity to absorb rain. The trees and their leaves, coupled with dead trees, soaked up all the rainwater. The soil was just right for bananas, cocoyams, plantain, cocoa, and climbing beans. These crops did very well during the wet years, but not Dad's yams. Yams do not like too much water nor too much dryness.

"It is a proud crop," Dad often said about his yams. Dad was concentrating on yam farming so much that he didn't put in any plantain or cocoa. He was trying to make yams a staple of the Chiaano diet. The people greatly encouraged him, because they love to eat yams. All our yams rotted within the yam mounds. We were very discouraged. Dad kept trying, hoping to raise the yam seedlings, but all efforts failed. He took to hunting, but it didn't work out well. Besides, the jungle was so infested with dangerous creatures that Mom was never happy about Dad's hunting.

Our family became very disillusioned about life as things

got worse and worse. We children began to sense disagreements between Mom and Dad. It seemed to me that my mother was quite hard on my dad. She was bitter, and deliberately asked Dad questions she knew he could not answer. It was during this difficult time that our brother Kwabena Kumah was born. Yaw and I thought that the birth of this new baby would bring peace to my parents, but it didn't.

Kwabena Kumah was only two weeks old when Mom and Dad had their final and biggest fight. The fight started before supper and escalated until midnight. We did not know the reason why our parents were acting this way. We were so sad to see our parents, who had loved one another so much, suddenly become so ugly toward each other. At one point Yaw tried to speak to them to calm them down, but his voice didn't account for much.

We sat in the veranda of our house and cried as they continued to insult one another and sometimes almost hit each other. Mom was very aggressive that night. She wasn't willing to calm down. It was as if she were possessed by a spirit. Finally, around midnight, they cooled off. The joy that once characterized our family seemed to have left us completely. It is so sad for children to see their parents fight. As I write these lines, I am aware that there are children in every part of the world who daily witness vicious quarrels between their mother and father. My heart goes out to them.

Since our new farm had never prospered, we were not surprised when Dad announced after supper one evening that we should return to Nepui, our original village. Mom left Chiaano with Kwabena Kumah while Yaw and I stayed with Dad, who was tidying up a few things before leaving. Yaw Kumah, our other brother, had left Chiaano six months earlier. Our grandfather Chaara Kwesi, Mom's dad, had sent a request, asking Dad to send one of us to him because he was getting old and needed "someone to hold his walking stick" as the Deg say when they need assistance in their old age. Grandpa's eyes had become rather dim, so he needed a younger child as a companion to help him in his sacrifices and at most of the daily chores.

When Mom left Chiaano with Kwabena Kumah, only Dad, Yaw and I remained. There was confusion at every meal time. The meals were either half cooked or burnt. Dad was learning to cook and, at the same time, putting Yaw and I through a crash course in cooking. The disasters we created were incredible.

We realized how ingenious Mom had been, because she seemed to know exactly the amount of salt, pepper or water required for each soup. Without watching, she simply dipped her hand in the salt bag and her fingers seemed to tell her the exact amount of salt needed. Such precision is very important because the African cayenne pepper respects no one. If you dared to put more in than required, it would make your nose and eyes produce liquid simultaneously.

Yaw and I were more careful than Dad in regard to cooking, even though he was the one teaching us. There were several times when we had to rewash all the food after Dad had cooked, because there was too much pepper or salt in it. By the end of the fourth week alone in Chiaano, we were holding our own very well. We also became very close to Dad. We became his best friends. He taught us many things and spent all his time with us.

We left Chiaano about five weeks after Mom had departed. The journey back to Nepui was a familiar one. We passed through Bendessa and said good bye to our friends there. Then we set out on the winding jungle road again with our luggage on our heads. The three of us carried all we possessed in the world: our mats, Dad's machete, two pillows, one set of outer clothes for each of us, one blanket, one towel, Dad's traditional cloth, two rat traps, the shirts and pants we were wearing and our gourd of water.

The only significant thing we had acquired while in Chiaano was Bo obia fa, our little dog. Yaw and I loved Bo obia fa and used to play with him each day. His name means "every created human being will be recalled by God." We had just passed Bendessa by about a mile when we saw someone calling us and running after us. We stopped. Papa Kramo caught up with us. We were happy to see him because he was one of Dad's friends, who had spent most of his time in our home in Chiaano. But his countenance wasn't friendly when he was close enough for us to see. His face looked as if he had been running after us all the way from Chiaano. We knew something serious was up.

"What is it, Kramo?" Dad asked while Yaw and I waited to hear the reason for Papa Kramo's anxiety.

"Kwame, you haven't finished paying for the dog," he said.

"What dog?" my father asked

"This dog, Bo obia fa," Kramo replied pointing to our travelling companion.

Dad was confused and so were we. The two men engaged in what became a very heated argument. Dad was sure he had paid the price in full. Papa Kramo was equally sure that he had more money coming. For two hours they argued. Finally Yaw told Dad that if that's what the man thinks, Dad should not worry but rather give him the balance. Bless his heart; Yaw did not realize that all we owned was the luggage on our heads.

After realizing that too much time had already been wasted, Dad decided to end the argument so that we could continue on our journey.

"Here, take the dog," he said with a calm voice, and handed Papa Kramo the rope. But Yaw and I couldn't accept the loss of our dog. Our ages (about ten and eleven) did not deter us from suggesting to Dad that he look the other way while we beat Papa Kramo up. Dad wouldn't let us.

"Let him go!" he said. That was painful! Bo obia fa himself did not understand why suddenly he had to part with our company. He kicked up a fuss as Papa Kramo dragged him away. Yaw and I broke down and cried as we watched our beloved friend disappear down the winding path.

"We'll get another dog when we get to Nepui," Dad finally spoke into our weeping, trying to comfort his two confused lads. Our crying became subdued sobs for the next several miles. Finally we stopped sobbing and faced reality. But one can never forget such a traumatic moment, at least not in this life.

Our exuberance and enthusiasm over the journey to Nepui completely vanished. Communication among us on the rest of the journey was very sparse. It became obvious that our Dad too was suffering because of the sudden loss of our pet.

On the second day of the journey we encountered another problem. We were just a mile away from a little village called Bewele when I told Dad I could no longer carry my luggage. I had been overcome by thirst and hunger. My legs refused to support the rest of my body.

"We are just about to enter Bewele," Dad said. In fact, we could hear the sound of women pounding when the wind changed direction. But even that sound failed to energize me. Each of us was so beat that neither Dad nor Yaw could conceive of taking on my load. While they were trying to convince me to "hang in there," the luggage tumbled from my head and I started to sweat profusely. Dad began to realize that I wasn't faking. He added my luggage to his, wondering whether he could walk the mile himself.

"This is *nkitin-nkiti,*" he said, referring to my loss of energy. *Nkitin-nkiti* is a condition in which one is overcome by starvation and thirst to the point that one could collapse at any moment and die. That one mile to Bewele was the longest mile of the whole journey. Dad put my hand on his arm and dragged me along until we met two women whose farm road joined ours. The women recognized the situation and quickly took Dad's luggage and split it among them. They were overloaded already, but they had fresh energy. They managed the luggage while Dad paid more attention to me. Occasionally, we would stop and Dad would fan me.

Finally we got to Bewele, and one of the women took us to her house. My situation was desperate. They quickly gave me water, while our landlady was busy preparing food as fast as possible. But Dad figured that I probably would not last until the food was ready. He asked the women if there was anything at all that they could give me to eat immediately. The landlady was preparing T-Z, a dish that takes at least two hours to prepare.

"There is *kuchoor* but no soup," she told Dad referring to the left-over T-Z from the previous day. Dad got the *kuchoor* and simply poured on water and salt to serve it as soup. Within a few minutes I had eaten up the *kuchoor* and was ready to carry on conversation, though still lying on the floor from exhaustion. By the time the landlady finished cooking, I had gained considerable energy and was able to gobble up the fresh food.

We spent the night at Bewele. Dad met some contemporaries of his and engaged them with tribal story telling. Tribal story telling is usually a happy time, though there are occasional stories that bring sadness or fear to the tender hearts of the young. We proudly sat close to Dad that night as story after story rolled from his lips. The other men were in no way lacking stories either. It became a competition as to who could end the night with the most stories. Sometimes the men got up and danced to the tune of the songs that were interwoven with the stories. The children were given the chance to respond to the stories as well. What a beautiful night it was!

My *nkitin-nkiti* had left me completely and my energy was back. Needless to say my giggles at the stories from time to time sounded like music to Dad's ears. He realized I had completely recovered. Yaw was very happy for my quick recovery as well and gently squeezed my hand any time I giggled.

Our people never forced children to go to bed. If a child was prepared to stay up until one or two in the morning to hear stories, the elders didn't mind. But, most often, our little heads betrayed us as they started to nod involuntarily. At such times we were dragged to the room to sleep. You could even get the odd tap on your backside if you resisted the elders' admonition to go to bed.

We listened to stories until midnight when Dad called it quits, realizing we had to continue our journey the next morning at around six o'clock. We went to bed and the six hours of sleep seemed to do the job. We felt strong when we woke up, ready to continue the trip. Our landlady gave us porridge to drink that morning before we left. Our kind of porridge is a good breakfast but it is not particularly good for travellers, because it leaves the body too quickly. One bowl of porridge usually makes a traveller water the grass at least two or three times every mile. However, these periodic stops were not bad at all, especially when one was carrying heavy loads. You were allowed to call for a stop any time, as long as you could justify it once everyone has put down their luggage.

"I want to water the grass," you would say. Then you step into the bush but not too far because the travelling companions want to hear whether your request was authentic or just an excuse to put down the load from your head. To help them hear, you direct the water to the driest leaf around, causing a rattling sound. As soon as the companions hear the sound, they feel satisfied and start blaming the porridge and calling it with many proverbial names like *baa-un ngwe*, "the porridge that cannot be stolen for it will show itself one way or the other." Usually these brief stops are good for everyone, even though the initial impression is that it is a nuisance to halt a journey for short stops.

Dad gave both the women who had helped us at Bewele a modest gift. We sure appreciated their help and their meals. We thanked them, especially the one who took us in. She had several children, but most were still asleep when we left that morning so Yaw and I could not say goodbye to them. "*Wii de bange*" (the sun is growing), Dad told us, so we must be on our way. Our feet led us to our friend – the winding path – again and we travelled on like nomads, which in a way, we actually were.

From Bewele to Yaara was a half day's journey. Two of my uncles lived there and Dad wanted the opportunity to introduce his brothers to his two oldest sons. Between Bewele and Yaara there are many villages and in every one of these villages Dad knew someone. So, we ended up arriving in Yaara very late. We walked in darkness from Tufuboi to Yaara.

Yaw was very upset about our lateness, since he really hated travelling in the dark. A fist fight almost broke out between Dad and him. I whispered to Yaw and assured him that, should Dad touch him, I would help him fight Dad. This was our usual way of supporting one another. We knew we could never pose a problem to Dad should he decide to fight us. When he starts expressing his anger, we usually ran out of his reach.

We managed to arrive in Yaara without a fight. Dad's brothers had just finished eating when we arrived. They were excited to see him and scolded him a bit for travelling so late with his children. We were so happy to see them, even though it was too dark to really see them well. They summoned their wives to give us water and feed us. Within an hour those dear women had accomplished both. The women were strong and enthusiastic and seemed to respect their men highly. After seeing them work that night, Yaw and I concluded that Mom had it too easy with Dad. We even considered telling Dad to beef up his authority at home. We knew we would never dare to tell him anything that implied that his wife was lacking in any way. He always warned us that we had no business in criticizing his wife. However, we often considered saying something negative about Mom just to see his reaction. We knew we could never do it. Saying anything against Mom was like touching a raw nerve.

We left Yaara at dawn and headed toward Nepui. We were very disappointed that Dad did not allow the day to break properly so that we could see our junior fathers (uncles) well. When Yaw is upset his questions are not very diplomatic. "Why were you in such a hurry to leave Yaara?" he asked.

"From Yaara to Nepui is a full day's walk, son," he replied. When Dad said it's a full day's walk, you had better believe it. That settled the question for us. We knew that the last leg of the journey was not going to be easy. Therefore, there was no point in being moody and making our long journey more uncomfortable.

"You should not worry; you will have the chance to stay with your junior fathers," Dad told us.

As the journey drew us closer and closer to Nepui, we were

excited to see our old town again. We arrived at sunset when most people were having their supper. Yaw and I would have to wait until the next day to see our former playmates and find out how much they had grown.

6

Alone in Nepui

WE HAD HOPED THAT MOM would be waiting at Nepui for us. Our anticipation and excitement soon changed to sorrow when we discovered that Mom had decided not to come to live in Nepui again. It was so sad for us. However, a cousin of my dad's prepared a meal for us that night and provided warm water for us to bathe. The next morning we saw a handful of our friends and visited places where we used to play and wrestle.

We also visited the Dawadawa trees of old-man Gbana, the crippled man. The old man had several fruit trees near his house, but because he was crippled, we often went there to steal fruit. Occasionally he caught us. He could move very fast on his hands. Sometimes he was able to sneak up on us and appear under the tree we had climbed. At such times we remained in the tree and started to cry until an adult would come and rescue us. We preferred other adults to spank us, because Gbana the cripple had such a broad chest and huge, strong hands. We often referred to his hands as "the iron bars."

Nepui had changed during our absence. It didn't look the same. Worst of all, Mom was not there to pamper or chastise us. Yaw and I missed Mom so much that we asked Dad's permission to visit her in Jugboi. He willingly gave it to us, hoping that Mom might change her mind and come to live with us in Nepui after all. From Nepui to Jugboi is about four miles, so it didn't take us long to get there. It seems to me that we ran the whole way because of our excitement to see Mom, Yaw Kumah and Kwabena Bichala again. It was a nice reunion. Our two younger brothers were happy to see us, although it took Kwabena Bichala a while to get used to us.

We stayed at Jugboi for a week and were thoroughly pampered by grandpa Chaara Kwesi and grandma Yobo. At the end of the week, we realized that Mom's decision to remain at Jugboi was final. We did all we could to bring her to Nepui, but to no avail. So we returned to our father empty-handed. Several more attempts were made to get Mom back. But grandpa at Jugboi insisted that Mom was needed to help him and grandma in their old age. When it became clear that Mom had no intention of coming back, Yaw and I took our domestic tasks seriously.

It became obvious that our lives would never be the same. Yaw and I had to work hard. We did the cooking, fetched the water, and did all the mundane chores around the house. Many times Dad tried to cook, sweep, or fetch water, but we always said, "No! As long as we are alive you will be cared for." He wiped the occasional tear from his face when he saw us doing things like washing our clothes. Dad believed that children should not have to do adult tasks, but circumstances forced him to compromise his principles.

He was a good father. In our culture, men were not supposed to perform certain domestic duties. He waited until everyone was asleep and then he would clean our cooking pots and do other chores just to give us a little break the next day. He made sure that no one saw him doing household chores. He was afraid of being reported to the chief for violating cultural values. His sensitivity to our culture and our need to preserve it was strong. At the same time, he loved his two young sons. It pained him to see us do all the work. He told us that he could not remarry because of his love for our mother. Therefore, he felt obliged to chip in as much as possible.

Yaw and I discussed with him our concern that tribal culture only permitted us to do household chores until our puberty. We asked him whether he would remarry when we reached puberty. Dad could not be budged on this point. There would be no second marriage. He told us that God would provide an answer to our problems in His own time.

Those days in Nepui without Mom were the most sorrowful and difficult days in our early years. When mother was at Jugboi, folks came from Manchala, again trying to lure Dad to take up the ugly practices at Manchala. But he refused. He started working for farmers at Nepui. They wanted to pay him for his labours, but he demanded yam seedlings instead. We went with him from farm to farm gathering the seedlings. The people we worked for were always kind. They gave us yams for our meals and two baskets full of yam seedlings each day. I remember one day when a farmer gave us several tubers of yam for our food, but Dad insisted that we take only what we needed for that day. His favourite Akan saying was, "*Didi daa-daa na ye*" – to have a little every day is better than plenty at once.

Several people were sympathetic to our plight, but there were others who teased us. It humiliated Yaw and I to work as labourers for farmers Dad had helped to get established in the first place. But Dad didn't care. His main worries were about how we felt rather than what people said about him. He was always concerned that his children should never beg for food.

We worked from our early waking to late at night. We really needed Mom. But there she was at Jugboi "sucking her Mom's breast," as Yaw put it with disdain. Such statements were said only in secret. We couldn't say such things in the presence of Dad. He continued to be very protective of Mom. We couldn't figure out why he never cursed her. Today, I realize that Kwame Sohn was a very good man who deeply loved his wife.

The harsh demands of both farming and domestic chores took their toll on us. We didn't look forward to coming home after a whole day under the severe African sun. We were always sweaty, dirty, smelly, and tired after work. When we got home, I lit the fire and Yaw picked up the bucket and walked half a mile to fetch water. After peeling yams and setting them on the fire to cook, Yaw and I would fetch more water. By the time we returned, the yams were well cooked. After eating, we boiled water and had a bath.

This daily routine was exhausting. Something had to change. Dad approached his cousin Borfu again and finally struck a deal with her: she would do our laundry and cooking in exchange for food and clothing. She thanked us and we thanked her. She was a faithful and considerate old lady.

Within two years of arriving back in Nepui, we had gathered and nursed enough yam seedlings for our needs. By the third year, we had enough yams to sell. During that third year, we started employing labourers in our farm. We also raised ducks and guinea fowl. People came from far and near to buy duck eggs and guinea fowl from us. Nothing pleased us more than seeing the restoration of our Dad.

At some point Dad decided he was going to send me to school. But he reversed his decision upon hearing that one of the teachers at Bamboi was an expert strapper. The children feared him more than any policeman or army officer. He was nicknamed *Me gua wu* (I will strap you). We heard that teachers from other villages came to hire his services in cases where students needed severe discipline.

"That goat will not strap my son," Dad said. Anyway, *Me gua wu* ended up providing a good excuse for my not starting school. At one point, Dad told me that I was bad enough already and didn't need to learn any more of the things that were going on in school. Stealing was as common as drinking water in school. Teachers encouraged students to steal eggs and all kinds of things for them. Dad figured we would lose all our chickens and duck eggs to the teachers if I enrolled in school.

Farm, farm, farm was all we did. We prospered again – according to the standards of the village. After three years in Nepui, we lacked nothing. We even started helping other farmers with yam seedlings. Then misfortune struck again. The village was hit by a severe drought that burned the crops. Our yams shrivelled in the yam mounds. What a shame! It was distressing to see Nepui farmers having to buy food from nearby villages. We never recovered from the drought. Yams that were planted the following year either rotted in the mounds or germinated and got burned a few weeks later. Our farm faded to nothing.

7

Another Good-bye

AT THIS TIME, MY FATHER was developing all kinds of illnesses. First, it was his eyes. Problems with his eyesight would flare up, recede, then return in full force. He also suffered from dizzy spells. Dad never liked using a cane, but circumstances gave him no choice. The day he accepted the cane, Yaw and I knew he was really suffering. As if that were not enough, he developed a bad hernia, which made him walk even slower. We spent our meagre savings in vain attempts to bring Dad back to health. With our resources depleted, Yaw and I had to work harder than ever.

Yaw was very good with the spear. He was able to hunt with the village men. I went fishing as well as labouring at other peoples' farms. Sometimes Dad was able to go farming with me, but, at this point, he was providing company more than anything else.

One day Dad ventured into the bush to hunt deer, and was bitten by a poisonous snake. He survived the snake bite without too much difficulty, but shortly after, he became very weak while returning home with us from a day of farming. We could hear his stomach rumbling. He started to sweat profusely. We stopped in the middle of the road and he sat down for a while. He got up with our support and said we should support him and walk along gently. We were still about two miles from home. His whole body started shaking and we knew he was in real pain.

We started to cry, but he begged us not to do that. We managed to get him home. He took off his farm clothes and went to lie on his bed. For a week, he couldn't eat well and had to remain in bed. By this time, the hernia protruded quite significantly at the lower end of his abdomen. The nearest hospital or clinic was over fifty miles away. Besides, we had no money to take him to the hospital. We sent a message to my aunt at Manchala, hoping that through her some financial arrangements could be made to take her brother to the hospital. Apparently she was suffering from the same disease we were: poverty. She couldn't find the two pounds necessary for the medical fee. The idea of going to a hospital was abandoned.

My Dad lay on his wretched bedding, tossing back and forth with pain. In the evening, Yaw and I sat by him like posts planted at his side, hoping that some miracle would come to help him. On Monday of the second week of the sickness, Dad called Yaw and me and said that his pain was quite intense. He thought that by Tuesday afternoon he would be dead. He also said that if the sickness did not kill him by the end of Tuesday, he would live for a long time. I was upset to hear him talk like that. The thought of losing him was too much for me. He was our father and friend. "Why would he want to die and leave us?" I said to myself. "Who will take care of us should he really die?" There were so many questions going through my mind.

At about two o'clock on a Tuesday afternoon a truck on the way from Kumasi to the north struck and killed a sheep belonging to one of Dad's friends in the village. It had rained that afternoon and the weather was a bit cool. Dad seemed to be more peaceful. He was not tossing and turning as he had been in the past weeks. He sat up half way, leaning on some pillows.

The friend who lost the sheep suggested that Yaw come and give him a hand in gutting the sheep, so that we could make a clear soup for Dad. Yaw left to work on the animal. He was gone for an hour. Everyone had left the room where Dad was, trying to give him some fresh air. I sat in the doorway in case he needed help. He called with a weak voice, and I stepped in. He asked me where Yaw was. I told him that Yaw had gone to help his friend prepare a sheep to make some soup for him.

"Oh, I wish he were around," he said.

"Why, Dad?" I asked quietly.

"I wanted to speak to both of you; but since he is not here, remember to pass this information on to him when he comes."

"What information?" I asked.

"You two boys have been very good friends to me and I thank you. I wish I had the power to change my situation, but it is impossible. It is clear to me that my time has come. Should anything happen, I want you and Yaw to go to Yaara. You, Kwabena, should stay with your junior father Yaw Boateng, and tell Yaw to stay with Asimbo. You will need to stop all your fights and team together at Yaara."

Then he told me to call his friend Yaw Wesseh so he could talk with him. I dashed for Yaw Wesseh's home. As soon as he saw me, Yaw Wesseh knew there was an emergency. He almost ran when I told him that Dad needed him. When he arrived at my father's bedside, I heard Dad tell him to make sure the debt was paid. I did not know what he was talking about. Yaw Wesseh, however, seemed to understand and agreed to take care of the situation.

Dad then acted as if he wanted to sit up. I took hold of his hand and his head, trying to help him sit, while Yaw Wesseh took his other hand. Dad suddenly started to throw up, but only some watery substance came out. Without much struggle, he breathed his last and we laid him carefully down on his bed.

Yaw Wesseh looked at me and started to sob heavily. I asked him why. I had never seen a person die, so I wasn't sure what had happened. Yaw Wesseh realized this, so he organized himself and told me that Dad had decided not to eat any more, which is the way the Deg people announce the death of a person. I jumped up and yelled, but he put his hand over my mouth to control me.

It was around 3:30 p.m. on Tuesday that Dad died, but in our culture all afternoon deaths have to be kept secret until everyone in the village has finished their evening meal. Once the death is announced, no one except infants and children is allowed to eat for two or three days. All those from fifteen years and up only drink water or locally brewed wine called *pito,* until the corpse is buried.

Yaw Wesseh did everything he could to prevent me from betraying the situation. He saw how emotional I had become as I tried helplessly to talk to Dad, who was lying there motionless. Finally Yaw Wesseh managed to calm me down and took time himself to wipe my tears so that no one could tell I had been crying. He knew the village would call him irresponsible if the news of the death leaked out early.

After he had calmed me down, Yaw Wesseh took me outside and brought my aunt and two other people into the house. After arranging Dad's body and much crying, they finally emerged with their faces all washed. They had locked the room that held my father's corpse. No one was allowed to enter. Secretly, young men were dispatched to call the village elders from their farms, as is the custom of our tribe. Others were sent to inform relatives who lived in distant places, such as Yaara and Manchala.

The saddest moment during my father's death was when Yaw returned to the house jubilant because he had managed to obtain some meat for Daddy. In fact, he had taken time to roast part of the liver, which he knew Dad would especially enjoy. When he approached the front door of our house I saw in his face how happy he was. He had also brought me a little piece of the roasted liver. He gave me my portion and for some reason I didn't have enough strength for my fingers to hang onto the meat so it dropped.

I had tried to help Yaw by fighting down my tears. I gathered some strength and told him, "Throw away the liver." I will never forget the look on his face as he saw my eyes filled with tears. He knew something was seriously wrong, but did not know exactly what. After all, Dad had appeared to be improving when he left. I was not sure whether I was allowed to tell Yaw or not, because of all the warnings I had received from my aunt and Yaw Wesseh that if my father was to get a proper burial, it depended on my ability to restrain myself until the village had had its supper. Here was my brother standing in front of me with his precious gift for our father in his hands, and a look of total confusion in his eyes.

At first, I just said that he couldn't see Dad right away. But I couldn't hold back the truth. I began to weep as I told him that our daddy was no more. Hardly had I got my words out when we were overpowered by our aunt and led to a secluded spot. The warning was repeated that if we wanted our dad to have a decent funeral, we must restrain ourselves for the time being. So, the two of us went and sat opposite the room where Dad's body was lying. We felt so alone, and yet we could not express our loneliness. We sat there like two little birds that had lost their mother. We could not talk or speak to one another, since our emotions would burst out. Tears rolled down our cheeks constantly. Darkness descended on the village at six, and still we sat there in silence.

Finally the time arrived for us to be able to cry. By seven o'clock people had finished their supper and many relatives had arrived from distant villages. After all the customary things were completed, my aunt began the "wailing chorus." Everyone in the village who could walk gathered in the inner courtyard of our house that evening for the tribal wailing. Emotions had climbed high by this time. By eight o'clock both Yaw and I had developed severe headaches from crying and wailing so much.

Our junior fathers Kofi Asimbo and Yaw Boateng arrived from Yaara at about 9:30. Their emotions were quite explosive when they saw us. My father and his brothers look a lot alike, especially my junior father Yaw Boateng. When we saw them, our crying erupted again. We wept and wept. However, our junior fathers took the time to comfort us and assured us that, as long as they were alive, everything would be all right for us.

We followed them around like anxious puppies. I told them what my father had said before he died, including that I was to stay with Yaw Boateng and Yaw to stay with Kofi Asimbo. They pampered us a little, and boasted that staying with them at Yaara would make us forget our father's death, because they would fill the gap. I was about eleven years old and Yaw around twelve when we were orphaned.

Mother arrived at Nepui the following morning with our two younger brothers Yaw Kumah and Kwabena Bichala. She was brokenhearted when she saw us. We looked so lonely and hungry. She knew she had no right to even talk with us, because she had abandoned us to live with her parents at Jugboi. Needless to say, she received a scolding from the older women for her "heartlessness." It was obvious that she was deeply troubled over the loss of Dad, but it was too late to make amends. Much of her sadness was because Yaw and I would soon be gone to Yaara to face life on our own.

If you are born male, you belong to your father's relatives, should your father die. If you are a girl, you go to your mother's family. The system was clear cut and allowed for no changes. Even to see his mother is very difficult for a boy who has lost his father. Once the father's relatives come for the boy, he is and remains their property. They can treat the child virtually any way they want without the mother being able to interfere.

My mom knew Dad's brothers and their unpredictable characters from past encounters. She knew we were in for real trouble at Yaara. But what could she do? She knew that she might never see us again – at least until we got married. My mom also knew that Yaara was a dangerous town within the Deg tribe. She cried and cried. Many of the elders understood the reason for her tears, but we didn't.

Yaw and I tried to comfort her and assure her that we would always visit her and that our junior fathers were very kind to us. The more her sons spoke, the more she cried. She knew we did not know what we were talking about.

By the third day after Dad's death, I had grown quite numb to the whole funeral "celebration," as we call it. Yaw and I were celebrities overnight. Much attention was paid to us. The whole village comforted us and gave us little gifts. During the years we were moving from place to place with Dad, we knew nothing but suffering. Even when we had returned to Nepui, our life had not changed. It was full of hard work and suffering. But during those three days, we had become like princes. Little did we know that the pampering and care would soon evaporate.

On Thursday morning it was time to bury Dad's body. As soon as the body was lifted up, the chorus of wailing started all over again. The wailers followed the corpse, and I was made to lead the procession. We walked slowly to the grave site and I was instructed to stand at the head of the grave. The body was lowered very gently until it touched the bottom. Then I was told to put the first shovel full of dirt on Dad's coffin. By doing this, I was signalling that permission is granted to bury the body. Putting dirt over my father was a most difficult thing to do. It hit me again that Dad was really gone. We cried and cried, Yaw and I. Everyone pampered us and escorted us home.

Mom spent the rest of the day with us, telling us how she regretted leaving us for so long. She was brokenhearted. She told us never to give up hope while in Yaara.

"Try to do all you can to survive," she said with tears rolling down her face. "Yaara isn't going to be one bit easy for you," she repeated. "Your dad was a fighter and you must fight until you achieve freedom for yourselves one day at Yaara."

Of course we did not realize the significance of these statements until we left Nepui to Yaara with Asimbo and his brother.

8

Yaara – A World of its Own

AFTER ALL THE FUNERAL CELEBRATIONS were over at Nepui, Asimbo and Yaw Boateng gathered the few possessions of their deceased brother and got ready to leave for Yaara. About ten of us left Nepui early that morning to walk the almost thirty-mile journey to Yaara: my aunt, our two uncles, Yaw and I, a cousin from New Longoro, and four others native to Nepui, who accompanied us as a form of tribal courtesy.

A non-human companion, greatly treasured by Yaw and me, was a beautiful grey dog. She had been given to us six months before Dad's death. The dog was especially fond of me, and we often played together. The only people she knew in the band travelling to Yaara were Yaw and me, so she stayed close to us. The journey was tiring because it was exceptionally hot that day. We stopped from time to time to eat some peanuts my aunt had brought along.

Once we left Nepui, we soon realized that our two junior fathers were quite harsh. The pampering was over. Instead of talking naturally to us, they snapped out orders. We missed the gentle way Dad used to talk to us; we didn't think much of our uncles' behaviour. However, since the years ahead were going to be spent with them, we decided we had to learn to cope with the situation. At some point, I managed to whisper that Asimbo and Yaw Boateng behaved rather roughly. As if he weren't concerned, Yaw replied, "I think the journey is getting to all of us. They will be okay once we get to Yaara."

We felt that part of the reason for their rough conduct was that they were disturbed by the loss of their brother. Little did we know that our uncles were still putting on their best behaviour.

By about five p.m. we reached Buseima, a village about a mile from Yaara. It was a strange, large village of about five thousand people. We saw mysterious carved images as we passed through the town. The people themselves looked strange and dirty. Very few had smiles on their faces. Even our dog, *Nso Nyame Ye* (God is able), felt the strangeness of the village. She stayed close by me with her tail tucked between her hind legs, her ears flattened back.

"We are all scared," I whispered to her. Eventually we picked up the Yaara road at the other end of Buseima. As we approached Yaara, I realized that Buseima was just a prelude to the extreme strangeness of that part of Deg territory. Something unfriendly, even vicious, seemed to hang over Yaara. The canopy of trees looked like mysterious images. Even the birds looked different and when they sang it sounded like music from a dark pit. The birds had such loud voices that they kept my heart thumping as we approached the village.

Finally we saw some women who had come to fetch water from Debeh stream. There was nothing feminine about these women. They were muscular and rugged looking. Entering Yaara was like entering a dark hole full of mice. Perhaps this was the reason why in the past Dad had brought us to Yaara at night and hurried us out before dawn. He wanted to shield us from sights that would frighten us. But now we were in Yaara to stay. As we walked to our future homes, we saw people leaning against the huge kapok trees. The dirt on them and their torn farm clothes blended together to look like death itself.

The trees at Yaara were very huge and the old men sat under them to chew tobacco and spit. Most of the old men had their own calabashes filled with ash. Whenever they wanted to spit, they picked up the calabash and spit on the ash. I almost threw up at seeing so many saliva-collecting calabashes.

What worried me most, the first day we got to Yaara, was Nso Nyame Ye. She was so confused and scared. I seemed to step on her leg or tail whenever I got up, because she was always digging to get under me.

We were thankful that evening for the water and food our uncle's wives brought us. There was a lot more fish in the soup than we could afford at Nepui. That provided some encouragement. My first public scolding came when I got up after we had finished eating to look for any broken earthen ware to put some food in for Nso Nyame Ye.

"Dogs are not treated like people in our town, and you better learn that real fast," junior father Yaw Boateng told me while pinching my ear. The dog did not eat that night. She quickly learned to scavenge for food.

During the third day after our arrival at Yaara, we were taken through a program that seemed like an orientation. Our heads were shaved clean and we were led to visit every house in the the village. We saw scary idols drenched in blood. Some of the blood on these images still looked quite fresh. At one point, we thought we would be sacrificed to these idols. We were shaking and weeping. People thought we were in that condition because we missed our dad. Forcing us to shave off our hair was a way of "breaking us in."

Our mother was now far away in Jugboi on the other side of the Black Volta river. Tradition made it impossible for her to visit us, let alone interfere in whatever happened to us at Yaara. The only person I knew really well was Yaw – and our dog. We were completely cut off from the rest of the world and were at the mercy of Kofi Asimbo and Yaw Boateng. From now on they determined our movements and everything. In fact, should they choose that we should die, there was nothing to stop them.

One thing we knew was that the people at Yaara, and the Deg Tribe for that matter, did not practice cannibalism. However, they were a ruthless people when they fought. They fought with guns, bows and arrows, and knives. They were unorthodox in almost everything. In short, Yaara was a world of its own.

Yaw and I were disillusioned and confused about our junior fathers, who we had thought would be such wonderful uncles. Dad's uncle, Yaw Sumaa, whom we were supposed to call grandfather, was the chief of Yaara. He prided himself on the number of dogs he was able to sacrifice each year. Heads of dogs were put on a string and hung in his room. When we entered we saw that three strings of dog heads already completely circled the room, and a fourth was nearing completion. There were about 150 to 200 heads. It was forbidden to count them. He alone knew the exact number.

It was not only the dogs' heads that were strange in grandpa Yaw Sumaa's room, but also his big calabash called *Chal Luh* (blood calabash). The blood of every animal sacrificed in that room was smeared over this calabash. The smearing had started long before my father was born. It was a horrible sight! However, we soon realized that grandpa was a harmless man, not vicious as Yaw and I had expected. In fact, he was kind. He gave Yaw and me nicknames. In some ways, he tried to help us adjust to the situation at Yaara.

Asimbo and Yaw Boateng followed tradition to the letter. They were also "men of war." They made it quite clear within the first weeks at Yaara that they would tolerate no nonsense. They were hard to please. Yaw was assigned to stay with Asimbo. According to tradition, the older son goes to the older uncle and the younger to the younger. Besides, Dad had already done the division before his death.

We were beaten daily, often unnecessarily. I remember one time when we were eating and I swallowed the soup down the wrong tube and started choking. I got up in a panic to get water. I was beaten for getting up while the elders were still eating. Our house and the one in which Yaw lived were only a stone's throw away, so I could see Yaw and sometimes hear him cry. His cries used to cut through me, but I could do nothing to help or comfort him. In fact, I did not dare even change the expression on my face.

As our time in Yaara grew, so did our stress. Everything we did was wrong. We were constantly told that Dad had not raised us well. Simple things such as playing games were discouraged. Whenever one of us was severely beaten or cruelly treated, we tried to meet somewhere in the bush to cry together and to encourage one another. Our junior fathers made us feel that we should not be together, so when we got together with other young children, we would play with them but not with one another. We lived like enemies, though we deeply loved one another.

In the evenings, after a hard day's work at the farm, we would come home and have to wait until everyone else had finished bathing before we could have our bath. We also received the short end of the stick where food was concerned. The wives of my uncles cooked the meals and sent the food to grandpa Yaw Sumaa's house, where we all gathered to eat. Yaw Boateng had three children and Asimbo had four. Asimbo had two boys and Yaw Boateng one who was grown enough to eat with us at grandpa's. No girl is allowed to eat with the men and boys. Half the time, Yaw and I left the meal hungry. Then we discovered that the women were reserving a substantial amount of food and the best meat for their husbands and children, which they ate privately after the public meal was done. Till we figured this out, Yaw and I sat night after night wondering why our uncles and their male children were spending so much time together in the room after our meal at grandpa's.

Yaw and I became thin and wretched. But we were not a unique sight in Yaara. There is a saying in the village that male children who lose their fathers rarely survive. Male orphans are regarded as "bad luck children," who were somehow responsible for their father's death. As a result, we were never completely accepted. Thankfully, some of these superstitions are now declining in practice in Yaara.

The village was full of superstitions. One reason Yaw and I got into trouble was that at our houses everything had a code name that was to be used as soon as the sun went down. For example, in day time a cow was called *Naaw* but after sunset it became *Mibo-paga-te*, which means "the one with wide nostrils." Chickens, cats, dogs, earthen ware, colours, and most other things changed their names after dark. Yaw and I couldn't keep up with the changes. There was so much to learn and remember. Thus we violated some of the rules daily and got our daily lashings.

I thought nothing could get worse. I was wrong. One morning Uncle Asimbo announced that his idol *Chamanwiah* had announced that he wanted my dog as a sacrifice. I begged him and said that Nso Nyame Ye was now my only friend. I told him I would do whatever he wanted, if only he would spare my dog. But he gave me a good scolding and went to the bush to look for the herbs to cook with the dog.

The hour while he was in the bush was unbearable for me. I did not know what to do. I tried to encourage my dog to run away, but, of course, she did not understand me. I hoped my uncle would change his mind, having seen my tears that morning. I should have known better. These people are not impressed by blood, let alone mere tears. They were hard men who had no time for remorse.

"Here he comes with the herbs," I whispered involuntarily to Nso Nyame Ye. He took the herbs to the shrine and performed most of the necessary preliminaries. After that, a few men joined him at the shrine as they often do.

I was sitting with my dog under grandpa's big kapok tree, hoping against hope. My heart was pounding. Suddenly Asimbo appeared and took the dog away from me. I tried to hang on to the dog, and cried – as if that was of any use. He simply kicked me away and took the dog to the shrine. It wasn't long before I heard a bitter yelp and knew it was over.

Then Asimbo had the nerve to command me to join the family festival in eating the dog meat. I told myself, a man dies only once; so my uncle can do to me whatever he wants – I will not eat. How could I betray the friend I so much cherished? I received severe lashes for my refusal, but, after all, that was routine in my life. My senior brother did not see any problems in eating the dog. In fact, he joined the others who chastised me for being so stubborn. At that moment I realized that Yaw had been completely "broken in" by the uncles.

I had always kept my mother's last words in my heart. She had said, "Try to do all you can to survive" and "fight until you achieve freedom for yourself." I remembered those words often in difficult times, and especially on that day when my dog was killed and I lost the desire to live. With her words I tried to dispell the thoughts that I might die in Yaara, knowing full well that the chances of an orphan like me surviving were very slim.

I should mention that Yaw did pay a very heavy price for eating Nso Nyame Ye's meat. Within hours after the feast, he was experiencing severe pain through most of his bones. By evening his hands had stiffened and his elbows locked up so that he could not stretch his arms. It took weeks before his hands loosened up again. Even today, at about age 41, he gets periodic visits from that dreadful disease. I still tease him occasionally that he should settle things with Nso Nyame Ye's ghost in order to receive a complete healing.

After the death of Nso Nyame Ye a new spirit was born in me. The agony and grief I suffered from the loss of the dog generated a "couldn't care less" attitude in me. Nothing could scare me anymore. Beatings did not decrease, but my skin had gotten tough to such mundane things. I expected to be beaten without cause. Many mornings I was awakened on my torn mat by my uncle Yaw Boateng pouring cold water on me because I did not wake up early enough. I would be shaking with a wet chill while my uncle's own children were still snoring in their beds.

The clothes we had brought from Nepui were soon worn and torn. But our uncles were so poor that they could not buy us new clothes. As grown as we were, they did not mind seeing our private parts dangling about. After a few weeks, I had had enough of that sort of thing, so I complained that I needed to be properly clothed and that I was their true brother's son. For some reason, they heeded the request with haste, which still puzzles me. I don't know whether the mentioning of "their brother's son" did it or my tone of voice. Anyway, I got away with it and was not even beaten.

I had become quite tough and had learned to steal. Whenever I was not properly fed, I stole smoked meat from Uncle Yaw Boateng's wife. They complained about the missing meat, but I denied any knowledge of it. I never had a permanent place where I slept. I moved from place to place in the village, to any friend who accepted me and gave me a place to lay my head. I had no sleeping mat or pillow. At one point I begged for an animal hide as a mat.

It was rough going but I started to enjoy the village. Although I had lost Yaw as a friend and brother, I did develop friendships with other boys like Yaw Bui, who sometimes brought me roasted yam from his family's farm. He and I often walked to Buseima to play. I discovered how nice some of the Buseima people were. I had also mastered most of the code names for things, reducing some of my beatings. I even had a girl friend, although a senior boy scared me off once he started to like the girl. At Yaara, life was according to the survival of the fittest. To survive, you had to be strong and hard.

Yaw's health had started to deteriorate. His hair was falling out and his legs and hands were getting thinner and thinner. Any time I got an opportunity, I urged him to remember what Mom said about "staying alive." I believe it was my encouragement that did keep him alive. Sometimes I stole for him. He was always too gentle, and had completely given in to our uncles.

Although we were treated like dirt, I did not mind. I was very alive inside. I fought with the boys and lost a hundred times, but that was Yaara life. You beat some and some beat you. In fact, the elders used to organize wrestling matches for us. They stood and cheered even when some of us were bleeding. We used to pound one another until our noses bled. I seemed to have the weakest nose for the games. Once the boys knew that, they always went for my nose, getting blood all over my chest. Broken hands and broken legs were common at such events, but the elders had medicine to heal victims quickly. This is the way the young are groomed for war and for fights against other villages.

There was also fun at Yaara, particularly during grasscutter season, when the bush is burned to drive out the grasscutters and then the elders spear them. When an elder spears a grass-cutter he may announce it by yelling, "*Ukaa ndaa ne,*" (the animal possesses the spear). Or he might say, "*Darg buu,*" (his spear is accurate on an animal). At the sound of those words, all the youth who happen to hear them start running for the grass-cutter, shouting "*min to sie ba*" (I heard it and arrived first). The one who gets there first gets to carry the animal home.

After it is carefully singed and washed, the grasscutter is sent to the home of the elder who killed it. The elder will cut off the head for you. The head may be cooked and eaten or you may request three cents from the man, if you prefer money. Usually the elders didn't have three cents, so one was always wise to settle for the head. I enjoyed the grasscutter hunts and developed the ability to run in the bush like a deer. Many times I had to give some of my animals to other boys who were not as swift. Yaw, for example, never got any grasscutters to carry unless he was directly following the elder who happened to spear the animal.

Asimbo and his brother were more interested in hunting than farming. They went hunting and stayed in the wild for three months at a time before coming home with their cargo. Asimbo had the smallest farm at Yaara. He usually traded meat for yams or cassava. During the lean months, when food was scarce in the village, his wife was unable to bring food to grandpa Yaw Sumaa's house. At such times, Yaw Boateng, who had a fair sized farm and usually had food reserves, complained that he was bearing the burden of feeding the family.

Usually, when they found that food was getting scarce, they would pack up and go off hunting. During their absence, we were supposed to take care of the farms. Uncle Yaw Boateng's farm wasin the bush, about eight miles from the village. It was my duty to weed half of the farm and provide cassava for his wife and children while he was away. It was scary to walk those eight miles by myself each day in the jungle, but I had no choice.

One day I was privileged to be taken on one of the hunting expeditions. While we were in the jungle, I discovered an unknown side of my junior fathers. I came to realize that they possessed supernatural powers. Every morning before they left to hunt, they chanted and poured libations on their talisman. I didn't understand the reason for these rites until I was in the bush with them. They had supernatural powers to vanish from the scene when attacked by wild beasts, such as lions.

It was not long before I realized that all the hunters at Yaara possessed similar powers, and that they miraculously vanished or changed themselves into other objects when attacked by wild animals. Hunters often encouraged their boys to hang on to their coats when dangerous animals were sighted. A boy holding a hunter's coat will vanish with the hunter when a wild beast attacks. Amazing! Such incidents confounded me. How could human beings act like gods?

This Yaara village was indeed the dwelling place of the devil himself. Satanic powers were displayed constantly in the village. My brother and I had heard strange things about Yaara, but now we were experiencing them. These supernatural events were hard for us to comprehend. But such things were commonplace to the long-time inhabitants of Yaara.

The powers of the supernatural were not restricted to the male hunters. The women also possessed certain unusual powers that made one's hair stand up. There were the women snake callers and the women soothsayers. These were powerful women who danced on red hot coals to foretell the future. The snake callers were able to suck snake venom from snakebite victims. My uncle told me that three-quarters of the witch doctors in the village were female. "What a mighty village this village is!" I often remarked to my brother.

Yaara – A World of its Own

At some point, Yaw and I began to take pride in our village. We came to feel that the powers that were in Yaara could protect us from anything. True enough, our uncles could kill us if they chose, but putting aside that unpleasant fact, we believed that there was no force that could harm us.

Despite our feelings of security, the nights at Yaara were quite scary. It was a common thing to hear muffled voices behind trees in the night as one went to the bush to attend to nature's call. Even the elders often went out in pairs after dark. The witches appeared to lurk around everywhere at night. Many times the fires of the witches were seen flickering in the bushes or hopping from tree to tree. The witches had the ability to shrink the lights they made to the size of tennis balls and then momentarily blow them up to the size of a big TV satellite dish. Such displays of power were not fun for the young. The nights were often filled with nightmares.

The death of an elder often created a terrifying environment for the young people of the village. When an elder died, the entire village gathered together to celebrate the funeral. It appeared that even the cosmic world was present. There was a special dance called *Gangan,* which only those who were older than seventy were permitted to perform. The youth and children were not even allowed to watch *Gangan.* How our imaginations were inflamed on nights when the *Gangan* was danced! We knew the sound of a particular drum, known as *Bentarey,* that was used during the *Gangan* dance. As soon as it sounded, we went into our rooms and put on our sleeping gear. The sound of *Bentarey* sent chills down your spine. It was an eerie-looking drum.

Yaara would not be Yaara without these things. It was a world of its own. The residents were lords unto themselves and appeared to have immunity from any organized law of the outside world. For example, several hunting mishaps caused the loss of life. The dead were buried and the funerals celebrated, but never did a policeman pass by during my years there.

The only thing that kept the community together was the sense of belonging and the taboos. The taboos were law. You risked your finger being cut off if you deliberately ignored or broke a village taboo. You were considered lucky if you were only fined a few goats and chickens to purify the land after you had broken a taboo. Children were not exempt from these rules. Your dad or mom had to pay if you broke a taboo. If a person murdered deliberately, he or she would be sent to a certain place from which they could not return to the tribe for eight years. During our years at Yaara, my brother and I never knew this "certain place" nor did we ever see a killer return after eight years. The same law of excommunication also applied to anyone who defiled his mother or was involved in any other case of incest. Usually the males paid the price, even if the offense was started by a female. It was an unfair practice, but that was Yaara. A world of its own!

My late aunt, Nendomajime, wrapped in cowrie shells, who used to dance on hot coals.

Grandpa Yaw Sumaa, the one who sacrificed so many dogs to his idols.

9

The Escape from Yaara

MY BROTHER YAW AND I BOTH KNEW the laws of our land, the land of the Deg people. We knew that as boys we had to stay with our uncles. However, we also knew that if a close relative on the maternal side is ill or dies, fatherless children are permitted to visit their mother.

One time Mom visited Yaara to see us. Tradition did not permit her to stay at our uncles' home. She stayed with a casual acquaintance at the village. Although she was in Yaara for over a week, we saw her only three times. Our hours at the farm were deliberately prolonged so that we came home very late at night. It was heartbreaking to have our visits restricted so severely. We were not even around to say goodbye to Mom the day she left for home.

A few years after this visit, Mom became very sick and felt that she was dying. She pleaded with our uncles, through a messenger, to allow her sons to visit her before she passed away. She should have known better. The message was treated as a joke. We didn't go, and Mom didn't die. Our uncles exploited the incident to mean that Mom was out to create a divided attention in Yaw and me so that we would not be loyal to them. We were teased as "the boys whose mother fakes." It did not matter to our uncles that everyone who had seen our mom during her illness said it was a miracle that she did not die.

Unfortunately, the episode ended any chance that we could see her in the following years. Our uncles also used this incident as an excuse to increase the harshness of our labours. Sadly, my brother and I came to blame our mother for the injustice. We hoped that Mom would leave us alone in the future, so that our condition wouldn't worsen any more on account of her.

During this time, I began to make serious plans to escape from Yaara. I fantasized every night about being free and having enough to eat. I even thought of school and how nice it would be for me to have my own pen to hang on my shirt pocket. Dad had planned to send me to school at Bamboi before he died. But he did not have the money to buy me a pair of khaki shorts and the shirt that were required by the Bamboi Primary School Board, though he blamed the strapper in order to save face. There was a strong desire inside me to fulfill my father's dream and attend school.

I secretly told my friend, Yaw Bui, that someday, when I was grown up, I would come to Yaara driving a car. He was carrying yams at the time. He laughed so hard, he fell and broke all of his yams. I couldn't blame Yaw Bui for his reaction. After all, Yaara had a rather unpleasant history regarding motor vehicles. Shortly before my brother and I arrived at the village, a man from Brong Ahafo drove a tractor to Yaara in search of someone who could sell him a large number of yam seedlings. The engine of the tractor scared the villagers so much that everyone, including the elders, took cover. The men of the village later warned the tractor owner never to bring his noisy monster to the village again. That settled the case. Yaara never saw a tractor while I was there. So, mentioning that I would be driving a car to Yaara some day was quite amusing to my friend.

There was another reason for his laughter. It was only the white people who were said to have cars in the cities, and not the black people.

Then an incident occurred that strengthened my resolve to escape. My youngest brother, who was living with Mom at Jugboi, lost an eye while playing with a nail. The case was reported to our uncles. They said it was an unfortunate incident, but Yaw and I would not be permitted to visit our brother. Then they changed their minds and said that we could make the trip after they returned from a three-month hunt. After all, they would be returning with meat that we could take with us for our relatives at Jugboi. For some reason, Yaw and I believed them. At the end of the three months, when they returned with a lot of game, no one mentioned the trip to see our brother. When Yaw and I brought the matter up, they kept on deceiving us until it became obvious that they were simply making fun of us. For me, that was the straw that broke the camel's back.

Yaw always wept whenever I told him I was planning to escape. He thought I would be killed by a wild animal once I left the village, or captured and subjected to brutal punishment. Those were realistic fears but I knew that I had to leave Yaara. There was no future there, only unjustified beatings and harsh work demands. But Yaw's consent to my plans was very important to me. Finally I got his approval.

"Make sure that when you leave, they can never find you," he said. "Die somewhere else, so that they won't blame Mom for it." He could not stand to see me make a fool of myself or to bring harassment to our mom.

We discussed some of the things I needed for the journey, such as roasted yams and a bottle of water. He didn't think it was a good idea. He felt I would be caught if I stopped for food and rest at any time during my escape. "This is about a forty-mile journey," he said. "You need to do the trip in one day. Otherwise you are doomed and I will be as well."

I knew his instincts were right, but I argued that an escape would be impossible without an occasional stop for rest and food and water.

"Then don't go," he remarked. I saw his point. To train myself, I started to deliberately not drink for twenty-four hours. Also, instead of using the trail leading to our farm, I often went straight through the jungle, pushing vines and tall grass aside to practice for my escape. I did this barefooted for months. I was encouraged by the fact that not once did an African python or any other wild beast confront me during my training.

Finally, the big day came. I told Yaw I would leave at dawn the next morning, a Friday. On Fridays we were not required to wake up by six a.m. because it was a sacred day and a day of rest for the people. I figured it would be around noon or evening before they started to miss me, unless for some reason, I was required to go to the farm very early to perform a special chore. Whatever the case, I had decided to make my move by the second cock crow, at four a.m. Yaw cried and at the same time told me not to be afraid on the journey.

"Just keep going and keep close to the trail to Bamboi. Only make sure that you don't walk directly on the path. Keep a few yards away and listen for dangerous sounds to avoid any meeting or confrontation."

I couldn't sleep that night, and by the first cock crow, I was up, sitting on my animal skin mat and thinking about the trip. At the sound of the second cock crow, I was out of the room with only my shorts and a khaki shirt. A few dogs saw me, but, for some reason, they did not make too much racket. I thanked them and moved past them. At first, I walked on the trail until it was light enough to see objects at a distance. Then I hit the jungle so that no one could see me.

By noon, I had crossed the Black Volta River without any interference from the crocodiles. That was a major accomplishment. The coolness of the river refreshed me from the severe noonday sun. I also drank enough water before proceeding. I was moving as fast as I could in the bush, getting cuts on my hands and thighs from the thick grasses. By two in the afternoon, I was getting quite weak from a loss of blood. But there were other things to worry about. My blood could be leaving a trail for my uncles to follow. They were specialists in tracking down wounded animals.

As it happened, they didn't miss me until late that evening when I was needed for a chore. Yaw told me this years later, when it couldn't do me any good.

By six p.m. I had covered the forty-mile jungle expedition from Yaara to Bamboi. What a relief! But I knew the battle was just beginning. My escape meant a loss of face for my uncles. They would not tolerate that indefinitely. I walked three miles from Bamboi to my mother's village. I got to Jugboi and saw Mom sitting at her open fire stirring T-Z. I was choked with emotion. I moved close to her and greeted her. She was at a loss for words. She quickly finished her T-Z and gave me a bowl of it. My, it tasted good! After that, she wanted to hear about what had happened. I related my story and how I had escaped and that I was not going back.

"No, no, no!" she said. "You are going back tomorrow. I am taking you myself." She was terrified because I had done such an abominable thing. "Do you want them to come and kill me; is that what you want?" She was close to panic.

She broke down and wept seeing the sores on me and how lean I had become. She would have liked to keep me. But tradition would not allow that. She called some cousins and told them of my arrival, hoping they would help keep me or give her some advice. They concluded that it was a bad thing that I had done and that I should go back. During the discussion, they mentioned that they were taking a nephew of theirs to Bamboi primary school the following day. I told Mom I would like to go to school. This announcement did nothing for her state of mind. She was outraged and felt I didn't know the implications and possible consequences of my actions.

On the following day I followed my cousins to Bamboi primary school, hoping I could get admitted. The cousins pretended they didn't see me. Their attitude stirred in me at the thought of being sent back to Yaara to face my uncles. I knew my life would end quickly if that happened. Even Yaw's life depended on the success of this escape. I stood on the compound of the Bamboi primary school and stared at the trees. All sorts of thoughts chased through my mind.

My two adult cousins left the school and started back to Jugboi without speaking a word to me. I felt abandoned and alone. I couldn't return to my mother's house. Her relatives would pressure her to send me back to Yaara. Where do I go from here? I wondered. After all the excitement of making it from Yaara, no one was prepared to keep me. I knew Mom would have loved to keep me. After all, I was her son. But I also knew the consequences of such an action, not only from my uncles at Yaara but from the Deg tribe in general. I concluded that I was not going back to Yaara. I would rather drown myself in the river than go back.

I was still standing in the school compound when a bell sounded and the children came out to play. They were all nicely dressed and tidy. They were happy looking. The girls were jumping and playing *Ampey*; the boys were chasing each other. I envied them and blamed my dad for dying and depriving me of such a life. It was comforting to watch them. Although I could not join them, I participated on my own at a distance. I laughed and pretended I was being chased. Then the bell sounded again and within a few minutes everyone had gone inside to their classes. I was alone again.

Then, like a revelation, a thought crossed my mind to look for Papa Kofi Kinto. Papa Kofi Kinto lived in Bamboi. He used to visit Dad in Nepui. The only problem was that he was a drunkard. People always made fun of him. Although Dad did not drink, Kofi Kinto appeared to enjoy spending time in our home when we were little kids. He would walk the seven miles from Bamboi to Nepui just for a visit with Dad, and often he would stay for supper. I was grown now, and I wondered whether he would recognize me when. Anyhow, this was the only real option left: to see Papa Kofi Kinto and to tell him of my problem.

I found him lying on the veranda of his home. He was drunk but he still recognized me. He also saw the sores and cuts on my body and shouted, "What has happened to Kwame Sohn's children? For goodness sake, tell me what has happened to you." I related my story of all the troubles at Yaara and how I had escaped. I told him my mom was afraid to let me stay and wanted me to go back.

"I understand your mom's point of view," he said. She can't keep you, but I can." I told him I had come to him because I wanted to go to school. It so happened that about this time the government of Ghana was urging people to send their children to school. Kofi Kinto felt I was doing well for taking the initiative on my own to comply with the government orders to be enrolled in school.

"I will look after you," he said. I mentioned that my main concern was that my uncles would soon be looking for me and would surely trace me to Bamboi. "Don't worry," he said. "I will take care of that when the time comes. Go to school and write your name."

Though Kofi Kinto was drunk and partially incoherent, I was so taken by his interest in me that I walked to the school that afternoon and actually had my name registered in the Bamboi Local Council Primary School. That evening I walked the three miles back to Jugboi with great exuberance and told my mom that I had registered at school and that Papa Kofi Kinto was prepared to look after me. At the mention of Kofi Kinto looking after me, Mom broke into gales of uninhibited laughter.

"Bless Kofi Kinto's heart," she said. "Son, Kofi Kinto has no penny to his name. He is a drunkard and his wife begs for food to look after their own children."

That didn't change my feelings. I told her I was taking Papa Kofi Kinto at his word and that I planned to stay with grandma Yobo at Jugboi and walk the three miles to school every morning. Apparently grandma Yobo was quite upset for the way I was being tossed about and had chastised Mom for "almost running away from her son in need." Although it was not lawful for her to keep me, she said that she was simply performing a job for Kofi Kinto. That was her technical explanation. That night, grandma Yobo spread some of her rags on the floor for me in the corner of her shack, and I slept like a log. I knew that once grandma had made up her mind to have me, my uncles from Yaara would have a tough time to move me from Jugboi.

There were about five boys from Jugboi who walked to Bamboi school, so I joined them. We ate breakfast at six a.m. and did not eat again until we returned home at six p.m. During the afternoon break, I often went to Papa Kofi Kinto's house. He gave me lots of encouragement but nothing to eat. Those were hard days, especially having to walk the three miles back to Jugboi after school. But Yaara had trained me for this sort of life. The other students struggled on the way home. Although I was quite lean and hungry, I would often trot or skip along, to their amazement. They thought I got fed at Kofi

Kinto's place during noon hours.

I took my lessons seriously and carried sticks home every day and counted them. In fact we used to call them "counters." The teachers were good instructors. They gave us lashes when they felt we needed them. Otherwise, they spent time with us, teaching us as best they could. All the teachers, of course, were from the south, and did not speak Deg. They were considered foreigners. The locals respected them, however. Every afternoon during break we went to fetch water for their wives. We also carried twelve fence posts each from Jugboi every other week to repair the school garden or to fix one of the teacher's gardens. At other times, they demanded eggs or yams, if one was unable to bring fence posts.

For some reason my uncles waited for a whole year before coming to Bamboi in an effort to get me back to Yaara. Our little class was sitting under a tree learning the alphabet when a senior student ran to our teacher and said that my uncles had come to see me and the headteacher wanted me at the office. It was as if my whole world was crumbling again.

I didn't take any chances. I ran to Papa Kofi Kinto's house, where I found him half sober. He got up, took the old exercise book he always carried, although he could not read, and grabbed his *Wing Sunk,* an old ball point pen that could no longer write. *Ya kaa* (Let's go), he said. I followed him to the office and before the headteacher could say a word, he reminded the headteacher that the district council of Bole was in the process of forcing all parents to let their children go to school and that he hoped the teacher was aware of that. The teacher replied that he was aware.

"Well, these men you see here have come to remove Kwabena from school and take him back to the jungle at Yaara," Kofi Kinto said.

The teacher, of course, was stunned and asked my uncles if Kofi Kinto's accusation was true. They lied and said that a school was starting at Yaara and that they felt I should come and attend that school since it would be easier for them to care for me. Of course, I knew they were lying and so did Kofi Kinto. He told the teacher that my uncles were lying and that if they should persist in trying to take me to Yaara, he would have them arrested immediately. The word "police" was always sufficient to scare our people, especially those from remote areas like Yaara. I am not sure whether Kofi Kinto meant what he said, but my uncles took him seriously. They left the office to start their forty-mile journey back to Yaara through the jungle. Kofi Kinto and the teacher laughed when they left.

The teachers took special interest in me after that episode, and did their best to help me read and write. I was bigger than most of the students and quite mature, so I sometimes felt shy to be in class one with the little children. I was provided with a special table and chair, since my legs could not fit under the tiny tables of class one. I worked hard at my studies at home. Grandma enjoyed seeing me do what I wanted to do. I also paid some of the senior boys in the school to give me extra help in the afternoons. They demanded wild fruit and dried fish in exchange for their tutoring. So, on weekends, I fished and hunted for *Kantalaga,* a wild fruit valued by the youth in those days.

Within a few months, the class one teacher told the headteacher he felt I could handle the work in class two. So I was promoted, along with one other boy. I was in class two for only two weeks, when that teacher said that I should be sent to class three. So, within a few weeks, I was promoted twice.

Class three, however, was quite a challenge. Again, I relied on my mates for extra teaching. This time, I paid my tutors by doing the chores that had been assigned to them by the school, such as weeding the teachers' gardens or fetching water for their wives. On some days, I had to fetch seven buckets of water from the river in a single afternoon. Fortunately, it wasn't long until I caught up with my classmates and could cut down on the tutorials. At the end of the year, when the exam results were released, I was third in the class.

A the end of the year, all the townspeople were invited to the school to hear the exam results. Parents came to congratulate their children. This occasion was always a bit sad for me, as there were no relatives to see me. My mother always claimed to be too busy with her groundnut farm. She never wanted to be accused of violating any cultural principles, so she stayed away from me as much as she could. Although she used her farm as an excuse for not getting involved with my life, I was aware that the real reason was her fear of what people might say, especially my cousins at Jugboi. However, the people of Bamboi were very kind. Whenever my name was mentioned for an honoured position in the exam results, they applauded as enthusiastically as they would for their own children.

Yaw Boateng, my father's junior brother whom I stayed with in Yaara after the death of my father. He is now called Abraham.

Kofi Asimbo (right), my father's other junior brother whom my brother Joseph stayed with in Yaara. At the left is Yonko, who was a revered hunter.

(See Chapter 8)

10

Homeless

IT TOOK A LONG TIME FOR ME to accept that I was free from the grip of my uncles at Yaara. I was always suspicious that someday they might still come and steal me away. Many nights I dreamed about swimming across a crocodile-infested river, with chains and ropes tied to my hands and legs. I had nightmare after nightmare. Even at school, any time I saw a stranger, I was worried that he might be an agent of my uncles. By the time I got to class four, or P4 as they called it, I began to accept that my uncles had taken Kofi Kinto's words about the police seriously. No surprise attempt was made to catch me and take me back to Yaara. Even my mother started to pass on little bits of information to me whenever she heard of someone coming from Yaara to Bamboi.

"As far as I can tell," she relayed to me through a woman traveller, "you have been forgotten in Yaara, so don't be afraid in Bamboi."

My reading and writing improved tremendously. With help from a friend, Noah, I frequently wrote letters to my brother in

Yaara. I never mailed them, fearing that mail from me might generate problems for Yaw. I was also unsure of who would read them, since there were only a few children from Yaara who attended school at Buseima, the village to the northwest of Yaara. I had piles of unmailed letters to my brother.

In spite of this limitation and my anxiety, I liked Bamboi and the school. School became my reality. I was proud of being in school and enjoyed it thoroughly. I even looked forward to the daily six miles from Jugboi to Bamboi and back. I developed many friendships at Bamboi and spent some of my afternoons with my new friends. We played soccer and other games.

After a while, I began to realize that Kofi Kinto was uncomfortable with having me visit him. He was embarrassed because he couldn't offer me any food. To remedy the situation, I stopped going to his place. It didn't bother him.

When I was in P4, a girl from Jugboi joined our little group in walking to school and back. For some reason, we disliked each other. We fought almost every day. Her grandma complained bitterly to my grandma Yobo that I should be reprimanded for my continual harassment of her granddaughter. But grandma Yobo was no pushover. You could get somewhere with her by using diplomacy, but never by threats. She responded that the girl should be pulled out of school. In her opinion, it was wrong to subject a girl to walking three miles twice each day. Besides, my grandma continued, the girl would not get far in school. She would get pregnant and drop out. So, why waste the girl's time and energy with all that walk

A few weeks after this altercation, I attacked the poor girl in a particularly violent, ugly manner. I broke her nose. The entire front of her school uniform was covered with blood. Her grandmother threatened to send me to the local police station, but the elders advised her not to take "a child of the Degs to the hands of foreigners." The police at Bamboi were all from the south, as were our teachers. The townspeople did not like them much. In the evening, the matter was brought to my grandma at Jugboi.

"I believe he was provoked enough to lash out in this brutal manner," was her response. However, my mother advised that they should send me to stay with a relative at Bamboi, to get me away from the girl. That ended my stay with grandma Yobo. The next day, I took my counter sticks, my catapult, and my after-school pants – in other words, my only belongings – and left Jugboi for Bamboi.

Moving to Bamboi was not difficult, since I already had friends there. I soon realized that my relative at Bamboi, Yaw Konyini, was a very, very poor man. He did not have enough food. But that was hardly a unique situation.

"I have seen his kind before," I said to myself. "As long as he does not beat me unnecessarily, I will be fine." Bamboi was bigger and more modern than Yaara. A main road passed right through town and you could frequently see large trucks on their way to Upper Volta. I figured that in a town like Bamboi, I could always survive.

I loved to fish. There was a major river in Bamboi that quickly caught my attention. A friend helped me to acquire a fishing line and I started fishing with a group of boys. Rarely did I go come back empty-handed from that river. It was as if the river loved me. Even when my friends failed to catch fish, I would still hook two or three. We fished every day after school.

I was a good boy at the beginning of those days, for I took all my fish home to the wife of Yaw Konyini, hoping I might be given food as a result. Sometimes I was, but many times they gave me no food at all. After the evening meal, Yaw Konyini would ask, "Oh, haven't you eaten?" He knew full well that his wife had not left me any food. I quickly developed the habit of roasting a fish myself and eating before I took the remaining fish to Yaw Konyini's house. Then friend's mother, who sold food at the roadside, said she wanted to buy my fish if I was willing to sell them. Boy, was I willing! I often sold most of my fish and took only one home. I used the money to buy porridge and rice during the afternoon break at school.

It wasn't long before Yaw Konyini reported me to my mother, saying that I was a good fisherman but a bad boy, since I didn't bring my catch home. My relative also chastised me verbally for this bad behaviour. I was deeply angered by this development and vowed to stay away from him. I started sleeping at the homes of some of my friends. Wherever I was accepted, I made it my home for that day.

I virtually had no home. It was sad, but I didn't let the situation overwhelm me. In spite of my troubles, my school work was always first class. I sat on people's verandas after sundown and did my assignments before they took their kerosene lanterns inside . Sometimes I was even given food. A few people got into the habit of keeping their leftovers for "Abena Fulamuso's boy," as they used to call me. Sometimes, when I was visiting the home of a very kind family, they would apologize for not having any food they could share with me that night. I moved from house to house. There were few houses at Bamboi that I didn't sleep in. As long as there were boys in any house, I made friends with them, so I could share the comforts of their home.

11

Lawlessness

I LOOK BACK ON MY YEARS IN Primary 5 and 6 with shame and remorse. They were years of lawlessness. In those days, I tried to rule the world. By the time I was in the middle of Primary 5, I was leading two local youth gangs at Bamboi.

Around this time, my mother's "brother," as we Degs put it, (a first cousin in western terms) who had been sick for several years and had left the Deg land to look for a cure from his unknown disease, returned to the village of Teselima, about ten miles from Bamboi. He was cured of the disease and was now visiting relatives to show them his new healthy condition. He was a charming man. He came to Bamboi to visit the relative that I had lived with for a brief time. They discussed me and I was summoned.

When I arrived, my mother's "brother" introduced himself and told me he had heard of all the troubles I had gone through. He said he regretted the hard life I had been forced to endure, and wanted to change things. Now that he was back with his tribe to stay, I should consider him as a father and come to him any time I wanted. He warned me that he had a rather large farm and that I would have to work hard during the holidays. I asked him if the work would interfere with my schooling.

"Not at all," he replied. "As a matter of fact, two of my own girls and two of my boys are in school. The government has said it is the thing to do these days." He smiled. He was nicely dressed and wore a beautiful hat. He put his hands in his pocket and brought out two shillings for me. "You are free to go now," he said. This was in 1967 when two shillings was big money. For me, anyway! *Who would be so foolish as to refuse to stay with this handsome, kind man?* I thought. I told him that if he is going to be a father to me, he should know that I would try hard to be a good son.

"A deal!" he said.

We immediately struck up an arrangement. I made peace with the relative I had lived with initially in Bamboi and agreed to move back in with him. My new father promised to send food to Bamboi so that I would have enough to eat. When school was not in session, I was to live with him in Teselima.

As soon as he left, I headed to Jugboi with my two shillings to show Mom and grandma. I was so excited when I saw my mom. And, for the first time in quite a while, she appeared very happy to see me. I discovered that my new father from Teselima had already been at Jugboi and had discussed my situation with Mom. She assured me that he was the best of all her relatives. He was hard working and had a big farm with plenty of cattle. She also said that her brother had many boys and girls at home. I couldn't wait till the term was over.

Finally, the term came to an end, and I was off to Teselima. My uncles at Yaara had released Yaw to come and say hello to this "new" relative and had instructed him to try to persuade me to come back to Yaara. So, the very first time I got to Teselima, Yaw was there! What joy that was to be able to talk with him freely and work with him, side by side – just like we had done as small boys. After a month's stay, a message came from Yaara that Yaw should return. He tried his best to take me along. I refused. He returned to his village alone and weeping. I wasn't afraid of my uncles in Yaara anymore, now that I had this new uncle to be my father. My time in Teselima went very well. I loved my new brothers and sisters and they loved me as well. There was plenty of food to eat. In fact, the dogs even got their fill each night. I couldn't believe it!

My new father was a fine and generous man. But there was a dark side to his character. In the process of finding a cure for his disease, he had become friends with many fetish priests, healers and rain callers. Witchcraft became a very important part of his life and his home contained several idols. It did not take long after his return to Teselima, for the village to realize that he was a force to be reckoned with. In fact, his own mother and sister feared his spiritual power. For me, his was the ideal home. Finally I had found someone with plenty of food and wealth and also spiritual powers to look after me.

People with spiritual powers could kill, heal, or cast far-reaching spells on people. Sometimes they were hired to destroy lives by spiritual power. The potential victim could be hundreds of miles away. All the fetish priest needed was the person's name. The fetish priest would sit in his shrine and chant and pour libations as he repeated the name. Usually that individual was dead within three days.

At our farm, thieves quickly took note and stayed away. Some people who stole from our farm were seized by a compulsion to return the stolen materials and confess. Other potential thieves found themselves suddenly rendered immobile as they tried to sneak off with their booty. It was always fun for us to catch such immobilized people. My new father wielded such incredible powers that I came to regard him as a god. I respected and trusted him as such. It wasn't long until he started showing me how the powers of darkness operated in the unseen world. I felt as if Yaara had followed me to Teselima, except this time I was emboldened by my encounter with witchcraft.

My heart became stubborn and hard. I became a ruthless young man in the area. I decided to merge my two gangs in Bamboi. During the school term we did all kinds of horrible things. I master-minded the burning of properties. We were occasionally hired by people to harass their enemies. Stoning animals was a daily routine. We also threw stones at men, women, girls, boys, and children just for mere satisfaction. I caused havoc wherever I went. I felt that no one could touch me, knowing that my home was spiritually fortified.

When the two gangs merged, we gave it the name "the Landary Boys." I am unsure why we chose this name or what it meant to us at the time, but the name was enough to scare any youth at Bamboi. The local police at Bamboi issued several warnings to us, but secretly feared our group. We were lords of the town. My nickname was Cob; my second ringleader was nicknamed Donbibin; the third one was Tika, and the fourth was Jumper. We were ruthless. One example will suffice. A deaf and mute man called Kojo Amumu lived in a half-collapsed building. For several nights we went in and whipped him severely without any provocation.

Not only were we brutal, we were also professional thieves. The Ewe tribe that resided at the bank of the river consisted of fishermen. They harvested fish, smoked them, and took them down south to sell. We often stole large numbers of fish from the Ewe, denying some people in the tribe their livelihood. We were never caught stealing. Perhaps people simply ignored us for the sake of peace.

The gang members were all ahead of me in school. They were in middle school. Things became worse when I also moved to middle school, form one. Now that we were in the same school, it was easier to coordinate our vicious activities. People called me dangerous wherever I went. Mom feared me and so did many of my relatives. Though we were a dangerous gang at night, we remained top students in our academic work during the day.

Our deeds were brutal and dangerous. Visitors in town had to respect us or leave quickly. Day after day, reports of our bad deeds poured into our relatives' homes. People told of cases of dogs being stoned; others reported swollen eyes because they were pelted with stones. We became the scourge of our town so that many of the elders felt they needed to do something about us.

But I knew that no one could seriously interfere with me. The boys all knew that any threat to us would be counteracted by the spiritual powers of my father. Therefore, we advanced daily in mischief and treachery. We practiced and trained ourselves so that we were always in top shape both for our misdeeds and for escape from the scene of the crime before the police could arrive.

My mother's "brother" from Teselima, who took me in as a son and amazed me with his spiritual powers.

Part Three: A New Life

12

The Mystery

ONE NIGHT, AS THE LANDARY BOYS were looking for trouble, we spotted a little crowd gathered at the village square. We decided we would disperse the group with stones. We drew near the crowd and found an old man in the middle. The words of this old man caught me off guard.

He was telling the group about Yesu, a man he said was God's direct son who had come down from heaven to help humanity. I had never heard such strange talk! The man had heard about Yesu from a friend of his who was working in the gold mines in ,in the southern part of Ghana. His friend was passing on information about Yesu that had been told to him by a visitor to the mines.

This Yesu is what every human needed to make his or her life complete, the friend had told him. He mentioned that a vacuum existed in the heart of every human being and that *Korowii* (the God Almighty) specifically reserved this vacuum for his son Yesu to fill. Any attempts to fill the vacuum with earthly things like pleasure, money, children, wives, husbands, and so on, would never succeed.

According to the old man, his friend told him that many people were unhappy because they have not permitted Yesu to take his lawful place in their hearts. Such people were living dangerously, because at death their souls would not be given a good home in the world beyond. When, however, Yesu fills the vacuum, people change for the good. The old man continued to speak, saying that, according to his friend, even younger people have this vacuum, which makes them restless until it is filled by Yesu.

The gang members were still waiting for me to give the signal for them to attack. For some reason, I could not give the order.

"What strange statements these are," I said to myself. It was obvious that the old man partly believed this strange stuff his friend had told him. I ordered my gang not to throw stones. The man spoke for a little while longer and then retired to his hut.

When I went to bed that night, I couldn't sleep. I thought about the man's words. *Do I really have an empty space in my heart? Who is this Yesu, anyway? Could he really give me joy every day as the man had said? And how do you get him to fill the vacuum in your heart? Would he fill my vacuum if he knew how bad I really was?* There were so many questions going through my mind that I tossed on my mat from side to side and could not fall asleep.

Before sunrise, I went to the old man and woke him up. He was terrified. I apologized to him for coming so early. He didn't speak a word, perhaps thinking or hoping he was dreaming. I explained that I had come to ask his opinion on whether he felt that Yesu would want to fill my vacuum. And could he help me find the town in which this Yesu lived. The man got even more puzzled and scared when he heard my questions. He gently tried to coax me to leave his room. I wouldn't leave. Unable to get rid of me, he sat down and repeated the story as he had heard it from his friend.

"Yesu," he said, "is an invisible man and does not live in any village."

"But how does he fill these vacuums in people's hearts?"

"You just ask Yesu and he hears, according to my friend."

After living in Yaara and Teselima, and knowing how one could be close to spirits and actually talk to them and have them reply without necessarily seeing them, I quickly understood that Yesu was a spirit. So, I simply spoke directly to him and said that I wanted my vacuum filled by him, if he didn't mind. I was waiting to hear his reply, as would have happened with the spirits at Yaara, but, instead, something happened that I cannot possibly describe clearly.

On the wall of this man's hut, a miracle occurred. It appeared as if a hand were holding some wide slate boards strung together. There was an opening and the hand was below the opening. The hand would pull the string and one of the slate boards slid into the opening so that I could see it clearly and brightly. Each of the slates contained some bad deed that I had done in the past shown like a movie. I saw myself clubbing a dog to death. Then that slate would be pulled down and another scene would roll past, showing exact details of my life.

I was so frightened that I began to beg and plead with the old man to stop showing me these scenes. I thought it was he who was showing me my past life. I promised him that I would not do these things any more. By this time, the old man had concluded that I had become mentally deranged. He didn't know what was going on. The pictures were clear and bright to me, but he saw nothing. I cannot recall how long this phenomenon lasted, but it was long enough to make me break down completely. I was sweating and exhausted after I regained full consciousness. I reached out and touched the wall where the pictures had appeared to me and pushed at it to make sure there was no hole in the wall.

I started to sob uncontrollably, again sending fear through the poor old man. He was terrified that I was going to get him involved in a spiritual confrontation with my fetish priest father. It was most amazing to me to find myself sobbing and sobbing. The last time I remembered crying was at Yaara, when my dog was pulled away from me and butchered as a sacrifice. Since then, I had become hardened and callous, a ruthless criminal. I could torture animals or beat up a helpless invalid without feeling anything.

But, here I was sobbing! The phenomena I had seen on the wall left its impact on my mind. Any time I thought of a dying dog or a deed of cruelty now, tears would roll down my cheeks as if fed by a fountain. I was sure that this Yesu had done something to my very core. The very thing that makes me a human had been touched.

When I left the man's room, I looked for my two gang ring leaders. When they saw me sobbing, they were dismayed. They could not believe their eyes. They had always relied on me as a tough leader, and here I was sobbing like a little girl. I told them I was no longer going to lead the Landary Boys. Stunned, they demanded to know the reason for my crying. I explained that the message we had heard from the old man the night before had changed me.

They began to charge toward the house of the old man to take revenge, but I stopped them. I convinced them that he was just a messenger. I said that Yesu was the one responsible. He had filled my vacuum. I said that Yesu didn't like the life I was living, so when he filled my vacuum he made me see how bad our activities had been. It wasn't long before they too asked Yesu if he would fill their vacuums. They spoke to Yesu just as

I had done. Not surprisingly, they were soon joining me in my crying and sobbing.

Within the next two days even the dogs at Bamboi knew that something had happened to me and my group. There was calm in the village. We didn't want to be identified as the "Landary Boys" any longer. What had happened to us was so real that we began to amend our behaviour. We found ways of helping people we had stolen from in the past. The deaf and mute man became our friend. We no longer assaulted him. The second evening after our conversion, we sat with him and made awkward signs in our desperate attempt to assure him that he was now our friend and that we would not hurt him any more. We told him that if ever he needed anything, he should tell us, and if somebody ever hurt him, he should let us know.

Indeed, Yesu had changed us. We were never to be the same again. When the fatigue caused by this whole experience left me, I felt a sense of joy. This joy was different from the feeling I used to have when supervising the stoning of dogs. It was a good joy. I felt so good inside myself that I spontaneously would leap like a little calf and smile to myself. It was as if I were learning to live anew.

The joy was so great, I decided to let my mom and family know. To my surprise, both my mom and my new father responded in a cold manner to the changes in me. Apparently, they thought that my involvement in the gang world had led me to a higher spiritual power that could be hostile to the ones they knew.

I was thoroughly amazed by their reactions. During my days of lawlessness, no one had spoken a word about the possibility of something being wrong with me. Now that I was changed for the good, they believed that I was "sick." I tried particularly hard to convince my mom that what had happened to me was a cause for rejoicing. I told her that Yesu had taken his place in my vacuum and that it made me feel wonderful. She remained cool on the subject.

It became obvious that my faith would face many challenges. My new father complained bitterly that since I had asked Yesu into my heart, his demonic powers had abandoned him. He could neither heal nor cast spells. This man, who had been so kind to me, began to regard me as a threat. He was convinced that I had connected with a strong spiritual force for the purpose of overwhelming his powers. For me, the reality of Yesu and his power to save and set us free began here. As immature as my faith was, my new father recognized a powerful spiritual force inside me.

The conflict at home grew greater as most of the sons and daughters of my new father gave their lives to Yesu after seeing the changes in me. At this time, my new father married his third wife, a Muslim woman who hated me intensely. The happiness I had had in living in Teselima faded rapidly. I became unwanted.

After I was chased away from home I received a bit of money from my poor relative in Bamboi. With this I was able to get on a truck that took me to Tamale, the capital of the Northern Region. Thus began the most difficult time of my life. Without family or relatives, I had to live like a street urchin, scrounging for food with the other orphans and widows.

But physical survival was not the biggest problem. I began to feel that I was being disobedient to my family for allowing Yesu to fill my vacuum. Perhaps I should return home and learn the fetish priest's arts. One thought sustained me through these times of confusion. Yesu had given me a complete change of heart. Although I was dirty and poor on the outside, I knew that Yesu had kept me clean inside. Every bit of cruelty had left me and been replaced by a love and respect for all people.

One of the people I was scrounging food from was the principal of a secondary school in Tamale, a devoted Muslim man who was kind in every way. His name was Mr. Gbedamoshi. One day, he met me and inquired why I was so lean, poor and wretched. I related all of my problems to him and then talked about my faith in Yesu. The principal mentioned that he had a staff member in his school who was a very devout Christian. He talked well about this Mr. C.K. Konadu and connected me to him. I will never forget Mr. Konadu's hug the first time I met him. He embraced me warmly and called me his "brother" even though I was so dirty and neglected.

"Indeed, this is a Yesu person," I whispered to myself, for no one had ever given me such a warm hug in all my life. My eyes filled with tears as he repeated that I was his brother in Yesu.

13

Mr. C.K. Konadu

CHARLES KWESI KONADU proved to be a wonderful saint of God. After my meeting with the Muslim principal, Mr. Konadu took me in as if I were his own son. He was unmarried then, and had to cook his own meals as well as prepare his lessons. Yet, he spent time with me and explained the Scriptures to me. It was through him that I came to truly understand Yesu. He read the Bible to me and took me to prayer meetings. He was the patron of the Scripture Union in the secondary school.

In fact, he loved the Lord and served Him so fervently on campus that the students nicknamed him "Bible water." Some students claimed that Mr. Konadu ate pages from the Bible. Others said he washed the back cover of his Bible, making sure that the water dripped into a cup. He would then drink that water with his evening meal. Of course, these stories were not true, except that Mr. Konadu did, indeed, feed his soul every day with God's word. He prayed and taught me how to pray. He would drive me on his motorbike to all-night prayer meetings. I wish that there were a lot more C.K. Konadus in the world. Here was a man who was not related to me in any way, yet, he poured his love on me unconditionally.

For me it was like heaven. I enjoyed our prayer times and Bible studies. I found myself identifying with the apostle Paul and the difficult times he went through because of Jesus. I used to admire Mr. Konadu's Bible and carefully studied the parts he had underlined. I did not own my own Bible then.

Mr. Konadu's interest in me extended beyond my spiritual growth. He was interested in everything that I did and encouraged me to study hard at school. I had enrolled in the secondary school where he taught. Mr. Konadu became my math teacher there. Tamale Secondary had well over a thousand students then, from all parts of the country. Mr. Konadu loved all of his students, but because of my situation, I felt that he always gave me special attention.

I wanted to know more about Yesu. I began to talk to Yesu about my folks at home. All bitterness had left me. I had good thoughts, even about my uncles at Yaara and wished to see them again.

Mr. Konadu quickly recognized that I could run. He encouraged my interest in athletics. He used to drive his motorbike at a low speed and I would run behind him. It was unorthodox training, but it worked. I became one of the top athletes in the school. I participated in almost every event until Mr. Konadu advised me to specialize in the 800 metres. I soon became good at this race. However, there was a member of the senior class at the school named Martin Kuiremi. He was an exceptional runner. All the long-distance events were his specialty, but the 800 metres, and 5000 metres were his favourites. He seemed to be unbeatable.

In 1973 we had what they used to call "inter-schools sports competitions" at a town in the Upper Region called Bawku. On the morning of our departure for the competitions, Mr. Konadu encouraged me.

"You can outrun Martin in the 800 metres." I gave him a puzzled look. "Yes," he continued, "you are fast and you have had good training. Win the 800 metres for your old Papa Konadu."

"How can I beat Martin?" I asked myself.

We left for Bawku, where I was able to meet the top athletes who were contending in the games. It was through these inter-schools competitions that the athletes were selected to compete in international events. So, everyone at Bawku had a very serious and intense attitude. The games at Bawku started very well. I was on the team that ran the 4 x 400 metres relay and we took first in that race.

The 800 metres was the last event, and Tamale Secondary School was tied with Navrongo Secondary for first place at this point. If Martin or I could win, our school would be first overall; otherwise Navrongo Secondary would go home with the coveted first place and the shining trophy. A cloud of tension formed. Schools that produced good athletes received generous grants from the government, which was anxious to make a good showing in Commonwealth Games and other international competitions. The "big race" was to be run on a Friday.

On Thursday night, the principal and teachers of our school summoned Martin and me to a special meeting. They told us that, "the future viability of the Tamale Secondary School in track and field depends on winning tomorrow's race." Apparently, the school was in need of a government grant. We were promised many things, if only we won the 800 metres. The two competitors from the Navrongo School were very good runners and we had heard all kinds of stories about their records. That night, several students served as security guards, standing outside the rooms where Martin and I slept. The competition had become so fierce that we feared that some overzealous Navrongo supporters might try to arrange for their school's primary competitors to be running with injuries. I woke up on Friday morning annoyed that I was a runner. The tension had mounted to a terrible pitch.

It was very hot and dry at Bawku. In those days I ran all my events bare-footed. The track at Bawku was a gravel track, which was not pleasant for my feet. Martin had been quite confident of winning the race until he saw one of the Navrongo boys do a warm-up lap around the field. Then he was as scared as I was, and started to argue with the teachers that they were putting unfair pressure on us.

At 1:30, I decided to do a warm-up and get ready for the race, which was scheduled for 2:30. I wanted to prove to that Navrongo boy that he would meet his match in an hour's time. Half way around the track my nose started to bleed profusely. I stopped and a Red Cross worker quickly escorted me to a doctor. Our teachers crossed the field and broke into the pavilion where I was being treated, cursing at the sun and heat.

"Bawku is not a good place for competitions. It is too dry," one of them said. "We should boycott this 800-metre event, if Kwabena Mensah doesn't recover from his bleeding," another joined in. The Red Cross doctor soon discharged me and told me to relax.

"How can anyone relax in this atmosphere?" I responded.

I was developing a headache and was very tense. Suddenly I thought, *I haven't told Yesu about this. He loves me and I bet he knows I am filled with fear and anxiety right now.* There were some tall flowers between the Bawku Secondary School and the track and field area. I went there and spoke to Yesu, telling him I was scared of the 800-metre race. There was a small patch of calm inside me as I walked out of the bushes. I heard our names announced over the loudspeaker. We were twelve competitors in total, two from each school. Martin and I wore red shorts and T-shirts. The principal came over with his entourage of teachers to give us advice on how to win.

"Run fast," he said. After a litany of similar insights, the advisors finally departed. Martin turned to me and said, "If they know all these things, why are they not running themselves?" As we took to our lanes, I experienced a sensation of complete calm. I felt that even if I finished last, I would do it with dignity.

The starting pistol fired and we were off. Hundreds of people had come to watch. There was cheering and yelling as we completed the first lap. Martin moved into second position behind a Navrongo boy, and I moved behind him into third spot. Then, the second Navrongo boy moved to first place, putting me fourth. Then Martin increased his speed and took the lead. I struggled to the third position. Martin and one of the Navrongo boys pulled ahead, leaving a few feet between them and the rest of us. I quickly moved very close behind the Navrongo boy.

Martin was running in the first lane, which is the best lane. Running in the second or third lane means you cover more distance. So all of us tried to stay on the inner lane as much as possible, except for passing. I was glad to see Martin in first place. *If he can just maintain that to the finish it will all be ours*, I thought. But then the Navrongo boy behind Martin appeared to be conserving energy to beat Martin on the last stretch. I could tell this by the way he was calmly following Martin. I was able to pull up behind Martin and, although I had to use the second lane to get to second place, I still felt strong.

I remembered Mr. Konadu's words: "You can beat Martin; you're fast and have had good training." I gave Martin a signal to let him know that it was me behind him. Sweat was pouring down his neck and back. He gave me a sign to keep up. *Maybe I* can *beat him*, I thought.

I shot ahead and passed Martin. There was a big roar all over the field for what the crowd regarded as an act of impudence. By this time we were on the last stretch of 110 metres. I gave every bit of energy left in me. I left the others several metres behind and, to the amazement of everyone, including myself, crossed the finish line first. It was unreal! Martin came in second and the two Navrongo boys placed third and fourth. But all four of us had broken the existing record. My time was 1 minute 49 seconds.

The joy of our teachers was quite a sight to behold. They carried me around the field on their hands. Our school won the games and received the grant. Martin and I were both selected for international competitions. Later on, I was able to improve on my time when I ran for Ghana in Upper Volta. There my time was 1 minute and 43 seconds.

I received athletic scholarships that put me through secondary school free of charge. My coach, E. Dwayne, was preparing me to run in the 1980 Olympic Games but Russia's invasion of Afghanistan deprived me of the opportunity as the Commonwealth countries boycotted the games.

Information about my running exploits reached Teselima. My relatives felt quite proud of me, and I received an enthusiastic welcome when I returned home for a school vacation. I had been home in Teselima for only a week when my new father's mother opened her life to Yesu. What a joy it was for me to gather with my siblings in Grandma's room for prayer, worship and praise. True love flowed among us and we encouraged one another. We gave our grandmother the name Grace. But Grandma's acceptance of Yesu renewed old difficulties. I had to leave Teselima prematurely.

Shortly after I returned to Tamale, Papa Konadu informed me that he was moving south to do further studies at the University of Cape Coast. It was a sad day for me. However, by this time I had grown in my faith. Papa Konadu had taught me to pray and to read God's Word on my own. I had also learned how to cook for myself. Papa Konadu had prepared me for this change.

"You must continue to grow and stand on your own feet in Christ," he said.

"Yes, I know how to talk to him now and he hears me."

Mr. Konadu left Tamale and I was alone again to face the vast world on my own – or so it seemed. This time, however, I had several Christian friends I could count on. Despite the presence of these believers, it was clear that I needed to stay close to Yesu at all times and not to rely on people. There were still deep questions I had to ponder. Would my relatives hunt me down and kill me through witchcraft? I knew they were capable of this. I had seen it work. What would I do if, while visiting Teselima, I was confronted by hostile fetish priests? If my new father's children were killed through witchcraft, would it not be my fault? I could not readily answer these questions. However, as I grew in my faith, I began to trust that if Yesu can change a heart like mine, he could also protect me and my new siblings back in Teselima.

Many nights in my dorm room, when questions came to mind, I wished that Mr. Konadu had not left. But, during those lonely, confusing nights, I grew increasingly dependent on Yesu as my source of comfort and strength. I was growing spiritually, without knowing it.

C.K. Konadu on the motorbike that taught me to run.
He and I were on our way to a Scripture Union meeting.

14

Sayibu, the Beloved Brother

IT IS CERTAINLY TRUE THAT WHEN GOD closes one door, he opens another. It was not long after Mr. Konadu left that I met a young, dynamic Dagumba boy from Yendi, a northern town. His name was Sayibu Imoro. He was a talented boy, brilliant in public debate and cultural activities. But the thing that attracted me to him was his fervent Christian faith. He had an intimate relationship with God that allowed him to enjoy life thoroughly. He was just like Mr. Konadu, except that he was about my age. He attended Ghana College, a senior secondary school. We met one day at a conference organized by the Scripture Union.

I was very impressed by a presentation he made at the meeting, and I talked with him after the program. I soon discovered that he was also an orphan who had faced difficult circumstances after his father's death. The selfless efforts of his brother Inusah made it possible for Sayibu to attend school, but hunger had remained an everyday companion.

Sayibu had been a diligent Muslim when he happened to meet a Christian development worker who had come to Yendi. Tom Ahima was an agriculturist. From the day they met, Mr. Ahima had tremendous compassion for Sayibu. He and his wife invited Sayibu to live with them. To Sayibu it was "manna from heaven." He was guaranteed at least two good meals a day. Mr. Ahima taught him the principles of rural development work. Sayibu felt very loved in the Ahima household.

Sayibu deeply appreciated that the Ahimas, despite their strong Christian convictions, never tried to impose their faith on him. They allowed him to worship in his Muslim way each day and even respected and preserved the sheep skin on which he prayed. They made it easy for him to develop his own mind. However, Sayibu felt that there was something about that man and his wife that was different from any Muslim he had met.

"They loved those who vehemently hated them and even prayed for the good of such people. I could never understand that," said Sayibu.

Sayibu began to feel that his own religiosity was rather mechanical. During a short vacation, Sayibu and a friend attended a youth camp in Tamale. They met young Christians whose faith attracted them so much that they both decided to abandon their Muslim faith and become Christians.

They faced several problems in their Muslim community as I had faced problems in my community. But Sayibu soon became convinced that God was calling him to live a life like his adoptive father and to help other young northerners who were in need of food, shelter and medical help.

I was very excited after Sayibu told me his story, because my dream had always been to have a development program to address the needs of orphans, widows and peasants. Sayibu and I became good friends. We encouraged one another in our Christian faith and prayed together. The Scripture Union selected both of us for leadership positions. I became the prayer secretary and Sayibu the student president of the Scripture Union. Little did we know that even though we were orphans, God loved us and planned to achieve much through us, both in Ghana and around the world.

15

A Faith with Passion

MY SPORTS CAREER GAVE ME A celebrity status. I rubbed shoulders with some of the most prominent people in Ghana. I was even privileged to have dinner with the president of our country. I became a "superstar" almost overnight. Many of the students at my school actually begged me to be their friend! The teachers respected and loved me. As I wallowed in the adulation, I began to forget about the suffering children and widows I had known, both at Bamboi and Tamale. My mind was set on "bigger things." My heart became foolish and my head became big.

One day, the regional secretary of the Scripture Union of Northern Ghana, Eric Asare, invited me to take a trip with him. We were to visit all of the Scripture Union groups in the Northern and Upper Regions of Ghana. Our trip took us to Navrongo Secondary School. The morning we were there, I met two young children who were so starved that you could count their ribs. They were holding a tiny head of raw millet that they told me they were going to roast once they had found a fire. I soon discovered that this was their meal for the day. I was so mad that I cursed the fathers and mothers who brought forth these children. The boys stood there and stared at me. I watched their chests rise and fall as their hearts frantically pumped what little blood they had through their veins. They probably wondered why I was so upset. After all, their kind of suffering was very common. For what seemed to me like a long time, the three of us just looked at each other in silence. Suddenly, the boys departed to look for a fire to roast their head of millet. "That head of millet couldn't fill the tummies of two large ants," I said to myself.

As sad as this encounter was, I am thankful today that it did happen, for it woke me up from the greed, pride, and callousness that had come to dominate my heart. I saw myself in the two boys and wondered whether I would not have ended up like them if men like Kofi Kinto and Mr. Konadu had not taken an interest in me. "Maybe I can become like Mr. Konadu to some of these poor ones," I whispered to myself in tears, for I knew that the two lads would not survive another month in their starving condition.

I came back to Tamale very subdued, with a constant picture of the two starving boys in my mind. I knew I would never be the same. I started to evaluate my ambition and my goals for life. I had a choice to make for my future. I could either live the rest of my life for myself, or I could live in solidarity with the poor and needy and show them Christian love as Mr. Konadu had done for me. I realized in both my heart and mind, that I should never allow myself to become the centre of the show in life. My Christianity must never lose its passion. It must be modeled after Yesu, who loved me so much that he died for me. Indeed, it was Yesu who had led me to the prominence I had been enjoying all too much.

The next time I saw Sayibu, it was in a bus station in

Tamale. I told him I had prayed to God for help with my future plans. I wanted to show true Christianity to those in need, as Mr. Konadu and Mr. Ahima had shown us.

"I couldn't agree with you more," said Sayibu. "That is exactly my vision too. We need to help our people with true love from Jesus."

As we talked in the bus station, we developed a plan to start working toward the acquisition of some property where we could implement a holistic ministry in the name of Jesus, whom we so dearly loved and wanted to serve. We acknowledged that first we must get to know our society and the needy. Being students, our time was very limited. We agreed that even among the students at our various institutions there were those who needed help. We could start from there. The distance between my Tamale Secondary School and Sayibu's Ghana College was about six or seven miles, so communication would not be too difficult.

Sayibu and I decided to pray and commit our thoughts and plans into God's hands right there and then. It had started to rain and people were crowding into the bus station. That did not stop us. We joined hands and prayed, telling God that we were available for his use. We also told him everything in our hearts concerning our plans.

It was a remarkable prayer meeting. I left the bus station with the feeling that I had signed up my life for war. I became frightened any time I thought of what we had told God. We did not have anywhere near the money or resources needed to make our plans a reality. I was also worried that, over time, I might lose my sense of commitment.

My interest in sports began to acquire a different emphasis. I still enjoyed running and, sure, I always ran to win, but I became indifferent to the glory that comes with being an athlete. This change attracted other runners to me. I became like a pastor to some of the athletes. Any chance I got, I told them of my faith and the importance of helping the needy. This was strange talk to their ears. They could not understand why I was thinking of the poor at a very young age. But to me, that was real life, to live for Yesu and to share my life with others so that they might be blessed.

Training for national sports competition.
Left to right: "Wicked," David, Audibil, Martin.

David and Martin.

16

Failures and the Birth of the Northern Evangelistic Association

By THE TIME I WAS IN MY final year of senior secondary school, Sayibu and I had started to care for some students who were in need of help. We supported needy students in both the Scripture Union and outside of it. Through the Scripture Union, we had come to develop several areas of ministry to students outside of Tamale. To get to these students was difficult. Sayibu and I met one day and asked the Lord to give us a bicycle so we could travel outside of Tamale and encourage the needy students we had come to know.

We knew of a CUSO woman who had come to teach at Sayibu's school. Her name was Allison, and she had come from Peterborough, Ontario in Canada. Allison had almost completed her duties in Ghana and was preparing to leave the country in a few months. She had a bicycle, and we knew that usually the CUSO people sold their belongings before leaving the country. It was not easy to find bicycles in Ghana at that time. Sayibu and I sent letters to all the Christian brothers and sisters we knew in and around Tamale, asking for their help to enable us to buy a bicycle. At that time, a new bicycle cost 50 cedis or about $24US, which was a lot of money – especially for two lads who were about nineteen. We figured that since Allison's bicycle was used, we might be able to buy it for $20. This was the amount we hoped to raise. At the same time, we prayed that Allison would not sell her bicycle to anyone else until we raised the money. The response to our appeals was completely negative. Our brothers and sisters in the faith simply lacked the resources to help. Many of them commended our efforts but explained that they were having trouble feeding their own families. We were very disappointed. Allison's time of departure was approaching very quickly and we saw the chance of obtaining the bicycle slipping away from us.

We met again to pray over and discuss the situation. We decided that Sayibu should tell Allison that we wanted to buy her bicycle. We hoped to borrow money from a rich individual and pay it off gradually through summer work. Little did we know that God had gone ahead and arranged things with Allison on our behalf. When Sayibu told Allison that we wanted to buy her bicycle, she surprised him with these words:

"Sayibu, I am not selling my bicycle. I decided long ago to give it to you and David. I've been meaning to tell you, but kept forgetting to do so."

I was in my dormitory when I saw Sayibu riding a red Tomos bicycle toward the building. I dashed outside to meet him. He was very excited when he saw me.

"God gave it . . ." he shouted while still quite a distance from me. I couldn't hear everything he said and was confused about what could have happened. People just don't give away bicycles in Ghana. He repeated his words as he got closer to me, and this time I heard the full sentence. "God gave it to us." As Sayibu jumped off the red Tomos bicycle, we praised God in loud voices and with great excitement. After the initial joy, we looked at the bicycle, then at each other and a sense of awe fell on us. It was as if God were standing between us and telling us that He supported our endeavours. We shook hands solemnly in acknowledgement of what God had done for us. Sayibu nodded and I nodded back and, with that, we parted. Sayibu rode back to his school in a solemn mood. The exuberance we had both experienced earlier was gone.

I went to my room and sat on my bed, wondering whether we really knew what we were doing. It was as if God had commissioned us to do some job for Him, which I felt we were too young to undertake. I was to find out that this God, the father of Yesu, could pick any person and use him or her. His Holy Book, the Bible, says He is omnipotent, omnificent, and omnipresent.

We travelled on that bicycle to all the schools surrounding Tamale, encouraging poor and struggling students, sharing God's word and sharing physical resources such as clothes and money with the needy ones. Several students gave their lives to Jesus and others had their spirits refreshed by our visits. It was a joy to see discouraged students strengthened. Gifts I received from my athletic victories, which I used to keep for myself, now became the means by which some students could continue their schooling. It was humbling to know that God was accepting my offerings through the lives of these students.

In 1976, bad days struck me again. I failed my final "O Level" exams, passing only in geography. I couldn't come to terms with the fact that God, to whom I had given myself and whom I loved so much, could stand by and allow me to fail so brutally. My failure sent shock waves through all of the Scripture Union groups in the Tamale area. I had not been a first class student during secondary school, but my grades were good enough that I had been allowed into the science program. At Tamale Secondary only good students were allowed into the sciences. So my marks at the finals were a great shock. I was so discouraged and ashamed that I found it difficult to visit other schools to see needy students. I had nothing left in me with which to encourage others.

When the news of my failure reached home, I was ridiculed. My new father said that he wasn't surprised at all. I felt that I had disappointed everyone who loved me and had invested in me, like Mr. C.K. Konadu. Of course, I didn't want Mr. Konadu to know that I had failed in such a miserable way.

A few good things happened in 1976. Sayibu passed all of his exams and transferred to my school to do his "A Level" courses. Now together in the same compound, we were able to pray together daily. We were also able to mobilize other young men and women who were interested in our vision for helping others.

Together, we began to evaluate some of the big government projects in northern Ghana. These projects usually worked for two to three years and then collapsed. In fact, some of them became what we called "death traps." An example of these "death traps" were the open dams, which provided water in the rainy season, but became low and muddy during the dry time. Cows, dogs, sheep and goats shared these waters with the people. They would "free" themselves into the water. People continued to drink such water, and diseases of epidemic proportions destroyed them. We came to the conclusion that if there was to be real help for our people, we the indigenous northerners would have to do it ourselves. We had come to realize that not only orphans, widows, and poor students were suffering, but thousands of peasants as well.

In those days, most of the key people in government positions in the North of Ghana were from the southern part of the country. It was they who collaborated with foreign "development" agencies, as they called themselves. These southerners never stayed in the North permanently. They transferred back to the South after a few years of "earning their spurs" in the North. So they never really got to know the needs of the people. Many of them simply didn't care. They viewed northerners as "backward" people and treated us accordingly.

These realities and the plight of our people weighed heavily on our hearts. Our group grew and we decided to form the Northern Evangelistic Association (NEA). A casual observer may have thought there was no need for our organization. After all, there were missionaries in northern Ghana. But the work of the missionaries was concerned almost exclusively with making converts. They didn't seem to care much about the struggling and destitute, or even about those who were driven out of their homes because of their faith in the gospel. We felt that it was necessary to start an evangelistic work different from that of the missionaries. It was a ministry that would involve preaching the gospel, caring for the poor, helping peasants and sending medical help to remote areas of the North.

This holistic vision of ministry did not change the fact that the Northern Evangelistic Association consisted of eleven poor students with scant resources. Where to begin? The first step had to be education and training. We pledged to help each other train in medicine, agriculture, theology and several other fields. Sayibu, Ben Anamoh and I prepared a detailed "blueprint" of how the NEA should function. Although we had no funds, we always felt that the Association should aim at becoming self-sufficient, unlike most projects in the country, which had to permanently rely on external support to survive.

We practiced self-sacrifice whenever possible. We shared our resources and worked to help one another. I gained employment as a laboratory assistant at Tamale Secondary. The principal, the same man who had connected me to Mr. Konadu, was very kind. He took time to visit me at the lab. The job provided funds for me and also for Sayibu as he continued in his A Level program. I was given a boy's hut as my quarters.

This small hut became the headquarters of the NEA. I made sure there was always some food there, in case any of our people visited. The hut also became a shelter for some students. I was never alone in my "bungalow" and frequently took on the responsibilities of chef. Some days I didn't know where the food would come from. My salary was 53 cedis a month, about $24 (at that time). Out of that salary, I bought food and helped needy students purchase school supplies. I also paid my tithe to the Scripture Union. Usually, by the second week of the month, the entire salary had been spent. But God always provided what was truly needed. Many days I was preparing to go to bed hungry, when Ben Anamoh would appear at the door with a loaf of bread. I would immediately summon Sayibu, with the news that it was time for a feast.

Brother Anamoh had been the first member of the NEA besides Sayibu and myself. He was married and was struggling financially. However, he had work in Tamale. The organization he worked for had its own bakery, so he could buy a loaf at a discount. There was a special method that Sayibu and I employed to put those loaves to optimum use. We put a little sugar into a cup, poured in hot water and stirred. We dipped pieces of bread into the sugar water before eating them. The hot water warmed our tummies and helped us to fall asleep.

In those days, Acts 2:42 became very practical and literal to us. We did exactly what the early church did; we, "broke bread together." Had we not cared for each other, we could not have survived. I became so lean that a man commented one day that he could use me as a rope with which to tie the end of his sack of grain. God was teaching us, first hand, what the destitute experience in life.

At the end of 1977, my salary was increased to 100 cedis a month (about $33). This increase was a tremendous help to us. In fact, I was able to save some money and we bought another second-hand bicycle.

I wrote the O Level exams again in 1977 and, again, failed them. It was very embarrassing for me, the Scripture Union and my friends. I was ridiculed wherever I went. Students laughed at me. Teachers blamed the Scripture Union for indoctrinating me too much on the gospel. Others felt that I was so obsessed with Jesus that I had become mentally incapable of thinking straight. The worst humiliation came from the students I was serving in the laboratory. These young people had all been two years behind me, but due to my failures, they became my seniors. Many of these students would deliberately dirty their beakers and test tubes and then, in a very sarcastic manner, instruct me on how to clean the items properly.

As bad as these "jokers" were, there was a science teacher who was much worse. He treated me like a slave. He hated me because I kept an account of all the science equipment in the laboratory. It had taken me a while to realize that one reason the principal gave me the job was to keep a careful eye on the lab equipment. It seems that the equipment had a way of vanishing. One day, an incubator disappeared from the lab. The science teacher accused me of knowing the whereabouts of the machine. Both of us were summoned to meet with the principal.

"David Mensah," the principal said, in front of the science teacher, " I employed you in that lab because of your honesty. I am confident that you know nothing about the incubator." On hearing that, the teacher walked out. I followed him to the lab, as the two of us were supposed to search for the machine. Once we were alone he around and gave me a vicious blow to the face. As I staggered backward and tried to keep my balance, he left the building in a huff. Two weeks later his six-year-old son innocently invited two students into his family's house to show them, "my father's new incubator." The students recognized the machine and quickly reported the news to the principal. The incubator was brought back to its rightful place in the lab.

Besides my status as an unofficial "watchman," I had another unpleasant duty at the lab – the gassing of rabbits before they were dissected. It was my job to put those poor animals into a small, air-tight glass box. Then I soaked a piece of cotton in formalin, threw it in with them, and closed the lid. The helpless creatures struggled for a while and then died. After having been delivered from the brutal killing of dogs, I never wanted to see another animal suffer. To make the situation even more painful, the rabbits regarded me as their "friend" because I took care of them. Watching those rabbits die was just horrible, I would whisper words of comfort to them, as if they could hear me inside that sealed box.

In spite of all the difficulties, I made up my mind not to quit. I felt that God was teaching me patience and humility. Besides, staying close to the school was important for me. I had registered for the O Level exams for the third time and I needed to use the school library to prepare. I prayed every day for God to help me pass the exams, because I needed them before I could move another step in my education.

Once again, the day came for me to jump over what was beginning to look like an insurmountable hurdle. The exam supervisors laughed as I walked in with my pens and pencils. I tried to be good natured and fake a laugh, but instead tears came. It was very depressing and embarrassing. I had studied hard and was sure that this was the time. I wrote the papers and was quite satisfied that I had done well.

The day the results were announced, I was visiting one of the student that the NEA had been helping. It was he who told me that the results were in. But he couldn't tell me anymore. The marks were kept confidential until all of the students who took the exam were informed about how they scored. I rushed to the exam centre with a feeling of excitement and confidence. But when I arrived at the centre, the man in charge of giving out the marks asked me to come with him into the privacy of an office. This was an unusual and, as we entered the office, I wondered what was going on. I found out soon enough when he showed me a sheet of paper that contained the test results. "Failed in every subject taken," read under my name.

"I didn't want you to feel embarrassed because of the people who might have overheard our conversation. That is why I called you in," the man said. "Sorry about what is happening to you, lad."

I stood there and stared at the ceiling. My eyes filled with tears. I wanted God to speak to me. I wanted him to tell me why I had to fail these exams three times. I was extremely dejected as I headed to my hut. On my way I met two teachers on their bicycles. They stopped and asked me about my performance. I told them I had failed again. "This is the first time I have heard of a student failing the O Levels three times in a row," one of them said and began to laugh uncontrollably.

The other teacher was more sympathetic. He came close to me and said, "Don't feel so downcast and don't listen to my friend. Most students don't have your kind of courage and perseverance. They usually drop out of education if they fail the exams twice. That is why my friend thinks you are the first one he has seen fail so many times." After those kind words, both teachers rode off.

I returned to my bungalow and discovered that I was out of food. That was just as well. I had lost my appetite.

Two months later, I attended a Scripture Union conference.

A young woman who had been a leader in the Scripture Union was absent from the meeting. No one knew why she wasn't there. After the morning program, I dropped by her home in Tamale. She had also failed her O Levels. In her case, it was for the first time. She was bitter when she met me at the front door. "I don't want anything to do with God now," she said.

"Why?" I asked her.

"I have prayed very much to God to help me pass the exams, but those who are not Christian have passed and not me. I have decided to stop being a Christian."

"Well, God's Word says, 'Believe in me and thou shalt be saved.' The Bible does not say, 'Believe in me and thou shalt pass thy exams.'" I tried to talk to her in an amicable manner, but she had already made up her mind.

She turned away and, indeed, abandoned the Christian faith.

As I returned to the conference, the words I had spoken to the girl stayed in my mind. It was as if the words were meant for me and not for the girl. "Yes," I said to myself, "Yesu has done harder things such as changing my heart. He could help me pass the exams if he had wanted. Perhaps there is a reason He wanted me to fail, and if there is a reason, so be it. He did not set me free so that I could try to manipulate him as my ancestors tried to do through witchcraft!" As I repeated these truths to myself, my own bitterness left me. God's spirit came upon my heart and Yesu became a friend again. "Regardless of anything that will happen to me, you will always be my friend, Lord," I prayed that night.

Vitality came into my life again. I went to the laboratory the next day with a renewed confidence. I did not allow the students to intimidate me. In fact, I started to help some of the students in their courses. Working in the lab for three years had helped me to acquire a lot of practical knowledge that the students lacked. But, because of my low self-esteem, I had not tried to help them. I was afraid they would laugh at me. But now I was able to assist the students in biology, chemistry, and physics. They were amazed at my knowledge and began to respect and appreciate my work. They also began to wonder why I had failed the exams.

Having failed the exams three times, however, study fatigue began to take its toll on me. I was sure that I needed to acquire more schooling in order to best serve the NEA. But as things were not going well in that direction, I became a bit desperate and began to investigate other opportunities. I turned to the principal of Tamale Secondary School for advice. This man knew a lot of people in high places. He was well respected throughout the North of Ghana. When I consulted him, he mentioned that he had a friend who was a principal in a teacher training college.

"If you would like to teach, I can get you there without any trouble," he said. While I was in his office, he telephoned this friend and explained my circumstances. He told him I was a good student and that he himself didn't understand why I was not passing the O Level exams. One did not need to pass the O Levels before entering into the teacher training college. In a way, going in that direction was like stepping backward in my educational plans. As I was thinking this, I heard my principal thank the principal of the teacher training college for accepting me. He hung up the phone and smiled, saying that everything was in place for me to start my training as a teacher in September.

Although this was a step backward, I was quite excited that at least I could become a primary or middle school teacher. I made all my preparations and saved money for my new course of studies. In September, I reported to the teacher's college, and introduced myself to the principal as the man his friend had told him about. He rejected me on the spot. He said the school was full and he was sorry for the inconvenience caused me. So I packed my luggage and came back to Tamale Secondary School to report the matter to my principal. He was taken aback. Fortunately, no one had yet been hired to replace me at the lab. I went back to work the following Monday.

While this incident was another big disappointment, it had helped me to save a full month's salary. I took this money and deposited it at the post office, where it could earn interest. The saving system at the post office was more reliable than at the banks. Besides, people like me were easily intimidated, and often robbed, by bank workers. My savings account grew and that made it possible for me to apply to Kumasi Polytechnical Institute in southern Ghana to study accounting. This school had a prestigious reputation and high fees to match it. I was accepted as a potential candidate, pending an interview that would take place at the school. I was very excited again, and even reported to my folks at home that I might be going to the Polytechnic at Kumasi.

While I was waiting to hear more from the school, an aunt died and I left Tamale to attend her funeral. When I returned two weeks later, I discovered that a letter had arrived in my absence, giving me three days to report to the school for an interview. The time had passed, and I had missed another chance to further my education.

I was becoming desperate about my future. I started to pray intensely for God's will to be done in my life. I talked to the Lord about my desire to help the poor. As my prayer life matured, my anxiety about the future diminished. Sayibu and I frequently prayed together. Sayibu was moved by my joy in being able to help him with his schooling, even though, by this time, he had left me far behind in our academic pursuits.

My friend and I stepped up our visitation program to the students and the needy. In 1978, I decided to register for the O

Level exams for the fourth time. Because of my savings, I was able to register for all of the courses without the usual financial problems. I worked at the lab during the day, and at night and on weekends I did visitations.

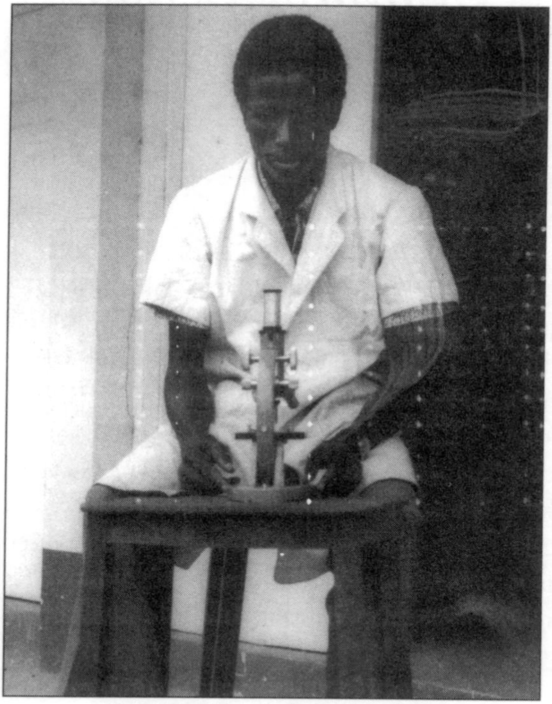

David working in the science lab.

17

Summer School

THE SECONDARY SCHOOLS USUALLY allowed the form five (equivalent of grade twelve) students to stay in school during the summer holidays, so that they could receive extra help for the exams they would be taking in the fall. However, in 1978, the schools were in such poor financial shape that they had to close their doors for the summer. The young people were told to go home and seek help on their own. Those who were hardest hit by this change of events were, of course, the poor students who could not afford to hire tutors.

I suggested to Sayibu that we should start a summer school to help the poor students. He laughed when I suggested it.

"Where are we going to get food to feed them?" he asked. "And even if we could feed them, where would we get the teachers to teach them? The fact is, we will never be able to do it. We don't have a laboratory for the science students and no money to hire a cook."

"You are right, it's impossible," I said. "Let's try it anyway."

After praying at length about the matter, we set out to organize a summer school. I still had some money in my savings account, which we designated for purchasing food. We knew two Christian brothers who were studying veterinary medicine in Nigeria. We wrote to them and asked if they would consider the challenge of teaching the sciences for our summer school. They agreed. Within a few weeks, many teachers in Tamale had volunteered their services. The minister of education in the North commended our efforts.

Before the term for the secondary schools was over, we were ready to go. We had rented a centre owned by the Presbyterian church. This centre had classrooms, and separate dormitories for boys and girls. Sayibu was chosen as the principal of the summer school and I was the vice-principal and bursar, along with errand boy, biology teacher, and cook.

It was great fun at first. But then cooking for a large number of students by myself began to take its toll. I brought the matter to the principal, and he suggested that some of the female students could help me with the cooking. A few girls were selected. It was also decided that the boys should do the dishes after every meal and clean the kitchen.

The school was so successful that the regional education officer made a personal visit to see what we were doing. After his visit, he begged us to admit his son. How could we refuse him? This school was meant for poor students, but the rich often have a way of getting what they want.

In the midst of all these activities, I was studying nights to prepare myself for my fourth attempt at the O Levels. Ironically, I was teaching biology, which I needed to pass myself. The students didn't mind.

The only setback at the summer school was that I didn't do my job as bursar very well. I ran the school into a deficit. The Presbyterian church gave us a loan, which helped us complete the summer. After school ended, we discussed the debt and Sayibu, the principal, and I, the vice-principal, unanimously decided that the bursar was responsible for the debt, so he should be the one to pay it off. It took me quite a long time, but I paid the debt in full to the Presbyterian church. When the time of payment came, I discovered, to my amazement, that the Presbyterian minister in charge of the matter had adjusted the interest rate in his favour. Nevertheless, we cleared the debt and kept our chins high.

The Presbyterian church suggested that we should keep the school going every summer. We declined. Sayibu and I were in no position to take on such a permanent responsibility. But we were very thankful to God for the school. None of the students who came under our care failed the exams – and, yes, that included me. On the fourth try, I passed my exams.

One could write a book about the events and adventures of the summer school. I will restrain myself and write only about one incident. One Friday morning I rode one of the NEA's bicycles into town to buy a few ingredients for lunch. The centre was about two miles away from town. Riding a bicycle in Tamale on Fridays is always a challenge, because the Muslims gather in their various mosques for worship. After the prayers are over, they block the roads as they walk home. Windy Fridays were especially cumbersome as the wind would lift the gowns of the Muslims.

On this Friday I was zooming down a slope toward a group of Muslims returning from prayer. As I got close to them, the wind lifted their gowns and my bicycle handle got caught under one gown. I dragged a poor Muslim man until most of his gown was torn, and he was bleeding from being scratched by the gravel road.

I stood beside him, feeling helpless and wondering just who or what was to blame for this mishap. I decided that it was all the wind's fault but didn't share my insight with the Muslim. The man was too confused to speak. He didn't want to admit what had just happened to him, especially right after holy Friday prayers. I remained with him and tried to comfort him. He pretended not to notice me and kept examining the torn sections of his gown. The way he was ignoring me indicated that he was up to no good. But I felt it was my duty to be with him and, if possible, to help him get first aid.

Suddenly he got up and, instead of speaking his native Dagbani, he spoke some sort of Arabic to the Muslims who were making their way to the scene of the accident. He proceeded to show them his torn gown. It was clear by his tone that he would seek vengeance. Most of the Muslims made exclamations that indicated they were in a very hostile mood.

Staying here any longer is like seeking suicide, I thought to myself. I made a dash to my bike, and sure enough, about five of the Muslims scrambled to grab me before I could get away. I was thankful for my two fast legs, which I could always trust – especially in times like this. Instead of mounting the bike right away, I pushed it as fast as I could until I had put a healthy distance between myself and pursuers. Then I jumped on the bike and sped away as they cursed and swore behind me.

I arrived at the school premises exhausted and frightened. Everyone knew something had happened, but I refused to tell anyone anything for fear that the Muslim man might have had a relative enrolled at the school. Hopefully, both the victim and I learned something from the accident. I, at least, had learned not to ride my bicycle into Tamale on Friday afternoons.

18

The Passport Ordeal

BY THE TIME SUMMER SCHOOL drew to a close, the members of the NEA were encouraging me to study theology in Canada in order to become the spiritual leader of our envisaged development project. The notion of studying in Canada had occurred to me three years earlier, and I had submitted an application to the passport office in Accra. For three years, I had been visiting Accra from time to time, checking on the progress of my passport application. It usually took a whole day to travel the 600 kilometres to Accra.

The only person I knew in that city was an NEA member, Zakaria Mahamadu, who was studying medicine at the Korle-Bu teaching hospital. Zak was poor but, somehow, he always managed to have food and boarding for me when I was in his neck of the woods. For three years, all the passport office kept telling me was "Your passport is still being processed." I knew no "big man" in Accra to help me.

Members of the NEA were fed up with the delays. At the end of summer school, they told me to visit Accra again and this time come back with a passport. I borrowed some money and went.

When I got to the passport office, I encountered unexpected trouble. I was greeted by a man who, I found out later, was posing as an official. This "official" told me that he would personally make sure that I received my passport that day. He asked me to give him a "tip" so he could see one of the key people. I explained that I had no money, that I had had to borrow money to make the journey from Tamale. Hearing the name "Tamale" made him more eager not to let me go. People in Accra often regard northerners as stupid.

The phony official was now determined to take every coin that was on me. His mood changed from friendly to hostile. He grabbed me and began to search my pockets. I managed to break loose and ran to the verandah. He followed me, determined to get my money. That money was my return fare to Tamale. I was so scared that I ran off and boarded a truck back to Tamale. I arrived very disappointed and, on top of that, was blamed for wasting money to go to Accra without the courage to find out what was holding up my passport.

Allison, the CUSO woman who had given us our first bicycle, had told me about a fine interdenominational Bible college in Ontario. I received brochures from Ontario Bible College (OBC, now renamed Tyndale College) and read them carefully. The fact that the school was interdenominational appealed to me and the other NEA members. I completed the application forms and mailed them to Canada. It wasn't long before I received word that I was accepted. What a joy it was to receive that news. Now that I had an official acceptance from OBC, surely the passport office would take me seriously.

I borrowed money again and rushed down to Accra with copies of my official admission forms. The passport office took the forms and said they would process them and that everything had to pass through normal channels. Being very naive, I thanked them and returned to Tamale feeling exuberant. Six months passed with no news from Accra. I had worked and paid off all my loans and had a little money left to travel to Accra again.

This time, I met a handicapped friend from the North who had come to Accra for medical attention. While in the city, he had been able to find a good job and had remained in Accra. He was very excited to see me, as I was to see him. I told him about my passport problem. My friend's legs were weak but his personality was strong and assertive. He was not a man who tolerated nonsense or took "no" for an answer. I gladly accepted his offer to accompany me to the passport office.

We arrived at the appropriate government building and quietly made our way to meet with the man who was supposed to be in charge of my passport. As we sat there and observed what was going on we became aware that, as my friend put it, "This is the most corrupt office on the face of the earth." Bribes were being offered and accepted everywhere. Money was constantly being counted out and changing hands. It was like being inside a gambling casino. People were so engrossed in their corrupt activities that it was some time before anyone noticed us. And even then, they assumed that we had come to offer them a bribe.

After a brief discussion, when the official we were talking to realized that we were not interested in offering a bribe, he shouted something to his co-workers. Suddenly, people began to shut their desk drawers and act like they were busy with paper work. But these "civil servants" were so angry with us that they threatened to report us to security. My friend told them to go ahead. That brought them to their senses, since any such action would expose the corruption of the entire office. They softened and promised that my passport would be ready to be picked up in two weeks. With that promise, they carefully coaxed us out of the office.

My friend was convinced that the two weeks promise was a ruse to get rid of us. The place was so corrupt that he thought I would never get a passport without paying a bribe. We were both thoroughly disgusted with our government in action.

My friend was right. The passport office had no intention of giving me the passport without a payoff. One month after my friend and I had departed that house of corruption, I decided to try once more. This time I planned on camping out in the passport office until they gave me my passport. I got up at four am. to get a ticket for the State Transport bus, which left Tamale at six a.m. One's chances of getting a ticket are often slim, no matter how early you get up. People often sleep at the station so they will be among the first in line. The ticket situation was aggravated by the fact that non-travellers often bought tickets and resold them for a profit.

However, I had travelled with this transport so often that my face had become familiar to the ticket agents. They knew I was a genuine traveller and made sure that I got a ticket. I arrived in Accra late that night because we had mechanical problems on the way. I slept at the bus terminal, a dusty, fenced-in courtyard. The next morning I wiped myself clean and made my way to the infamous passport office.

Arriving at the now too-familiar building, I climbed a few steps and went through two doors into a huge courtyard. From the courtyard doors led to various offices. In the courtyard there were the usual peddlers. The place was crowded to capacity. I made my way straight to the room my friend and I had visited weeks ago. To my amazement, the officers recognized me and someone even mentioned my name.

"What do you want now?" one of them shouted. "Get out! Your passport will be ready in two weeks."

The intimidation was quite strong. I felt burned out by the whole corrupt process, and decided to forget about Canada and a passport. As I was making my way through the door, one of the men called me to come back. He took me to his desk, which held a large pile of passports – mine was on top of the heap. I reached out for it, but he slapped my hand.

"We don't do things like that here," he said. "Do you think we are fools who work for nothing?" He kept repeating this phrase for quite a while as he flipped through my passport. I got the message, but my Christian convictions prevented me from engaging in bribery. I tried to explain my convictions to the young man. He burst into laughter.

"If you are not willing to pay, why do you want a passport? Even in London people give bribes. It is not a new thing, my friend."

Before I could respond, a phone rang on the third desk to his left. The phone call was for him, so he left his desk to take the call. For some unknown reason, he left my passport on his desk. I stood there gazing at the passport. The officer watched me carefully as he talked. I started to reason within myself. "If I took the passport and ran, would God consider that stealing?" It didn't take me long to answer that one, since I had fulfilled all the state requirements, including the payment of 400 cedis for the processing of the passport. I grabbed the passport and made my way quickly out of the room to the big courtyard. I looked back and saw the young man in serious pursuit. I made my way quickly out of the crowded courtyard to the road. He was still following, cursing. Once I got to the road, I knew the game was mine.

"You are going to pay for this when I catch you," he yelled.

"You can't catch me," I yelled back, putting a greater distance between us.

"You just wait and see," he shouted as he took his wristwatch off his arm and put it into his pocket. He clearly intended to go all out to catch me.

"Come and get me, then," I told him, and put myself into 800-metre gear.

Within a few seconds, he realized I was not the kind to be pursued on foot. I was gone, never to be seen by him again. I ran until I got to the traffic circle in the centre of Accra, a distance of several miles. What a joy that day was! I went to the market place and bought a special covering for the passport. I celebrated the episode with good goat meat at a roadside "chop bar."

The next morning I headed off to Tamale with great excitement. As I sat in the bus, I was filled with thanks to God for the phone call that came just at the crucial moment. I felt that God had honoured my determination not to resort to bribery and had provided His way for me to get the passport. It was as if my whole athletic training was for this occasion. The brethren in Tamale laughed to tears when I described the whole episode. They agreed that I hadn't stolen the passport and, for that matter, that I had not sinned. After agreeing on that, we celebrated some more.

19

New Obstacles

OBTAINING MY PASSPORT BROUGHT ME UNTOLD joy as it became clear that I would, indeed, be able to travel to Canada. I began to wrap up my activities in Tamale. I sent a special thank you letter to Mr. Gbedamoshi, the head teacher of Tamale Secondary School, for his help in getting me the job at the laboratory, and I asked him to release me from that position. It was quite a sad time when I next saw the head teacher in his office. Mr. Gbedamoshi was happy to see me go to Canada but, at the same time, he was sad to see me disappear from the campus of Tamale Secondary.

"I will certainly miss seeing that red Tomos bicycle and its young rider plying the campus road," he said. "Keep up the running, if you can." He wished me the best of luck and said I should pass by and give my final goodbye when I was ready to leave Ghana.

As I visited friend after friend in Tamale to say goodbye, I realized how much I had become a part of Tamale, this Northern Dagomba capital. Some friends felt that the track and field races in Tamale would never be the same after I left – a prediction that actually turned out to be true. The sports program in Northern Ghana collapsed just after my departure, due to a lack of funds to support the games.

After making certain I had covered enough ground in my preparations to leave for Canada, I decided to make the "big" trip to Teselima to tell my new father, Mom and my close relatives that in a few weeks' time I would be leaving for *Abrokyire*. *Abrokyire* means "overseas," but my Deg people always interpret the word as "the end of the world." It is that part of the earth where people speak in muffled voices. People who live there are said to have cat eyes and are scary looking. We also heard that they flame at night on their beds. When they die, due to the excessive heat in them, they turn completely black like charcoal. These and other stories were often told about the *Abrokyire* people, although no one in our tribe had been to *Abrokyire*.

I arrived on a Friday night and broke the news to my new father early Saturday morning. He was excited, but expressed serious doubts as to whether my mom would allow me to travel to *Abrokyire*. He quickly dispatched his eldest son to Jugboi, seven miles away, to fetch her. My new father often acted like a military man. He liked to advance quickly on a target. Within hours, my mother was brought to Teselima. After she had a chance to rest, my new father summoned the family together. Mom realized immediately that I was connected to whatever the fuss was all about. Once the meeting began, my new father lost the courage to break the news of my plans to Mom, and uncharacteristically kept circling around the issue. It was my mother who got to the point.

"Tell me what is going on. I didn't make my way here in the hot sun to listen to this!"

"Take it easy, you women are sometimes too anxious about

things and in the process you lose all your cool," my adopted father replied.

"You have your nerve to mention the word anxiety. We all know that anxiety lives and sleeps with you," my mother responded. With that, we all laughed. This was my adoptive father's tactic to loosen Mom up, so that she could take the news positively.

"Well, our son Kwabena has been blessed by His God and our ancestors with an opportunity to go to *Abrokyire* next month. I could not keep the good news to myself, so I sent for you all to come and share the joy with me." Silence descended on the group. After several minutes, one of my uncles spoke up.

"Has any Deg person ever gone to see this place since the creation of our tribe – I mean the place he is going to?"

"As far as I know, no!" responded an aunt.

"Maybe His God wants him to be the first person from our tribe," my mother said, to our surprise.

What a release that was to me! But a barrage of questions were poured on her from all sides of the family court: "Won't he forget our language when he goes there, without any other Deg person living there?" "What kind of food do they eat?" The whole thing got out of hand, as people kept asking irrelevant questions and giving flimsy excuses for keeping me in Ghana.

Someone asked, "Will you remove your teeth and put in gold teeth like the *Abrokyire* people?" That question was too much and I burst out laughing. But I was quickly rebuked for making fun of the question.

"You will look very scary to the children if you did that," one uncle said.

"Not only to the children. I will run away from him, if he puts in gold teeth," added an aunt.

I maintained a sober demeanour for the rest of the meeting, and kept my humorous notions to myself. My discretion paid off. After everyone had their say, the family wished me all the blessings from, as my adopted father put it, "Your God and our ancestors." It became an emotional meeting as it suddenly dawned on me how deeply my people loved me. They were very poor people and had no knowledge about the world beyond their domain. Yet they were full of rich love, the kind of love that seems to be available only in rural communities. It is so deep that it cannot be expressed in words.

By Saturday afternoon, one of the best family cows was sold to raise funds for my trip. My adoptive father further declared to the family that he would support me while I was abroad through the sale of cattle – for by then he had many cattle. That was a big relief to me, because that was the next thing I had wanted to discuss with them. He also agreed to travel to Accra with me to see me off. It was a miracle. This was the man who couldn't stand me because of my Christianity, but even though he knew I was going to a Bible college, he was still prepared to sell his cows to assist me in my theological training.

After receiving my "clearance" from the family in Teselima, I travelled to Accra to seek a visa to Canada. The Canadian high commissioner gave me medical forms, which several doctors in Accra had to fill out after examining me. After the physical examination was completed, the forms were returned to the High Commission which sent them to the Ivory Coast to be formally processed. I was told that the procedure would take two to three weeks. So I left to spend that time in Tamale. At the end of the second week, I returned to Accra to check on the forms. The forms hadn't been returned yet, so back to Tamale I went.

The whole process of obtaining a visa suddenly turned into a nightmare. For some reason, the Canadian High Commission kept deceiving me about the medical forms until I requested to know the reason my forms hadn't been returned from the

Ivory Coast for over a month. A woman who was filling in for the visa person told me that my medical forms were in – they had taken only two weeks to be returned from the Ivory Coast. She further said I had a clean bill of health, but that she couldn't give me the visa until her superior returned to work. I went back to Tamale very angry that even the "white man" was going to treat me as did the Ghana passport office. I was very frustrated and discouraged.

Another two weeks passed and I went to Accra again. This time, the boss of the visa department was in. She spoke to me in a cold, authoritarian manner. She asked me how I was going to be sponsored while in Canada. I showed her the papers that indicated that I had been approved by the government of Ghana and that they would transfer funds to Canada, while my adoptive father paid the cedi equivalent to the government.

"That seems to be a good arrangement, but you will not be granted a visa by this office until you have an account in a bank in Canada with at least $1,000 in it. After you have saved that much and deposited it in Canada come and see us." With that she asked me to leave.

She was so hostile! I decided that I should forget about Ontario Bible College. I felt that if the people in Canada were this mean, I shouldn't bother to go there. But on my way out from her office, I met another young Canadian woman who told me she was from New Brunswick. She was very cheerful and lively.

"Why do you look so discouraged, my African friend?" she said, putting both her hands on my shoulders and gazing into my eyes. I didn't have enough courage to tell her about the visa problem. But I left the Canadian High Commission with a good attitude toward Canada because of the caring spirit of the New Brunswick woman. "Not every Canadian is like the one in the visa office," I said to myself.

I was so depressed by the whole ugly episode that when I got to the medical student hostel at Korle Bu, Zak wondered whether I was sick. I told him about the new policy at the Canadian High Commission concerning the deposit of one thousand dollars.

"Why is everyone making things so difficult for us?" he asked. Then he suggested that we should have a special prayer for God to open the doors wide so I could travel to Canada. We prayed and I left the next day for Tamale without much hope of coming to Accra again. It seemed as if the door to Canada was firmly and permanently closed, because, unless God decided to work a miracle, it would be impossible for me to raise one thousand dollars and deposit it in a Canadian bank.

I worried about how to tell my friends and family that the Canadian trip had been cancelled. There was also the humiliation of asking for my job back at the lab. On the day I was to begin this unpleasant process, I met Bernadette Bonnin, a Christian sister from Minnesota, who was in Ghana teaching French through the American Peace Corp program. I told her of all my problems concerning the visa. She was very concerned. She told me that her time in Ghana was over, and she was leaving for Accra the next day on her way to the United States. She asked me to accompany her to Accra and see her off. She offered to pay for my transportation.

Bernadette was a very good Christian sister who attended the Tamale Fellowship prayer meetings. She identified with Ghanaians, wore Ghanaian clothes, and was obviously at ease when socializing with Ghanaians. I felt honoured when she asked me to see her off. I mentioned the proposed trip to Sayibu. He decided that both of us should go to Accra and make Bernadette's last two days in the country pleasant. We wanted to help her shop for Ghanaian crafts, so that she would not be cheated. Ghanaians have the habit of doubling or even tripling prices of commodities for a white customer. The white people tend not to bargain when prices are quoted and the Ghanaian merchants take advantage of that.

We arrived in Accra on a Wednesday evening and Sayibu and I went to stay with Zak, while Bernadette stayed at the Wycliffe Bible Translators' headquarters. Before we dispersed, she told me to meet her at eight a.m. at the Canadian High Commission, and from there we would go to Accra centre to shop. Nothing crossed my mind when she made the suggestion, because the High Commission was a central point to meet when one wanted to go and shop.

Bernadette was already there when we arrived the next morning. Sayibu had a few personal things to do that morning so he couldn't come on the shopping expedition, but promised to meet us at the local crafts area by eleven. Instead of looking for a taxi right away, Bernadette asked me to follow her to the Canadian High Commission.

"What do you want to go there for?" I asked.

"I want to talk to those people and find out for myself what is holding up your visa."

Panic overtook me. I had known Bernadette as an unassuming, quiet and gentle woman. She was also so tiny and frail that we used to tease her that one day the monsoon winds would sweep her off her feet and carry her into the Sahara desert. I was sure she would mess up what little chance I had of getting a visa in the future. I told her not to go, but she just laughed at me.

"You can't just walk in without an appointment," I said, trying to stop her.

She pulled a pair of sunglasses from her purse, put them on, and walked steadily toward the High Commission building. I gave up my resistance and followed her like a tamed pup. She told the receptionist she wanted to see the person in charge of visas. The receptionist went inside and returned to say that we could see the visa woman in fifteen minutes. We sat down to wait. After twenty minutes we were called in. As soon as we sat down, Bernadette asked the lady, "What is the real problem holding up this young man's visa approval?"

"The new policy here is that visa applicants must have at least one thousand dollars in a Canadian bank before a visa can be issued," the official answered.

"Be reasonable," Bernadette replied. "How practical is this new policy to people like this young man who doesn't know anyone beyond this city? How in the name of truth can he have one thousand dollars in Canada?" Bernadette questioned, really fuming.

Bernadette's tone scared the Canadian woman so much that she asked whether I was Bernadette's son. I quickly glanced at my skin to see whether sitting with two white women had suddenly changed my skin colour. Within fifteen minutes of entering that office, a Canadian visa had been stamped into my passport and we walked out.

It was one of those days when I could not contain my joy. I was so happy that tears came from my eyes. That night, before I fell asleep, I began to reflect on God's kindness to me. I thought of Yaara and how God had been with me as I swam across that crocodile-infested river. I reflected on how the Lord provided Srakpo to take me in at a crucial time, and Kofi Kinto, the drunkard, to scare away my uncles from Yaara. I thought about the phone call that allowed me to grab my passport and run away from the passport office. And how, only a few hours before, He had used a quiet woman like Bernadette to secure my visa. I felt overwhelmed by God's kindness, and burst into sobbing. As I wept, I remembered a portion of Scripture Mr. Konadu always quoted, "Not by might, nor by power, but by My Spirit, says the Lord of hosts" (Zechariah 4:6 NASB). This text became very alive to me. I was brought to a renewed understanding that God was with me and that I must trust His Spirit to direct and lead me.

The next day I saw Bernadette off at the Kotoka International Airport, then made my way back to Teselima to confirm to my mother and all the relatives that the trip to Canada was now a sure thing. Since I had only two weeks left before my departure, I felt I should spend only one week in the North and the last week in Accra. My brother Yaw, my adoptive father, and two of his daughters decided to accompany me to Tamale and Accra to see me off.

While in Tamale, I took my passport around and showed my Christian friends the stamped Canadian visa. The passport and visa were physical representations of God's answer to the many prayers that had been made on my behalf. I used this gesture as a way of, once again, thanking all the dear people who had prayed for me. The brethren organized a little party for me and the entourage from Teselima. After a few days in Tamale, I finally said my good-byes to friends, teachers, and the Christian brothers and sisters. We left for Accra safely and without any hitch.

20

Last-Minute Complications

IN ACCRA I WAS WALKING ON CLOUDS. I had only seven days left before the big take off to Canada. My passport, visa, and air ticket were all ready. Everything looked positive. Nothing could go wrong – or so I thought. Then someone told me that, since I had my air ticket, visa, and admission papers to study in Canada, I was entitled to $40US from the government. She went on to explain that this is money the government gives to people leaving the country, especially those going to study abroad. I just needed to take my passport to the Bank of Ghana, show them my visa, and collect the money.

"The whole process takes only a day. So there is nothing to worry about," she told me.

It sounded great, especially since the only money I had was $10US that Sayibu had given me for the trip. That $40 certainly would help to tide me over until my adoptive father could plow through the necessary paperwork and send funds to me in Canada. So off I went to the Bank of Ghana. I met other students in the building who were going to places ranging from

Moscow to Copenhagen. We all queued up and waited our turn. The building was air conditioned so I became quite chilled and hoped my turn would come quickly so that I could get back into the tropical sun.

"You shouldn't go to Canada, you know," the guy behind me whispered. "I hear Canada is very, very cold, even colder than this room."

I took him to be one of those people who love to exaggerate. *Anytime I feel cold in Canada, I will just go and stand in the sun and get warm*, I thought.

Finally, my turn came and I presented my passport to an officer, who passed the collected passports to his superiors. He came back and told us that we should come back tomorrow morning for our passports and the $40, since they had to process the applications from the day before. We signed our names in a book for identification purposes.

I was thrilled that, for the first time in my life, I had been inside the Bank of Ghana building. I excitedly told Yaw and other friends about the experience. Everyone wanted to know what it was like.

By eight o'clock the following day, I was back in the bank, waiting to receive my $40 and my passport. One of the clerks asked my name and then went into another office. He came back to tell me that, unfortunately, my application was not approved because the boss had left for home early the previous day.

"It will be approved today," he assured me, "So come back at four o'clock."

I returned promptly at four.

"The boss, for some reason, hasn't approved your papers. Please come back tomorrow morning. Don't worry they will be ready," he added when he saw the puzzled look on my face.

As I walked home, I became very concerned and decided that the next day I would simply ask for my passport and forget the $40. I started remembering stories of how people in Accra sometimes stole passports with visas and used them to travel. I knew that something was fishy in the Bank of Ghana.

The next morning I was there when the bank opened, but again I was told that the papers were not ready. In desperation, I began to demand my passport but a security guard sternly told me to calm down. I opened my mouth to speak, but he shoved me out of the building and slammed the door. I sat on the steps of the bank building and began to cry, cursing the woman who had told me about the $40 in the first place. I felt completely helpless.

The next day I decided to wait until after three o'clock before going to the bank again. That way, the people at the bank could not claim that I hadn't given them adequate time to prepare my passport and visa. On my way I stopped in at the Ghana Airways office to confirm my flight. I mentioned to the Ghana Airways woman that I was on my way to the Bank of Ghana to check on my passport.

"Hurry up and go. At four o'clock today the office that approves such matters will close for the week," she said.

Panic descended on me. I had only two days left in Ghana to leave for Canada. "If I don't get my passport this afternoon, it means game over for my travel plans," I said.

"Run," she said with real concern on her face.

Time to put my running skills back into use. I had only forty minutes to get to the bank. I worked up a great speed on the crowded Accra streets, swerving among pedestrians, cyclists, and market women. It would take me at least ten minutes to get to the bank, even at top speed, because of the crowded streets. I am sure that people who saw me running, regarded me as a thief or a madman. Nobody in his right mind would run that fast on the busy streets of Accra. But I had no choice.

As I got close to the bank, a very big Makola market woman carrying a huge 40- to 50-pound pan of cassava flour on her head walked right in front of me. I thought I could swerve by on her right hand side, but a friend of hers saw my speed and cautioned her to get out of my way – good intentions but bad advice. She moved right into my lane and we collided. Boy, was she heavy. Both of us hit the ground and were buried in cassava flour. Several helpful citizens gathered around and helped the lady and I onto our feet. My nose was bleeding a bit. When the woman saw me standing there, my body painted white by flour with eyes blinking and a little stream of red blood coming from my nose, she broke into laughter. The crowd immediately joined in. But it was not a laughing matter for me. I had to press on to the bank.

I took off again, trying to wipe myself off while I ran, but cassava flour can be a very stubborn substance. When I got into the bank, my appearance drew excited glances. People sprang up from their desks to look at me. I provided a bit of diversion from the everyday routine. Everyone laughed, including the security guard. They all wanted to know why I was so white and why I was at the bank. The security man didn't even recognize me until I explained my identity.

The man who was in charge of the passport situation came out of his office to find out what all of the fun was about. He overheard my conversation with the guard, and took me into his office to find out what my problem was, but his amusement over my appearance slowed things down. He asked for the country I was preparing to travel to, but before I could say "Canada," he started to laugh hysterically. We went through this procedure three times before he could stop laughing and listen to me. But once he settled down, he proved to be a very nice man. I told him my story and how I needed the passport to travel within two days' time.

He reached out to my passport.

"No,"he said. "We can't allow you to travel. All contractors are supposed to declare their assets before they leave the country."

"But I am a student. I'm not a contractor."

"Your papers indicate that you are a contractor."

"No, sir."

A contractor's papers had mistakenly been put into the middle of my passport together with my own papers. When I insisted that I was a student, he started to sort out the papers carefully. He separated two sets of papers with different signatures.

"I am very sorry," he said. "I mistakenly added the papers together and never took the time to sort them out." He approved my papers and called one of the clerks to fill out a form and give me the $40. Once we were in the clerk's office, he said they had just run out of the forms. I knew this was his way of asking for a bribe. I took my passport and left the Bank of Ghana without the money I was entitled to. I wasn't going to fool around with that passport anymore.

I went home and stirred up another round of laughter when Yaw and others saw me. I looked funny to them, but I was very happy, because I had my passport. The episode also made me treasure the ten dollars Sayibu had given me.

Now that I had my passport back, planned to enjoy Accra for one final day with my friends and relatives and say goodbye to them the next day. With only one day left, I could not foresee any problem. The only possible thing that could crop up would be if the single Ghana DC 10 aircraft had a breakdown and needed major repairs, I reasoned to myself. This faithful aircraft had been serving Ghana on all international flights, so there was always the possibility of a day's delay so it could be serviced. Otherwise, I was sure to be bound for Canada as scheduled.

We woke up the next morning to find ourselves in an unprecedented situation. The government had been overthrown by the army. "There is a coup," was on everyone's lips. The radio told civilians to remain calm and to observe whatever the new leaders would tell us through the Ghana Broadcasting Corporation. There were army personnel all over Accra. Terror crept into my heart as I thought of my travel plans. We were told that security at the airport was extra tight and that no one was permitted to leave the country. A new law was quickly passed that all who planned to leave the country must report to a special office, where they would be interviewed by military personnel. My new father urged me to forget the Canada trip. We were all panic stricken.

I started to feel overwhelmed by all of the problems that seemed to rain down on me constantly. In my discouragement I remembered a verse in the Bible that says, "The Lord is good, a stronghold in the day of trouble, and He knows those who take refuge in Him" (Nahum 1:7, NASB). This verse brought renewed strength to my weak knees.

"If there ever is a day of trouble, this is it," I said to myself. "I'll bet these are the kind of days the Bible is speaking about." One thing that was clear in my heart was that I had genuinely given my life to God through accepting His Son Jesus Christ. I knew that the love of God and the desire to follow Him took precedence in all that I did. I took refuge in God and depended upon him as " a stronghold in the day of trouble," such as the one I was facing now. With that conviction, I told the Methodist minister we were lodging with that I was going to the army to tell them of my travel plans to Canada.

"I wouldn't go there, if I were you. Every soldier in town is insane today," he said.

My adoptive father and everyone else agreed that I shouldn't venture to see the army. We were all so scared that we couldn't eat. But I insisted that I would visit the army with my passport and papers. Indeed, I did, after a time of prayer.

When I arrived I was briefly interrogated by a junior officer. When he realized I was from the North, he began to laugh.

"You people from the bush, you don't even understand what a coup is." He sent me into a room where I met several more army personnel. There was a man crying in front of three army officers as I got in. I was frightened but kept repeating to myself the text that God was my stronghold in the time of trouble. A senior officer looked at my papers and cross examined me in detail.

"Do you know what is going on in this country right now?" he asked.

"Yes."

"Give me your address in Accra."

I was very scared but gave him the address. He told me to go home.

I left, wondering what would be the next step. When I returned to the home of the Methodist preacher, everyone was anxious to know what had happened. I told them the army had questioned me extensively but that their attitude had been reasonably friendly.

"So, do you think they will allow you to travel or not?" the preacher asked.

"I don't know. But they took the address of where I am staying."

"You mean to say you gave them my house address?" He was so panic stricken that within fifteen minutes, he made four trips to the washroom. His fear was shared by all who were in the house. It was as if I had revealed our position to the enemy in a time of war. Everyone made sure I got the message that giving out the address could bring untold hardship to the preacher and his family.

At about 6:30 that evening a black police jeep arrived in front of the house. This added confusion to our fear. I had talked to the army, not the police.

"What do they want?" I wondered loudly.

"You tell us," was the general reply.

The policeman walked to the door. I was trembling as I went to meet him, but since I was the cause of the problem, I felt I should face it.

"I want David Kwabena Mensah," the police officer said.

"Here I am."

"You ready go for Canada?" he asked in broken English.

"Yes, sir."

"Well, make you hurry up. Chief say I come bring you quick."

I was unsure whether this was some kind of trap. But I had no choice. Everyone helped me to quickly pack my few things. I took my suitcase to the jeep and climbed into the back.

Before we started, the policeman asked, "Your papa no de come say bye bye?"

I told him I was not sure whether my dad and relatives would come to say good-bye because they were scared.

He got down from the jeep and went to them. I heard him ask, "You no de come to airport say bye bye to *pikin*?" (your child).

My relatives reluctantly squeezed themselves into the jeep. We were driven directly to the airport and the army processed my papers. The Ghana Airways DC 10 was taking army personnel to London, but again God had ruled that I should be taken along to start my journey to Canada. At the airport my relatives were a bit relieved, but they still could not understand why the army was treating me like a prince.

"What did you give the army?" my new father asked.

"Nothing," I replied.

"You mean they drove to pick you up for no reason?"

"There is a reason," I said. "God had told them to do so they were acting on a higher command."

"Your God never gives up," he replied.

Realizing that God was involved in my travel plans, I took the liberty of asking one of the officers to drive my relatives home after my departure, since it would be late.

"OK, sir," the officer said. I found out much later that, indeed, my relatives were driven home after I flew off.

I was thrilled and full of tears as I climbed aboard the DC10 and took my seat. "God is a sovereign God," I said to myself. It wasn't long until we were in the air! I relaxed as I heard the hydraulics retract the landing gear. I looked down and the whole of Accra lay beneath me with its beautiful shore and the ocean looking still.

"Beautiful Ghana, I am leaving you for a while, but I will come back home some day!" I was choked with emotion. For the first time, I realized how deeply I loved Ghana.

The flight to Heathrow airport in London was smooth. One of the army personnel in the aircraft happened to be a former student of Tamale Secondary School. He came to my seat quite often to entertain me and make sure I was enjoying my flight. We had a brief stopover at Rome. When I looked through my window and saw quite a few white people I realized that we had left Africa and were now in the white man's land. Within forty-five minutes we were airborne again, penetrating the deep blue skies on our way to England.

After several hours of flight, the pilot announced that we were making our final descent to Heathrow airport. I looked through my window and thought the pilot had made a mistake. "Where is London?" I whispered to myself. All I could see through the window of the aircraft was thick clouds – a type I had never seen. The clouds were so thick it was as if one could touch them. Thankfully, the experienced Ghanaian pilot squeezed the aircraft through the clouds and landed the DC 10 professionally in the busy Heathrow airport.

21

Heathrow Airport

THE REAL NIGHTMARE OF THE TRIP started here. Once we got off the aircraft, I found myself totally alone. Everyone appeared to know where to go and what to do – except me. I followed the army boys for a while, until a security guard turned me away and pointed to where I was supposed to go. I rushed in that direction, half running and half walking until I came face to face with a conveyor belt for passengers. I had never seen one before. The way it moved scared me. It was like one of our African pythons moving with its head and tail hidden.

I ran back until I met the same security man. He yelled at me in such a deep English accent that I missed every word. One thing was clear though; I knew I was facing the wrong direction and he was telling me to turn around and carry on. I tried to explain to him about the belt but I could tell he was getting quite angry with me. So I turned and walked toward the python-like creature, hoping that it had slithered away. But there it was, still moving on its journey.

I rushed toward the security guard again and this time it was evident that he was ready for a confrontation. He stretched out both arms and all I could hear him say was, "Go on, go on!" He proceeded to usher me along. He was a tall, strong-looking guard – probably in his fifties. He made sure that this time I obeyed him because he was right behind me and any time I tried to stop or look back he shouted, "Go on!" and stretched out his two hands, indicating that I could only go forward. He kept at me until we got to the narrowing path leading directly to the long creature again. He was still shouting his "Go on!" when we arrived at the lair of the beast.

This time, I was brave and decided to test the thing by putting one foot on it to see if it was something one could walk on. Immediately, the creature began to drag that foot away (or so I thought). It felt like the monster was trying to swallow me. I screamed and half scared my English friend.

"This is why I didn't want to pass here," I told him. "I want another road!"

"This is where you have to pass to make transfer arrangements for your next flight," he replied. "Come on, let's go!"

But I was too frightened to jump onto the beast. The Englishman finally realized my problem, and his harsh attitude towards me immediately changed.

"It is a conveyor belt. It won't hurt you," he said. He took my hand and tried to help me take a step. In my panic, I jumped onto the conveyor belt and landed flat on my back screaming. He managed to lift me up and then burst into laughter.

"Haven't you seen one of these before?"

"Not at all, sir." He laughed really hard.

"There are lots of them in Canada where you are going." He knew my destination because he had checked through my passport. He was very kind after this ordeal and led me to the passenger transfer counter and made sure that the woman at the desk was aware that I was a first time traveller and needed to be treated as a special case. With that, he made a few jokes with me, patted my back and left.

The ticket woman at the counter was equally nice, and after checking through my passport and air ticket, directed me to a place where I could sit and wait.

"You may even snooze if you wish and I will wake you up when it's time to go," she said. I curled up and not only snoozed but slept soundly. The next thing I knew I felt a gentle tap on my back and a kind female voice was saying, "My African friend, it's time to go. Your aircraft is boarding now." Thanking her, I proceeded to the gate she showed me, and joined the line for the final checking to board the aircraft.

I could not believe how silent the people were. No one spoke. People kept to themselves. It suddenly dawned on me that I had left Africa. Nowhere in Ghana would people be in such a line without chatting and laughing or even having the odd fist fight. I began to experience the first pangs of homesickness. We finally got to our seats in the aircraft – a 747 jumbo jet. It was cold in the aircraft – both the temperature and, in my opinion at that time, the attitude of the passengers. Even the people sitting next to me acted as though they didn't notice me. I managed to say a "good afternoon" to all of them, only to receive a nod from some and no response from others.

I became uneasy and began to remember some of the questions my family had asked me the day I had announced I was leaving for Canada. My relatives had many reservations about these people with, "cat eyes." They warned me that white people often don't talk for days and live in unbearably cold places. I had brushed these notions aside as being nonsense. However, sitting in that cold jumbo jet, surrounded by white people, all of them silent, caused me to ponder what the folks back home had said. But it was too late for second thoughts. The jet was firing its engines. There was no turning back. I was now on the white man's terrain. So I braced myself for the worst as we sped down the runway and were lifted up, up and away.

It was the biggest aircraft I had ever seen. It was like a city to me. There were so many people. I continued to ponder over the quietness of my fellow human beings. My fears were a little bit relieved once we were in the air. The stewardesses came to offer drinks and there were smiles on their faces. I relaxed and asked one of the women what to do in case I needed to go to the washroom. She led me by a large number of people, even that seemed intimidating – to walk down the aisles and notice everyone looking at you but not talking. Soon I got to know what to do in the aircraft and accepted that this would be my home for a few hours until we touched down again. I did all I could to enjoy the aircraft.

At some point, I started to talk with one of the people beside me. His English was very limited. Until then I thought that anyone who was white could speak perfect English. I began to wonder if it was my accent that was causing the problem. I soon discovered it wasn't my accent for when he spoke to the stewardess he was having great difficulty getting his request across.

As we talked, I found out he was from Italy. His family had migrated to Canada and this was his first trip to visit them. This was a very exciting trip for him. He was full of anticipation. He asked me why I was going to Canada. I told him I was on my way to study. He asked how many people would be meeting me at the airport. I told him I didn't know anyone in Canada but I was sure that someone from Ontario Bible College would be there to meet me. We managed to carry on a little bit of conversation and I shared with him some of the story of my life and my Christian faith. He didn't believe in anything but it was interesting to him and he said he wished he understood English better so that we could talk more. He was a delightful man and I was glad to have someone to converse with.

It seemed like such a long journey. I was tired but could not sleep, perhaps because of the mingled excitement and apprehension I was feeling. From time to time the pilot would announce that we were passing over some country, but each time I looked out the window to see land, it somehow reminded me that I had left home, and that I was very, very far away. A deep sadness would flood over me. Although I appreciated the pilot's courtesy, I decided not to look out the window.

We were served meals that looked very nice but to me they tasted flat. I was already missing the hot pepper and spices of home. I was too excited to eat anyway, so I drank a lot. I was always asking for water or orange pop. At that time in Ghana it was very difficult to get a "Fanta" but here I could have it whenever I wanted – free. I really enjoyed it.

It was announced that we were going to watch a movie. I wondered, *How is that possible?* Down came a screen right in front of us. If my people from Carpenter, Teselima, Jugboi and Yaara could only see one of their own sons sitting in the air and watching a "Cine," how amazed they would be! I thoroughly enjoyed the film. It was a story that had been filmed in Africa. But I was puzzled as to where the man was that was showing the film. I looked behind me, behind the screen, everywhere trying to figure out where he was. It was most amazing to me.

After a few hours, the signal came on to fasten our seat belts and the pilot announced that we were approaching Toronto airport and were about to land. Oh, the excitement I felt. Soon I began to see tall buildings. I strained my neck to see as much as I could see from the windows. I found it difficult to sit still. Toronto, a city that I had been preparing myself to come to for years. At last, I was here! I could barely contain my excitement. Down, down, down, finally we touched the ground, with the engines screaming louder than ever. We came to a stop and disembarked.

Those who were not Canadians were directed very politely and nicely to a special area. One man even addressed me as "sir" and advised me where to turn. I was flabbergasted to hear a white man call me "sir." Toronto seemed like the nicest place in the world. I was led into a small cubicle where I saw "Immigration" signs all over the place. I found out that our aircraft had been delayed quite a bit. It didn't matter to me that we were late, what mattered was that I was actually in Toronto and talking to the people of Toronto.

22

The Mysterious Man at Toronto Airport

MY EXUBERANCE SUBSIDED QUICKLY once I began to speak to the people at the immigration office. First of all, I was told that my luggage had not arrived. I was very worried over this development and wondered if the bag had been stolen. I kept telling the woman in charge that I needed my luggage. She escorted me back to a small cubicle and went to check on my missing suitcase. She soon returned to inform me that a mistake had occurred in England and that my luggage was on its way in another airplane that would arrive in two or three hours. She assured me that there was nothing to worry about and that we should go ahead and process my papers.

Then the woman started to go through my passport. There was a paper missing in my passport which, of course, I was not aware of. Apparently, after my visa was given to me in Ghana, the officer at the Canadian High Commission forgot to add my student authorization paper and clip it inside the passport. That omission was about to become another challenging hurdle for me.

The Toronto official kept asking, "Where is your visa?" All I could do was point to the stamp that appeared in my passport.

"No, not this. Where is your student visa?" I could only say that this was all the Canadian High Commission had given me. After we had gone through this routine three times, she stated very emphatically, "I want your student visa!"

"I don't know what else is needed because I thought this was my student visa in the passport."

She closed the passport. "Anybody who comes into this country to study gets this kind of stamp in the passport like you have, but a certain paper accompanies that stamp telling us that you are here to study. We call it a student visa and you need to have one."

"Well, maybe in Ghana they don't give out those papers because the Canadian High Commission gave me this but they didn't give me anything else."

The woman stomped away from her desk, obviously in a rage, then she circled back. "Are you trying to tell me that I don't know what I'm talking about?"

"No, I'm just trying to reason that if the Canadian High Commission knows about this paper they should have given it to me before I left." I tried to speak calmly but that didn't seem to have much effect. She mumbled some words I didn't understand then declared, "No, it's not the fault of the Canadian High Commission, I think we have to send you back."

"Send me back where?"

"Back to Ghana because you've entered this country illegally!"

The great joy and anticipation with which I had arrived in Canada, suddenly dissipated. I just didn't know what to do. My voice took on a frantic tone.

"I am here legally. I have done all I could. I went to the Canadian High Commission in Ghana. I took my passport. I went there with an American woman and my passport was stamped. The paper you're asking for I know nothing about and I just don't think it's fair for you to say that because I don't have this paper that you have to send me back."

"You need to have it and only people who come here illegally come without it."

"Well then, how did I get this stamp in my passport if I came here illegally?"

The woman's anger took on a haughty tone. "That's what I want to find out, how you got that stamp in your passport. It could be that you have a friend there that could take your passport in and stamp it for you."

This absurd accusation deeply angered me. "So you think I'm a crook. Is that what you think of me?"

"I'm doing my job and you don't have a legal paper to enter my country. I need to make sure that only people that have correct papers are accepted into the country. I have no choice but to send you back to Ghana."

That was the only solution she could see. I realized that I had not handled the situation well. By becoming confrontational, I had only added to the anger of an official who, at that moment, wielded tremendous power over me. I talked to her gently and apologized for losing my cool. I explained, once again, that I knew nothing about the student visa. I was sure that my lack of such a visa resulted from an oversight by the Canadian High Commission in Ghana. They had simply forgotten to give it to me. But I was sorry that I had arrived without it and caused her a problem.

"'Sorries' don't explain things to Immigration! We have to process people into the country in the way that we have been advised. So there is no way I can take your 'sorry' for anything. There is nothing I can do but send you back on the next available plane. As soon as your luggage arrives, we will make further arrangements for you to go back to Ghana."

She took my passport with her into a different cubicle to talk to another officer. The area we were in was a collection of cubicles. In her absence, a young man popped out of one of the other cubicles. Apparently, he had overheard the discussions. He quietly whispered, "Don't worry. No one is going to send you back to Ghana. We will do all we can to find out what is the matter. Don't pay too much attention to her and don't be too scared."

That was advice I really couldn't take. I was exhausted and disoriented. The excitement had quickly dissolved and the reality that I was in a foreign land had set in. I knew I had to abide by new rules and to listen carefully to what was expected. I appreciated the young man's words and attitude. As I watched him return to his cubicle, I hoped he would get involved with my case.

The woman returned, more determined than ever to deport me. I was certain that a representative of Ontario Bible College, would be at the airport to meet me. I had been corresponding with the secretary to the president of the college. She knew about my arrival. I asked the immigration officer to have the woman paged. She complied but several attempts reaped no response. The officer was now even more suspicious of me.

I was carrying a recent letter from the secretary that contained her home phone number. The officer phoned the secretary, who confirmed that she knew about me, that the school was aware of my coming, and that I was enrolled as a student. But apparently there had been some misunderstanding about my date of arrival. The secretary said that I had arrived two weeks early and she couldn't come and get me because she didn't drive or have a car. There was nothing she could do. Of course, I could only hear one end of the conversation but I could tell from the weary look on the face of the immigration officer, that the situation was getting very complicated.

After she hung up, the officer's mood seemed to change. She seemed to be struggling with the problem of what to do with me. To be fair, neither OBC nor anyone else was giving her much help. Her frustration came through in her voice.

"Look, school does not open for two weeks. Where are you going to go for those two weeks? You have no acquaintances in this country. If we approve this visa where are you going to stay? The woman that you count on very much says she can't be here, she can't drive and there is nobody here from the college to meet you and we can't send you to the college because it is locked up." She gave me a weary grin. "Now, where do you want us to keep you?"

"Maybe immigration can find a place for me to stay until the school reopens," I replied.

She laughed. "It's closing time, but we don't sleep here, you know. None of us have rooms here. We come here to work and we have homes that we go to." I suggested that perhaps one of them could take me to their home until school reopened. That suggestion inspired a long, loud laugh.

Our aircraft had arrived at about nine p.m. It was now about eleven and we were advised that my luggage had arrived. My suitcase and a few smaller items were brought to me. Seeing my luggage revived me a little. It was like having an old friend with me. The suitcase was thoroughly searched, which seemed to reassure the immigration officer that I was not a crook but a bona fide student. I suggested that perhaps Immigration could phone the Canadian High Commission in Ghana and have the necessary paper sent to me instead of sending me to Ghana to get the paper.

The immigration officer informed me that I was being placed on bond for twelve days. During that time, they would establish whether or not I was in Canada legally. When the twelve days were up, it was my responsibility to report back to that immigration office. I would then be told whether or not I could remain in the country.

Then the officer began to zero in on where I would stay for the next twelve days. I was becoming increasingly tired and could no longer deal with the questions. I began to think that returning to Ghana might not be such a bad idea. After all, this woman, who was a government official, had treated me with anger and suspicion. What would happen when I got out on the streets? When I spoke, my voice was a hoarse whisper. "Madam, I agree that you should send me back to Ghana, because I don't know anybody in this country and I don't want to be here anymore."

She looked at me and said, "I have already written things down saying this is the way we will deal with you, that you will be allowed in here for twelve days. So we won't send you back now."

I was too tired to argue. The woman told me that she needed to talk to some other officers about my case. I could just sit and wait for her to get back. I sat on the floor, leaned against my suitcase and fell asleep. She returned, woke me and advised me that they were not equipped to look after me. I would have to find a hotel. She gave me a telephone number to call to let them know of my whereabouts so that they could monitor my situation for the next twelve days. She then told me that it was time for them to close the office and that I would have to leave. She gave me my temporary twelve-day paper.

It was a most difficult thing for me to hear that woman tell me to go out of the airport and find a hotel. Who do I contact to help me find a hotel? Where do I go? Besides which, I had only $10 in my pocket. How could I pay for a hotel? She showed me where I could exit the airport and get a bus to town. My emotions seemed to let loose. I had faced hard times before but in Ghana everything was familiar to me. I felt tears escaping down my cheeks, as I picked up my luggage and headed for the exit.

I saw a washroom close by. I went in, toting my luggage. My first prayer in Canada was in that washroom.

"Yesu, you have done so many things for me. You have delivered me from many dangerous situations at Yaara. You cared for me when my father died. You provided for me in Accra; you helped me to get my passport at the last minute; you helped even the army to provide a means for me to leave Ghana for Canada. Now, here I am at midnight in a country unknown to me. I don't know anybody in this country. The only person that I have written letters to is not here and cannot drive. I am here all by myself, but I know that you are here with me – you who have cared for me so much. I am stranded. I am really stranded in a foreign land and at this time it is only You that I can rely on to find meaning for me even this night. Where do I go this night when even the lights in this airport are all going off?"

As I came out the bathroom, I saw a young white man, his arms folded across his chest, leaning against the wall. I put down my luggage, approached him.

"Sir, I am stranded. I have come from Ghana and I don't know anyone in this town. It is very late now and the immigration people are telling me that I need to leave the airport and that I have to find a place to stay until I can contact them because I don't have a certain paper. I need any help that I can get. If you can just help me to even find a way to Ontario Bible College. I understand that it is not reopening for two weeks but I would like to go to a place very close to it and stay close to it so that when it reopens I won't have far to walk to get there."

He looked at me. "My friend, I am also a visitor in town, but I will try to help you." I felt very lucky to have encountered this man, a visitor who was willing to help someone who was obviously lost and desperate.

My luggage consisted of one suitcase, which was heavy because all I had was in it, a small radio, an African straw hat, and a little pouch with all my papers. This man took the big bag, leaving me with my straw hat, my pouch and the radio.

As we went out the door, I felt terrified. I saw so many lights and at a distance I could see Toronto. The buildings looked like giants stretching to the sky. As I gazed at them, awe fell over me. It seemed as if the city had no end and, as late as it was, there were bright lights in those tall buildings, bright lights coming from left and right as if these lights were touching the skies. What a contrast between this place and Ghana. As soon as the sun went down, Ghana was dark.

As I was staring at the Toronto skyline, the young man said it was time for us to leave. A bus immediately pulled in front of us and opened its door as if the driver had been responding to instructions from my friend. We boarded the bus for a trip that took at least thirty minutes. Finally, the bus stopped and we got out. I offered to pay the man because I had seen him give money to the driver. But he refused. "Oh no, don't worry about it. I know your problem." I didn't take that to mean much. I just surmised that he had accurately pegged me as a poor African boy with meagre resources.

We were now in the middle of the city. It felt strange to be standing in the midst of so many tall towers. But the strangest part was yet to come. The man guided me to a concrete stairway that led underground. He told me that we were going to board a train. After making our way down the stairs, we approached a set of turnstyles. There was a booth in the middle of the turnstyles where a man sat silent and motionless. His eyes were partially closed. The lighting in the booth was a garish white, making the man inside look like a ghost. My friend dropped a few coin-like objects into the turnstyles and we passed through. We walked down another set of stairs into a tunnel that contained a long platform. There were two other people there but they were standing quite a distance from us.

Suddenly, I heard and felt a rumble. The entire earth seemed to be moving. There was a blast of air and a train appeared to whip into the tunnel. The train was actually travelling underground. This really was *Abrokyire* (overseas)! I was so glad to have someone with me who knew what was going on but, at the same time, I began to have suspicions about this man. There was something strange about him. How foolish I was to go with a complete stranger who could, for all I know, be a dangerous killer. It was late and I had already told him that I didn't know anybody in the country. If he killed me that night – who would know?

The train opened its doors, we entered and I sat down while he stood and held one of the upper bars. As the train pulled away, my suspicions about this mysterious man increased. He couldn't be a "visitor" in Toronto. After all, he had perfect knowledge of the bus route from the airport, and appeared very much at home in the underground. I reasoned that this man knew exactly what he was doing. In fact, he was probably operating in accordance with a plan. I remembered a story that a friend in Ghana had told me about a vicious gang of killers that lived underground in *Abrokyire*. These underground people made money by committing all sorts of horrible crimes. The name of this underground organization was the Mafia.

Now, looking back, I can view my fear with a certain amount of amusement. But, at that time, there was nothing funny about it. My fatigue had vanished. I was wide awake and terrified.

I wanted to learn more about this mysterious gentleman in hopes of placating my fear. I asked him what his name was. He didn't answer the question but began to carry on a very general conversation. As he did, he must have seen the anxiety in my face. He took hold of my right hand as if to comfort me. That act sent chills down my spine.

I tried to remain calm as I spoke. "Sir, I would like to pay you for the money you gave to the bus driver and I would also like to pay you for this train fee."

"Oh, I know your problem. Don't worry about it," he replied.

What did he mean by that? I kept trying to learn the man's identity.

"I know you know my problem, but I would at least like you to tell me your name so that I could write to you some day and tell you about myself and send you a note of thanks."

Once again, he avoided the question about his name. He began to ask me about my life in Ghana and about my family. "How is your relationship with your people now?"

For many years, as the previous chapters have indicated, I hadn't been getting along very well with many of my family members because of my Christian faith. Before leaving Ghana, I had reconciled with those relatives. But how could this man on the underground train know about the problems with my family? I began to feel cold. My fear increased. Then as I looked at him, with my hand still held in his, my thoughts moved in a different direction. Maybe that prayer in the airport washroom had received a very quick and direct answer. Could this person be an angel in disguise?

He was certainly a very mysterious man. He would not tell me his name,; he knew my problem; he paid all my fees for the bus and train and he was asking about my relationship with my people in Africa. I couldn't figure it out! But there was something inside me that began to encourage me, a voice or a feeling that said, "This is a friend. This is Yesu's person. He is here to help you and you needn't fear him." The thought that Yesu had dispatched someone to help me was completely overwhelming. I began to cry. I didn't want my companion to see me crying, but that wasn't a problem. He was looking the other way at the moment.

I had just brushed away the tears, when the man suddenly turned and spoke to me. "Don't be afraid of this country, and don't be afraid of this city." At that moment, I knew for sure that my positive speculations were being confirmed, that, indeed, Yesu had given me a friend, someone to guide me. Then a different kind of fear gripped me. I was sitting next to an angel! I didn't ask any more questions. That hardly seemed necessary. I decided just to listen and follow him wherever he took me.

After a ride of less than fifteen minutes, we left the train and took a taxi to Ontario Bible College. It was past midnight when we arrived. As my friend was paying the cab driver, a green van pulled up. The van held no passengers, just a driver who got out with an armload of boxes and a key dangling from one hand. He unlocked the front door and took the boxes inside. My friend approached the driver and spoke in a kindly voice. "This boy is from Africa and has come to this school to study. He has a room here, please help him to get to his room."

The driver asked my name, then ran up to the third floor, to look at a chart posted there. He quickly returned.

"The school is not to be reopened for a while," he said, "but his room is here and his room number is 316."

My friend gave the driver a serene smile. "Please help him to his room."

The mysterious man then turned to me, handed me a map of Toronto and explained how the traffic lights worked. "If you see the palm of a man's hand on the screen, don't cross the street, but if you see a white figure of a person, then you can cross. Be content and be happy, and pay attention to the reasons why you have come to this land." With that, he turned and walked away.

The bus driver helped me carry my things to room 316, then he left. From my window, I watched the mysterious stranger slowly disappear into the night. After he was gone, I lay on the bed and thought of how Yesu had designated somebody to care for me. Yesu knew where I was and what I needed. A sense of strength began to overtake me. I knew that I was going to be all right. The man said I should be happy, content and not to be afraid of the town or the country. Yesu had asked him to tell me that. How could I be afraid again? I cried for awhile with a sensation of joy and awe, then peace engulfed me, tiredness overtook me, and I slept.

23

Ontario Bible College

THERE IS PURPOSE AND MEANING IN suffering. I was to come to a deeper understanding of that truth during my stay in Canada. Preparing myself for the challenges that waited back in Ghana was to be a difficult task. If the Lord had not toughened me up during my childhood and youth in Africa, I might have run from the problems that had to be overcome in, what was for me, a strange and different world.

I awoke the next morning, and took my chewing stick into the hall. Chewing sticks are small pieces of wood that Africans use to clean their teeth. We chew for awhile, then spit out the splinters, chew again and spit, chew and spit. I realized very quickly that the halls were too clean to use my chewing stick. I couldn't spit on those beautifully polished floors. A friend who had once visited Nigeria had given me a tube of Pepsodent toothpaste as a going away present. I decided that it was time to begin using western customs.

I walked up and down the hall and found the washroom and showers. It was the first time I had seen a shower that had hot and cold water. I couldn't get the hang of it right away. I would turn on the water and it would either be too hot – and I would run out – or too cold. But I fiddled with the knobs until I finally got the right temperature. After my shower, I used my new toothbrush and toothpaste and cleaned my teeth. I felt refreshed, but also very hungry.

The past few days had been full of traumatic experiences. I was emotionally drained. The smallest thing could cause me to break into tears. But there was joy in me each time I remembered the mysterious man's words to me. The memory of those encouraging words set me to whistling that morning as I returned to room 316.

Before I left Ghana, my mother had given me small bowl of *gari,* a food we obtain from cassava. The cassava is a tuber that we harvest from the ground and shred into fine particles. We put these particles into a big sack and dry them for a week to get all the starch out of the cassava. After that, it is dry fried, and once it is properly prepared it will keep for over a year without spoiling. It is an important food for Ghanaians, for it can be ready to eat very quickly. One only needs to pour water on it and it tends to expand, so even a small amount can help you in an emergency.

When my mother gave me the *gari* "just in case," I told her, "Don't you know I am going to the white man's country where there is everything?" But my mother pleaded with me to take the *gari.* I did so to keep her at peace. Little did I know that this gift from my mother would save my life. Sitting alone in my room at OBC that morning, the reality of my situation began to set in. The school was closed. It would be two weeks before the cafeteria began to serve food. I would have to survive on the gari. I had no bowls, or cups to mix it in, nor did I have sugar to put on it, I just chewed it from time to time when I was unbearably hungry. At the sink I made a cup of my hands cup and drank water. The *gari* lasted for about six days and when it was gone, I had nothing except water.

For awhile room 316 became my whole world. I could hear people coming and going in the building but I was too frightened to venture off of my floor. I was scared that something would go wrong and I would end up outside the school and unable to get back in. Even more frightening was the prospect that an official from immigration might find out that I could not support myself, and would use that as an excuse to deport me. But as I stayed in that room day after day, growing hungrier and thinner, it became obvious that if something didn't happen very quickly I might not survive.

Fortunately, something did happen. On the morning of my eighth day at OBC, I heard a lot of noise and the voices of young people. I headed toward the activity and found a lounge where there was a large gathering of students. It was about nine a.m. One of the students was a black boy from Jamaica, who I later found out was the student president. They called themselves "RAs" – resident advisors – and had arrived early to prepare themselves to handle the rest of the students. Several professors were with them.

They could tell that something was wrong the moment I stepped into the room. I was very lean, very quiet, and my eyes were beginning to sink a bit. I felt as though I was dehydrating, even though I had been drinking a lot of water. Everyone was very kind. They welcomed me to the school, and asked why I was there so early. When they learned that I had been in that building for over a week, they asked where I had been going for food. I told them that I hadn't been eating. They were shocked. Such a thing doesn't happen in Canada!

Every one of them felt terrible. They assured me that lunch would be served in a few hours. As they showed me where the dining room was located, they apologized over and over for the negligence of the school. Among them was a professor named Douglas Webster. He was there to teach the resident advisors how to assist the rest of the students. But that morning he spent a lot of time with me; he seemed to have a gift for communicating with a brother in Christ who had just arrived from a far away land. I returned to 316 with the assurance that I would be informed when lunch was served. I fell asleep for a couple of hours, and was awakened by the Jamaican boy.

"My friend, lunch is ready and we want you to come and eat with us."

I went downstairs, and, indeed, there was food all over the place. They heaped my plate with rice and chicken wings cooked in honey. After about three or four mouthfuls, I started to gag. I was quickly escorted to a washroom, where I emptied what I had just put into my stomach. The food was so sugary and oily I thought, *Goodness, what a country to come to. Is this the kind of food I will have to eat while I'm here?* I wished I hadn't come to Canada. I wondered how that boy from Jamaica was not having problems with eating. He actually seemed to like the stuff. How was that possible with such terrible food? I decided to go back to my room and, somehow, survive on water.

But the students and profs remained very concerned about me. They gave me several cans of soda pop (the only lunch item I was able to handle). They informed me that breakfast, lunch and supper would be served every day, and urged me to keep trying to eat. For three days I tried but, except for the soft drinks, I couldn't keep down any of the cafeteria food. I vomited so much that my ribs began to ache.

Somehow word got to Doug Webster that this African boy couldn't handle the cafeteria food and something had to be done. Doug came to my room, talked to me about my background and tried to find out why I couldn't eat. Student complaints about the food in the cafeteria were hardly unique, but Doug had never encountered a situation quite like this.

That evening he talked with his wife, Ginny, about my situation. Ginny had spent her early childhood in Zaire, where her parents had served as missionaries. She had a good knowledge of African culture. She instructed her husband to fetch me from the school. That night Ginny cooked corn, along with some North American dishes. I didn't even look at the other things but ate that boiled corn like a pig. I ate and ate and ate. Doug and Ginny could only watch in amazement. Preoccupied though I was, I did notice the joy on their faces. At last, this young man from Africa was able to take nourishment. The food settled comfortably into my stomach.

The professor informed the cafeteria manager and from that day on, corn was always available at OBC's cafeteria. I ate the corn and gradually started adding small portions of North American food. I am grateful to Ginny Webster for being sensitive and helping me to get used to western food. I am also thankful to Yesu. At every difficult juncture in my life, he provided some very special people to help me. People like Doug and Ginny Webster.

When the twelve bond days were up, one of the students volunteered to take me to the airport immigration office. The woman who dealt with me before was there – full of apologies for her earlier rudeness. A telex had arrived confirming that I had gone through all the legal channels to enter Canada. It was not my fault I had arrived without a student visa. She continued to apologize on behalf of Canada and the Canadian High Commission in Ghana. She wished me good luck and told me that the bond was lifted. I was issued a student visa that was renewable every year on the basis of my financial position and my progress in education. This time I left the immigration office feeling good.

The student drove me back to OBC and during that drive through the city I appreciated my mysterious stranger even more as I realized how long the distance was. The young told me the trains were called subway trains and tried to chart the route I would have taken that night. He was full of awe that, late at night, someone who said he did not know the city went out of his way to bring me to the college. That day, I saw how difficult a journey it must have been.

Back at the college I wrote a letter back to my pastor in Ghana, Pastor Daniel Kwame. He had been praying that Yesu would help me on my journey. I told him how his prayers had been answered, that God sent a mysterious person to lead me from the airport to the school. The pastor replied that he had no doubt that the person was an angel. He had been praying and praying on my behalf and said that he was not surprised that God had sent an angel to guide me.

Even before school officially started, a good relationship developed between Professor Webster and me. He dropped by my room almost daily to make sure that I was doing all right. I enjoyed several more dinners in the Webster home. How grateful I was for this kind man who was later to become my teacher and helper in many ways. We were kindred spirits and a bond formed between us. The more he visited me the more I relaxed and began to think that some of the stories I had heard about these people with cat eyes were not true. This man was taking the initiative to visit me. As we talked and laughed together, I realized that he wanted me to feel at home at OBC. Canada was still a strange country to me, but it was a country with many genuine Christian people. Sometimes, when I was alone in my dorm room, I would sing and dance for joy at being among Yesu's people.

As the school prepared to resume classes, I discovered that I was not the only African student at OBC. Two young men from Kenya arrived to begin their studies at the college. One Zambian boy had been at OBC for two years and a Nigerian boy had been there for three years.

A couple of days before classes started, the five of us got together. The ones who had already studied at OBC did most of the talking, warning the rest of us not to take anything for granted. They told us that there were kind professors and kind workers, from the library to the bookshop, from the switchboard to secretarial offices. They told us we would find many wonderful Christians among the people at the college, but warned us not to let down our guard, for we would also find those who did not share our faith. They explained that occasionally we would be appalled by the conduct of people who called themselves Christians. They encouraged us to keep our eyes focussed on God. We ended our meeting with a time of prayer.

When classes started it was quite interesting. For me, it was fascinating to be in classes where most of the students were white. I wished my people in Deg land could have seen me sitting in a classroom with white students and, in most cases, having a white teacher. There was much excitement in me during those first days. The fellowship among the students was wonderful. Most of the white students were colour-blind in the very best sense of that term. There was a real sense of Christian community at the college, and it was a joy for me to be a part of that community.

Then the roof fell in – or so it seemed. I received letters informing me that I would not be receiving any funds from Ghana. The new military government would not permit money to be sent out of the country. The fact that I was attending a Bible college made the situation all the more impossible. So, no money was coming from home. What was coming was a date when I was supposed to explain to the financial controller of the school how my fees would be paid. I had been looking forward to explaining how my relatives back in Ghana were going to help me. Now all I had was that ten dollars that, somehow, I had been able to hang onto. The controller wouldn't be very impressed. Once again, I became haunted by an age-old question – why me?

I felt like a thief when I attended my classes. I was stealing an education I couldn't pay for. I felt as though I was robbing the school of essential things. I had been given my first month's meal card without paying. Every time I walked through the cafeteria line and had my card punched I felt guilty. Shouldn't I explain to the school that I was without funds and couldn't ever pay them for the food? By this time, I had adjusted to North American food and liked it very much, but, despite this, my appetite vanished.

Sleeping became very difficult. I would lay on my back and stare at the walls and wonder how I was going to pay for my education. My student visa did not allow me to get a job in Canada. I knew no one, which made borrowing the money impossible. The problem seemed insurmountable.

My close sense of community with the other African students did provide some comfort. One evening when I was feeling very discouraged I went to a friend, Jacob Kibor, a Kenyan student in the Master of Divinity program. I asked if he would join me on a walk around the campus. I intended to share my financial problems with him and ask his advice.

We hadn't walked for long when we saw a gathering of some kind in the campus chapel. It looked like a church meeting. There was a man from England, a man with white hair, speaking with such zeal and wisdom that I felt compelled to sit in one of the pews close to the door and listen to this man. He was speaking about spiritual virginity and purity of life. After a few minutes, Jacob left and I began to feel uneasy. I was among strangers. But the speaker was very good and I wasn't about to leave. He continued to speak about purity of life and how one could dedicate oneself to the service of God.

The meeting concluded, but the people stayed in the chapel, visiting with one another. My eyes began to focus on a lively young man who almost seemed to bounce around the sanctuary. I watched him move from one person to another, shaking hands, embracing people. He was full of smiles and warmth. I envied the joy that obviously dominated this man's heart. Suddenly he walked straight to me, shook my hand and embraced me. It meant so much to me. Imagine this white man hugging me, like we had been friends for years! He was smiling and asked me all kinds of questions. He spoke English with an Italian accent. We began to discuss the sermon and he seemed surprised by my knowledge of theology.

He asked my name, introduced himself as Vince, then whisked me to another corner of the chapel to meet another gentleman.

"This is Gene Paisley," he said. "Gene is a dairy farmer." Gene was also a giant. The man was tall, robust and strong-looking, with huge hands. I was more than a little intimidated. I stood there trying to look calm, while Vince explained to the giant that I was from Africa.

"When did you arrive in Canada?" Gene spoke in a surprisingly soft voice.

"I came recently. I haven't been here a month yet."

"Who do you know here?" he asked.

"Actually I don't know anybody here, I just came to the Bible college to study," I answered.

Gene insisted that I visit his farm when I had a break from my studies. He wanted to show me how farming was done in Canada. It was gratifying to have this man invite me to his home. But I noticed that when Vince heard that I was a stranger in Canada, his mood became a bit more serious.

"There will be another meeting here tomorrow night. Please come. I want you to meet my wife. She is from Trinidad. I know she will want you to visit us frequently. You will not be lonely again."

The next evening, I was the first person to be at the chapel, even before the others arrived for the conference. When the meeting concluded, Vince introduced me to his wife, Barbara. Barbara too was very warm, and they both showed a keen interest in me. I realized they were not just being courteous; the invitation to visit them as frequently as I could was genuine. Vince assured me that if I wanted to visit he would pick me up at the school. Vince explained that he was a new Christian.

"Actually, my wife brought me to Christianity," he told me. "This group that is meeting here, we are called the Stouffville Christian Fellowship. Stouffville is north of Toronto. We came to this chapel to show our active Christianity. We hoped some of the students would join us to hear our speaker." I certainly appreciated the "active Christianity" of these fine people. That night, I slept a little more soundly.

The next morning, about six o'clock, I heard a voice by my bed saying, "Good morning, my African friend, do you remember me?"

I stared at my early morning visitor through eyes heavy with sleep. I must confess that, at that time, all white people looked the same to me. I feebly muttered, "Sure, I know you."

"I'm Vince. We met at the chapel last night. You remember?"

"Yes, of course I do, ah, now. I'm just not a morning person."

"Last night when I went home, I couldn't sleep. God told me to bring you this. Take it. I will come back after work, at six p.m. Barbara and I want you to join us for supper." I mumbled an agreement, took the envelope he gave me, tucked it under my pillow, then dropped back to sleep.

That afternoon, while I was eating lunch, the thought came to me that someone had come to my room in the early morning and left me a gift. Of course, the whole thing could have been a dream. I wasn't sure. I rushed upstairs to my room, shook out my pillow and an envelope fell out. I opened the envelope and there was $1,600 in cash that Vince had brought to me because the Lord had told him to do it. Although I didn't have a complete understanding of Canadian money, I knew that this was a lot. I was so excited!

I took the money downstairs to the accounting department. I rushed in with such exuberance that one of the accountants asked me what was going on. I just spread all the money on her desk and said that this was for my tuition and other fees. What a joyful time that afternoon was for me!

I left that office singing one of the Scripture Union songs we had learned in Ghana:

Keep praising the Lord, when the skies above are gray.
Keep praising the Lord, for the answer's on the way.
Do not despair, for the Lord will answer prayer.
To those who endure, the victory is sure.
Keep praising the Lord.

I sang that song over and over again as I climbed up to my room. I didn't even bother to go back to finish my lunch.

In my room, I began to feel very sad as I pondered my life. I was sad because I had refused consistently to accept that, indeed, God was with me and that He cared for me. Yesu had promised to look after me and had shown his faithfulness in so many ways. Why did I continue to forget that God was sovereign – even in times of trouble? Why, when the going got tough, had I not been able, as the song I had been singing said, to keep from despair and keep praising the Lord, believing that the answers were on the way?

I felt so ashamed. I began to relate my life to the stories in the Bible about the people of Israel who were travelling from Egypt to Canaan. I thought of how God parted the Red Sea for their escape from the Egyptian army and how the Lord had provided all their needs. And, yet, despite all the miracles they witnessed, the people of Israel became angry and discouraged whenever trouble appeared. They acted as if God didn't exist. I identified completely with the Israelites. God was disappointed with those people and I was sure that He was disappointed with me. He had opened the Red Sea in my situation; He had done the impossible and, yet, I had consistently behaved in an ungrateful manner.

For a long time I pondered these things and the money that Vince had brought. $1600 was a substantial sum of money in 1979. It completely covered my fees for that term. Didn't Paul tell the Philippians, "My God shall supply all your needs, according to His riches in glory, in Jesus" (Phil. 4:19)? That verse took on new meaning for me that afternoon. I began to realize that this verse was not written just for the Philippians but also for me. I understood that supplying my needs might mean that sometimes I had nothing, so that I would trust Him more. Perhaps it might mean that sometimes I would go hungry, if plenty was taking me away from Him. I saw that supplying my needs does not mean that I would get everything I wanted instantly, but that my needs would be met in different ways. I was very thankful. I cried and thanked Yesu for His kindness, love and faithfulness.

I walked out of that room feeling like a prince. I was swinging my arms and whistling as I came on two students who were staring at me, wondering what was happening to me. I could only tell them that I was happy; that God hadn't forgotten me.

Vince came as he had promised. What a lovely meal his wife had prepared for me. Barbara had searched all over

Toronto to find things that I might like. She found plantain, yams and crabmeat. It was just like being in an African home. I can still remember the joy on their faces as I ate that meal. They felt so fulfilled.

Vince told me that he had a scrap yard, that he had money, and that I shouldn't worry, they would look after me. He told me that it would be their delight to be able to help me. He looked at the clothes I was wearing and said that it was going to be getting very cold in Toronto and that my clothes would not be warm enough. He then ushered me to his closet. There was a very extensive wardrobe. Vince told me to try the clothes on, and everything fit me like it had been made to order. Vince had been tiny like me, but had begun to put on a little weight and could no longer wear much of his wardrobe. I tried on one item of clothing after another. Everything fit me so comfortably that Vince just stood in the middle of the room clapping his hands, as excited as a child.

"I didn't know what to do with these clothes. Some of them are almost brand new. I didn't realize it my African friend, but God was having me buy those clothes for you! They are all yours!" With that, he threw his arms around me and gave me a hug.

When I went back to school that night, I was carrying a trunk filled with a dapper new wardrobe. When I went to class the next morning, most of my fellow students stared at me. Until they found out the whole story, they kept staring and wondering if I had suddenly become rich. Vince had exceptional taste in clothes – and suddenly his wardrobe was mine. I looked like I had stepped off the cover of a magazine.

There I was, someone who had been feeling so cornered, now feeling so released. Day in and day out, I kept praising the Lord. God had finally made me understand that truly, He is the Lord.

Several times I went to my mailbox and found gifts from anonymous givers. Once there was a large cheque from someone in Montreal. His or her name was not on the cheque, and the signature was illegible. That cheque alone covered my fees for another term. Through miracle after miracle, God assured me He had brought me to this land to study and that I should not worry. I felt so privileged that Yesu had reached out to me in Africa, and had cared for me also in this land that neither I nor my ancestors had ever known. He not only provided for my food and tuition but even my clothes.

From 1979 onward, I determined in my heart not to be reckless in my thinking patterns – trusting God only when my needs were being supplied and then becoming melancholy when I ran into hurdles. I did not want to treat Yesu that way.

Life became more meaningful as the days went on. I was able to share my deepening commitment and determination to walk with God with my friend Vince. I slowly came to realize that Vince and Barbara needed me as I needed them. They were both new Christians. God had brought me into their lives so that I could help them to mature in their faith. We began having Bible studies together, trying to understand what the Scriptures were saying to us. We trusted God and wanted to live for him, but what did that mean in terms of how we conducted our everyday lives? Together we addressed some pretty hard questions. Those were special days; we grew as Christians and moved closer to God.

One day, while we were having lunch at a restaurant, Vince told me he was leaving his scrap yard business. My first reaction was that my friend was also taking leave of his senses. After all, Vince had worked very hard to build up that business and was now almost a millionaire. Barbara was pregnant, hardly an opportune time to shop around for new career options. I asked him why he would do such a bizarre thing. He sat quietly for a moment.

"My friend, I started that business with a very crooked heart. I know how to cheat, I know how to take things almost for nothing from people's scrap. I know how to go into areas where I should not be. I have cheated so many people in building that organization up. I have never been fair with my prices when I had to pay people for their scrap. God has been speaking to my heart that this is not the way he wants me to go. He has spoken to me clearly that I can no longer cheat. Just as you have determined to live an honourable life for Him, so have I. I plan to speak to my associates and my employees that I have to resign as president."

When Vince delivered the news to his business partners, they were shocked. Here was Vince, the best wheeler-dealer of them all, suddenly talking to them about the importance of running a business in a manner that would be pleasing to Christ. But after awhile they began to see his point. It was not enough to simply be honest in terms of the law (which they had always been) but it was also important to treat everyone in a fair manner. Today that company operates on strong principles of integrity and is doing better than ever. But Vince is no longer a part of it. He is serving as a missionary in Italy. He and Barbara now have two children. They are happy because they know they are where God wants them to be.

As I observed the changes in Vince's life, I was reminded of II Corinthians 5:17, which says, "If any man is in Christ, he is a new creature. Old things have passed away, behold new things have come." Here was a young entrepreneur, just beginning a life of increasing wealth, having every material thing a young man like him could desire. And, yet, inside he knew God was calling him to take a new path. Vince was willing to let go of that business. Such faithfulness was a challenge to me. It was also a reminder that life does not consist in the abundance of things we have, but in the true spirit of Christ, which liberates us from greed, from selfishness and opens our eyes to the hurts of others. Vince was walking, as I had, into "an unknown land." He did not know exactly where God was going to lead him.

Vince and Barbara did everything they could to make my life at OBC pleasant. It wasn't always Bible studies that brought us together. Sometimes we would go out just for fun. One such time was the day we packed a large picnic basket and headed for Centre Island, a ferry ride from downtown Toronto. It was a beautiful place. There were gardens everywhere. It seemed as though people from all over the globe met there to have picnics. This was my first visit to this pretty place and I was excited as we boarded the ferry.

While we were sitting on the boat I noticed a young man dressed in jeans, leaning over the railing. I saw him move as though he was trying to jump overboard. I bolted toward him, and got there just as half of his body was over the railing. I grabbed him by his jeans and managed to pull him back on board. His face was flushed with anger. He told me he was fed up with life and wanted to end it. In a very sarcastic manner, he asked if I would have the courtesy to leave him alone. I refused the request and asked him if he knew where he was going after death. When he said no, I shared some of my own experiences with him and emphasized that there is life after death and he needed to think about that before committing suicide.

The young man's mood began to change. He told me his name was Roger and he asked how he could reverse his life as I had reversed mine in Africa. As I was speaking with Roger, a woman who had been watching us drew closer and began to pray as I talked. Roger opened his heart and said he wanted to see the leading of God in his life. He assured me he would not attempt suicide again and actually thanked me for saving his life. Roger spent the day with us at Centre Island. The next day we directed him to a pastor who could help him further. What a joy was mine to know that, through God's love, I had been able to keep that man from death and, even more important, that I had been able to lead him to a meaningful life.

At the island, we played like young children. While we were wandering about, a police officer approached on his horse. I was still a little apprehensive about police officers and was preparing myself to run should the need arise. Vince called to him and he rode in our direction. My heart began to pound and I wondered why Vince had called out to the policeman. But my friend was completely relaxed as he explained to the officer that I was from Africa, and asked him to pose in a picture with me. The officer graciously answered yes. The policeman took a few minutes to get the horse set, then beckoned me closer and reached down to put his hand on my shoulder while Vince snapped our photograph.

The officer was very kind. His friendliness gave me a different feeling for the law officers of Canada. I compared that man's attitude with the attitude of officers I had seen in Ghana. The police in Ghana are usually concerned with receiving bribes and making things very difficult for civilians. But, from that day on, I felt comfortable and even happy to see police cruisers passing by. From that first impression, I came to understand that the Canadian police were approachable and genuinely concerned with being helpful.

Vince and Barbara always wanted me to feel at home and part of their family. I took that freedom very literally. I was never afraid to open their refrigerator to have a snack. Their home truly was a home to me.

Life at Ontario Bible College was quite exciting and I studied hard. I even managed to complete a British correspondence program in journalism while keeping up with my other studies. My Bachelor of Religious Education program was scheduled to take four years but I took extra classes and completed it in three. I was not worried any more and, indeed, God always met my needs at the school. My love for God grew every day as I continued to see the way he cared for me.

In my early days in Canada, I began to hear all kinds of stories concerning racial issues.I took a special course to study the relationship between whites and blacks. The study was recorded in a fifty-page paper and supervised by a South African professor. In my study, I conducted interviews with police officers, black and white pastors, and a variety of other people. I saw some discrepancies in the attitudes of both races. I found that both blacks and whites had their own racist ideas, but these unfortunate notions were not very pronounced. It would be misleading to say that there was absolutely no racism in Ontario or Toronto. But I must say that I, personally, encountered very little. I found Canadians to be very accommodating and loving people.

There was only one occasion when I was subjected to an overt act of racism. OBC's choir was touring Ontario. I was in the choir along with another African student from Mauritius. One night our tour took us to a Baptist church in Leamington. After singing, it was our habit to go into the crowd, meet the people, shake hands and visit. For the other African student and myself, meeting the people of Ontario was the best part of the tour. It really did seem to make Canadians feel good to see two Africans singing in the choir. Many people would ask us questions about Africa and we were always delighted to provide answers. In this church, however, there was one woman who would not shake my hand. She shook hands with the white students in front of me and those behind me. In fact, she made a conspicuous show of ignoring me and the other African student.

I felt very sad, especially sad because that woman was in the church. Racism has no place in the church. How could someone call oneself a child of God and yet not be willing to touch my black skin? But upon thinking about all of the churches we had been in, I was able to single her out as an extreme case. I should add that her attitude was certainly not typical of the people in that Leamington church. I didn't let that isolated case spoil my view of other Canadian whites, or, for that matter, Canadian blacks, Chinese, Japanese, Latin Americans or any of the other nationalities who make Toronto their home. Toronto is truly a multi-cultural city. It amazed me how much I could learn of other people and cultures in this one place! It also made me think of what heaven will be like with people of every tribe and nation.

At college the most exciting times for me were the chapels. They were remarkable. There we met many people of different nationalities, and missionaries who had been in various countries. Not surprisingly, I took special interest in the missionaries who had served in Africa. It was fascinating to hear them report on their missions. They gave me a better idea of how Africans are perceived around the world.

At other times we would hear from a new believer about his or her spiritual journey. I will never forget a Cambodian boy who told us of how he and many other young people were prisoners in a concentration camp during the war. Every day, soldiers would select one or two people from the group and shoot them in front of the other young people. No one understood why they were doing this. The area around the camp was mined and the few who tried to escape were blown up.

Our speaker described the horror from which there seemed no escape. Each day he knew that either he would be killed or he would watch a friend be murdered in front of his eyes. Finally, he decided to chance an escape. As he left the camp, he looked up and spoke in his own language to, "The one who is up there, the one who made the moon, the stars, the sun." He said he didn't know if anyone was there but he just asked, "Is there any way that you can help me?" He began to walk through a mine field. Miraculously, he made it through and travelled many miles until he came to the ocean.

As he stood on the beach, he saw an ocean liner passing. He waved to call attention to himself. The ship dispatched a small boat that picked him up and returned to the liner. On the ship he met Christians, who prayed with him. Some of the Christians began to tell him about Jesus. The Cambodian boy told them, in a kind way, that they shouldn't speak to him about Jesus as though Jesus were a stranger to him. For it was Jesus who had saved him from death the night before. Before the ship docked in Canada, he had begun to realize that the unknown God whom he had spoken to in that dreadful camp was a mighty God indeed. Such stories deepened my understanding of the greatness of God. I realized that God has absolutely no limitations. He is everywhere, moving, searching hearts, looking for those who will cry out to him.

24

The Paisleys

I MAINTAINED A CLOSE CONTACT WITH Gene Paisley, the friendly farmer I met at the OBC chapel. Gene was fascinated by the plan that our Christian group in Ghana was developing to help people in the north of the country. Gene invited me to spend my summers working on his farm. He felt I might learn some farming methods that could be used in Ghana. I could not be paid because I was on a student visa, but Gene checked with Ontario Bible College to see if it was legally permissible if I were to work on the farm and he were to pay my fees. The college assured him that the arrangement was perfectly acceptable.

Working on the farm was interesting. I remember that my first assignment was helping to clean the barn. I also remember that the smells in the barn were difficult to handle, although I adjusted in a few days. Coming from village life in Africa, I loved being in a rural community. I felt so at home and enjoyed learning about the land, when to sow crops, and how to milk cows – with machines. I watched the milking system with wonder – machines taking the milk and pumps drawing the milk to the big bulk tank.

Not all the work was fun though; there were certain jobs that everybody wished they could be excused from. Picking stones was one of those. One person would drive a tractor, pulling a wagon up and down the fields. The rest of us, walking beside the wagon, picked stones from the soil to keep them from ruining farm machinery. Often one of us managed to get our fingers caught between two stones and watched our fingernails turn black. It seemed that we would never get to the end of the fields. It always amazed me that year after year new stones would come to the surface and the same fields would need to be cleared again. I was not alone in my dislike of this activity. It seemed that everyone looked for a legitimate reason to be exempt.

Haying season could also be a pain. When I came to the farm, each individual bale of hay was thrown on to a wagon, where someone loaded them neatly, seven layers high. The bales weighed about fifty pounds each and I weighed about 115 to 120 pounds. Each bale was wrapped with two pieces of twine. I didn't quite have the knack of getting my fingers out from under the strings at the right time, and on several occasions as I tried to throw the bale up I ended up rolling on the ground with the hay on top of me. I would get up and look at my friend Gary, Mr. Paisley's adult son, and wish he would find me something else to do. But Gary had confidence in my ability to learn, a bit too much confidence perhaps, and never changed my assignment.

I tried my best not to lag behind the other workers. After the wagon was loaded it carried the hay to elevators that took the bales into the barn, where we neatly stacked them again. Once again, I wasn't the only one who didn't care for the task. Everyone who worked on the farm was delighted when Gene purchased a baler that kicked the bales into wagons with high racks. This technology released us from the most difficult step of the haying process.

Baler or no baler, there was always plenty of work to do at the farm. An electric fence in the pasture deterred the cattle from getting more grass than they needed. There was a fairly strong current passing through this fence, which had to be moved daily. Before going to the field for this assignment, you made sure you unplugged the fence. You always did this yourself so that you would be sure not to get "zapped." Even as you walked to the field, you kept looking over your shoulder to make sure no one had plugged in the fence looking for some fun at your expense.

One day, I was sent to the field with another student who was working there for the summer, a girl named Renee. We were to bring in a new calf that was lying right beneath the dew covered fence. I told Renee that some of the guys in our summer crew might be up to no good and that we had better be careful. She confidently told me that she had unplugged the line and there was no need to fear. The young lady continued to brush off my warnings, and when we got to the calf, she didn't give the fence a second thought. As she pulled the calf up, it pushed her against the fence. Lo and behold, I was right – the rascals had plugged it back in. Did Renee yell! She wiggled free and sat on the ground, looking a bit dazed. I told her she must not have unplugged the fence correctly. But Renee knew the truth. She had been tricked. For the rest of the summer, she was more cautious and even instigated a few of her own dastardly deeds.

We had lots of fun and lots of food. We always looked forward to lunch time. Elenor, Gary's wife, prepared wonderful, hearty meals for us. All of us had ravenous appetites but Elenor made sure that we left the table feeling happy and full. I knew I was a long way from Ghana.

Whenever I was on vacation I came and stayed at Gary's house, which was located on the farm. We woke up early in the morning and often there seemed to be a competition to see who would be first to the barn. Usually we were up by 5:30 and I often dreaded the sound of the alarm clock for, like I said, I'm just not a morning person. For the first hour I felt like I was half asleep.

The worst job on the farm, however, was neither the stone picking nor the haying, but being sent for the chain. It was long and very heavy. It was required when a tractor had problems in the field and needed to be towed. Being designated to go for it was the most dreaded job of all. At such times one examined oneself to see if there wasn't something you had done wrong and wondered whether in fact this was a punishment.

At the other end of the scale, my favourite job was working with the animals. They became like friends to me, and knew what times of day were feeding times. When the young heifers in their fenced yard would see me arriving with two pails of grain there was such excitement. They would run back and forth, jump and kick with glee. I talked about the farm life with other students who were there for the summer. They agreed that being on the farm with the people, animals, and a lot of land was a great contrast to more than nine months of studying.

There were other dimensions of summers on the farm that I cherished. For one, I knew that Gene Paisley and his wife, Laura, deeply loved me and cared about me – as did Gary, Elenor and their children, Lynnita and Matthew. They were all Christians and it was a joy to work with them. The good relationships made all the difficult jobs seem insignificant. We prayed together and had Bible studies together.

There was another element. The Paisleys' daughter, Brenda, had returned from serving in France with a Christian organization called Operation Mobilization and was now working at a bank in nearby Unionville. Brenda and I enjoyed talking together and discussing the problems that Christians face in different parts of the world. We seemed to have many things in common and developed a strong friendship. Ours was a healthy friendship that showed no signs of becoming anything more. After all, I was engaged to a girl in Africa and she was almost engaged to a Canadian boy.

Circumstances began to change. I had not adequately prepared my fiancée for the difficult times that would face both of us while I was in Canada and she remained in Ghana. Oh, I certainly communicated my joy and excitement about studying in North America but, looking back on it, I'm sure she did not realize all that was involved. How could she? Northern Ghana, as I have already indicated, is a very isolated part of the world, where knowledge about *Abrokyire* consists mostly of tall tales. Having a loved one travel to *Abrokyire* to study for several years was almost unheard of. My fiancée had absolutely nothing in her background, or that of her family and friends, to prepare her for what was happening – or even to really understand it.

She began to think that I was spending too much time in pursuing an education. It must have been difficult for her to watch her friends get married and start families while all she had was a stack of letters from Canada. The best solution was for her to visit me in North America and find out what *Abrokyire* was really like. But those plans got mired in the inevitable trials that come with trying to get a passport in Ghana.

That was a very difficult time for me, as the letters from home became increasingly unpleasant and my relationship with the girl I was going to marry collapsed. I tried to deal with the situation by becoming even more involved with my studies. However, the breakup caused me to spend more time praying with Brenda. We prayed for my former fiancée and asked for God to keep His hand on her as she planned for her future.

Then, a few months later, Brenda's relationship with her "almost" fiancé ended. Originally, both Brenda and her boyfriend had felt a strong commitment to foreign missions. But her boyfriend's goals in life began to change and Brenda felt that their lives were no longer moving in the same direction. The end of this relationship added new dimensions to our friendship.

I feel uncomfortable writing that Brenda and I were brought closer together by a shared misery over failed romances but, on reflection, that seems to be what happened. We began caring for each other more. Our friendship cushioned us against the extremes of heartbreak. As the days went on, I began to realize that my affection for Brenda was very deep. I remember saying to myself, after a visit with Brenda, "My goodness, it's just too bad this girl is white! If she had only been black, she would have been a masterpiece of a wife!"

I quickly began to recognize my attitude for what it was – racism! I came to realize that I deeply loved Brenda and it was wrong to deny that love because of race. Yes, I guess you could say that I finally understood that love is not just skin deep. But the whole situation was so awkward. What if Brenda didn't share the depth of my feelings? I could be ruining a very special friendship. What about Brenda's family? Would they think that I had exploited their kindness? What about my family? How would they react when they found out that I wanted to marry a woman with cat eyes?

First things first, I felt that I needed to find out if Brenda was open to the possibility of marrying someone of a different race. My chance came one evening, when Brenda and I attended a lecture by George Verwer, the director of Operation Mobilization. He spoke about church and missions and how the church needed to expand its vision to other parts of the world. On our way home, with heart pounding, I spoke.

"You have been enthused about missions since before I met you. We've been challenged by hearing this message tonight. I wonder, what would you do if God led you to Africa, and you became attached to a black person and he wanted to marry you?" She calmly turned around and replied, "If God wanted me to work in Africa and led me to marry someone, skin colour would not be an issue to me."

Wow! I thought. *What great news!* Brenda had no idea why I was asking this question. But from my standpoint the question was very important. For I had come to realize that many people are open to those of all races and nationalities as friends, but draw the line at inter-racial marriage. Her answer was a delight to me. But I couldn't allow myself to get carried away. After all, she had only said that she was open to the possibility of marrying a black man. That was a far cry from saying that she would marry me.

I felt that, before pursuing matters with Brenda any further, I needed to consult with my mother. I had been writing to my mother regularly, of course, but this particular letter was written with special care. After all the traditional greetings, I delicately asked what she would think if I brought home a white girl as my bride. I told her I had been socializing with a wonderful Canadian girl. She was nice in every way, the only "problem" being that she was white. I told my mother that the relationship was still in a very early stage and I would appreciate her thoughts on the matter.

I received the most beautiful reply from my mother. At that time, my mother was not a Christian, but she wrote with great wisdom and sensitivity. She said she had great respect for me, primarily because of my faith in God. She knew of many people who thought I would deny my faith when hit by hard times but they had been proven wrong.

"You know what it is to be hurt. You know what it is to suffer. You have also learned what it is to trust your God in difficult circumstances. The God that you serve, and because of whom you have lost so much in our society, your God has made all the colours in the world. He made the white people. He made the black people. I don't even know all the people he has made but I know His people are many. It would be a very silly thing, David, for you to reject God's offer to you on the basis of a colour, one of the colours that he has made. If you are going to choose a wife, your choice should be on her character, and should be someone who would be prepared to go all out to serve your God the way you are, because I know you will never settle down with a woman who does not believe in God the way you do. Let that mind guide you. For my part, I will embrace anyone who proves to love your God and has good qualities in her character."

When I received that letter, I felt empowered. My mother had written with such insight. How lucky I was to have such a wonderful mom. I knew that if Brenda consented to marry me, my mother would make it her task to persuade the rest of the family that my choice was correct. My family was no longer a problem. Now, it was up to me.

My love for Brenda continued to deepen and grow. I felt like an athlete who had trained hard and was now on the mark, waiting for the gun to fire so he could move. But getting off that mark was proving to be tough. Brenda and I were having a lot of conversations about a lot of topics, but I couldn't seem to bring the conversation around to marriage. Finally, I decided I could stall no longer.

At that time Brenda was typing all my papers for me and felt that, by reading my work, she was understanding me better. She certainly understood my sensitivity on race issues. I gathered enough courage to ask her out for dinner. She thought the purpose of the invitation was to show my appreciation for all the typing she had done. I was grateful for the typing, of course, but the purpose of the dinner was to propose marriage. I would just speak what was on my mind and let the chips fall where they may.

The big night arrived. I took her to a charming restaurant located near the college. It was a difficult night for me. We ordered our meals and I found I couldn't eat well. I kept picking at my food, occasionally looking at Brenda, and from time to time squirming on my chair. Every time I had the thought of breaking my news, my heartbeat doubled its pounding and I coiled back. I would get ready again and the waiter would come. Each time I would prepare myself to speak, I would feel as though beads of sweat were going to break out on my forehead. Brenda, oblivious to what was going through my mind, thoroughly enjoyed the meal.

We finished our dinner, and by the time we got to the car I felt like kicking myself. *What is the matter with you?* I thought. *You've missed your chance.* I continued to chastise myself on the drive to the college. *You thought you were a brave person. You haven't even been able to open your mouth! How could you be such a chicken in front of a little girl?*

When we arrived back at the college, I asked her inside for a brief visit. I thought that perhaps I could function better in familiar surroundings. We went to the library, to a small room called a quiet room. We talked for awhile and I finally thought, as the Ghanaians would put it, "do and die." That means you say something even though it means your death. I cleared my throat and spoke.

"Brenda, what I'm going to say, it might be wrong, it might be inappropriate, but I just feel I should say it and whatever happens, just forgive me."

Tension appeared on her face; she didn't know if she had offended me or what was happening. I kept going.

"I've been thinking – our relationship as friends has grown in so many proportions, and more and more I've felt deeply in love with you and I felt that I should let you know, so that if it is inappropriate then we can all pray about it and squash it. But I'm feeling very deeply about it, and every time I see you I'm beginning to feel guilty of my thoughts about you and having you as a wife in the future."

I kept speaking fast without giving her a chance to reply because I wanted to get everything I'd kept inside out in the open. I even came to the point of saying, "I'm going to graduate next year and I thought we could get married in May and then I would like us to go to Winnipeg for me to do a Master of Arts program and after that we would go to Ghana and start the mission work that our group had established before I came to Canada."

I kept nothing back. And what a release I felt that I had been able, finally, to say everything that was inside my heart. My good feeling didn't last long. It occurred to me that I had no idea how the woman I loved was responding to my monologue.

Brenda sat very still for a moment, and then said," Yes, I too am deeply in love with you. You're the most wonderful person I've ever met."

I suddenly felt as though I was in dreamland. I didn't know what to do, whether to get up and dance or what. I was too excited to say anything. She said yes – she had just agreed to marry me! She had agreed to go to Winnipeg with me – she had agreed to go to Ghana and work with me – she is in love with me! Someone walked into the room, searching for a book. I hardly noticed he was there. He noticed we were having a serious conversation and offered to leave. We, however, decided to leave, and went to the lounge. At this point, I was walking like an army captain, not the timid David who had been feeling so sheepish for the better part of the evening. I had opened my heart and its outpourings had met with favour, dispelling all my fear. Brenda and I talked into the night, then I saw her off.

From the parking lot, as I walked back to OBC looking at the buildings around me, I felt as though God had given me the whole world and put it at my feet. I started to leap exuberantly and even performed some African dances. I was so excited I didn't know what to do. I moved along the halls of the school whistling like a bird. When I returned to my room, I thanked God for what had just taken place.

I sat on my bed before sleeping and began to think. *I wonder if Brenda's agreement was just a polite way to keep from crushing my spirit.* I knew how she had tried so much in her previous relationship to help the boy she was dating. I wondered if she really meant what she had just said. *Was she just being kind to an African boy so as not to hurt me?* I hoped this wasn't so. As these things were going through my mind, I began to think, *Actually, if she said anything just to calm me down, it was because I had spoken too much. If anybody spoke to you in the near-hysterical manner that you spoke to her, what would you have done? Here you were, the very first time you had spoken about your love for the girl, you started by proposing, giving wedding dates, talking about your career and moving to Winnipeg, leaving Canada and going to Ghana to work there. You spoke about everything – how could anybody give a reasonable answer?*

I didn't sleep well that night and the next morning I phoned Brenda to find out if, in the cold, sober light of morning, she still wanted to marry me. I was so happy when Brenda reaffirmed that she deeply loved me and thought I would be the most wonderful husband. To my amazement, she told me that rather than frighten her, my future planning and vision had won her.

"You know what you want to do. Our goals are one. You are not someone who will change directions on a whim. I know you are the type of man I want to follow, to live with and to work with."

Brenda explained that for some time she had been telling her family and friends that she was deeply impressed by my character, but she had been surprised herself when something had changed within her that took her feelings for me beyond friendship. She began to miss me when I was gone for even a short period of time. Brenda always regarded herself as a cautious type, someone who makes important decisions only after careful deliberation. But when I had proposed marriage, she knew that her only answer could be, "Yes!" Hearing this caused me to shout, "hallelujah" within myself. I began to float on clouds. Life somehow was different. Everything was perfect. I could hardly wait for graduation, when we could be married. I was the luckiest guy in the world. This beautiful woman with a beautiful character, from a home I had felt very much a part of already, would be mine.

But there were serious obstacles that had to be overcome. As I have already explained, the Paisleys had always been very kind to me. Their farm had become my surrogate home. But when Brenda and I announced our plans to marry, her parents were deeply troubled. There were many difficult questions for them to deal with. Would an inter-racial marriage subject their daughter and, for that matter, their grandchildren to a life of cruel comments and covert discrimination? Was a life of serving in Ghana really the right thing for Brenda?

Mr. and Mrs. Paisley sought counsel from other Christian friends and missionaries. Brenda and I were surprised to hear that some missionaries ended their work when their children became teenagers, out of fear that the children might marry a native of the country they were serving in. Only one missionary gave a positive outlook on inter-racial marriage. In fact, Gene and Laura Paisley were bombarded with negative opinions about what would happen to their daughter if she married me. When I visited the farm, the unhappiness and anxiety was apparent. Everyone continued to be nice, but I could tell that Gene, in particular, was deeply distressed as he tried to work through this problem in a way that was pleasing to Christ.

Brenda and I would meet on Friday evenings for the purpose of praying specifically about this problem. We also decided to talk with Dr. Sikakane, an OBC professor from South Africa. Professor Sikakane was a man who knew something about racial problems. He had seen the harshness with which the whites dealt with the blacks in South Africa. This black man used to be called from time to time to speak at a white church in South Africa, but when he applied to become a member, the congregation voted against him. When we told Dr. Sikakane our story, his first reaction was to get up from his chair, kneel down, and call us to pray. After he had prayed for us, he advised us that if two people decide that they will work at their relationship, with Christ's help it will work. Despite all the ugliness he had seen in interracial dealings, he told of us of three interracial couples who had excellent marriages.

"My son and daughter, do not allow colour to prevent you from pursuing a life that is worthy."

With that, he prayed for us again. Then he talked about how marriages between whites fail, marriages between blacks fail, marriages within other racial groups and cultures fail. If people are not willing to serve one another, their relationship will not last. The backgrounds that people come from are not what determines a good marriage. For a successful marriage you must have a man and a woman who truly love each other and are willing to live together in a spirit of give and take. Brenda and I left Dr. Sikakane's office feeling very content. What he had told us made a lot of sense. Skin colour was no guarantee of a happy and lasting marriage.

But none of this changed the fact that Brenda's parents remained skeptical. One Sunday evening a very heated discussion developed while I was at the Paisley home. While the tone of the discussion was unfortunate, it was also, perhaps, inevitable. It was also very valuable for me. I learned that there was much more to the resistance of Brenda's parents to our marriage than the colour of my skin. If Brenda married me she would, in time, be moving to Ghana. They would see her very rarely. Brenda's parents wanted only what most parents want. They wanted their daughter to live nearby, where they could interact with her frequently. They wanted to be able to enjoy their grandchildren and watch them grow up, step by step. Nothing was resolved that night, but I left with a better understanding of how deep and intense was the love of this father and mother for their daughter.

A few weeks later, I phoned Brenda's father. "I know you have reservations, but this is the course I feel I should go. Brenda feels the same way. I would like us to become officially engaged."

Mr. Paisley was quiet for a moment and then said, "If this is what you both are convinced of and feel you should do, I don't have much to say right now, but I wish you every blessing in your endeavour."

The next day, Brenda and I went out for supper with two friends, Dan and Brigitte. I had Brenda's engagement ring in my pocket. The story of her ring is an interesting one. Early in our friendship, acquaintances of ours, Michael and Primrose, told me, "We see you and Brenda as really nice people and we don't know whether we are speaking out of turn, but we just felt that if some day you feel like you are interested in one another, please give us the honour of buying an engagement ring for you."

At that point I responded that we were not interested in one another, we were just good friends. A few nights before taking Brenda and the two friends out for supper, I was praying with a friend in the school. Afterward, I told the friend what Michael and Primrose had said to me long ago, offering to buy a ring. I said I wished they would get in touch again. That night, I was called to the phone. Lo and behold, it was Michael.

"You know, David, we spoke to you a long time ago and offered to by an engagement ring for you to give to Brenda, and we just wanted you to know that the offer is still open." I couldn't believe my ears. My response was very different this time. I told him I was ready. He asked when we could get it.

"Tomorrow!"

When I put down the phone, I knew I had just experienced another of God's miracles. Brenda knew nothing of the ring. Early in our engagement she had told me it was not necessary for me to struggle to buy her a ring, but we did wonder how to make our engagement public without one.

The next evening, Brenda, Dan, Brigitte, and I went to a special restaurant for dinner. I again found that timid side of myself. I became nervous and unable to get that ring out of my pocket. I went to the washroom about four times. On my last visit, Dan decided he would follow me. He saw me just standing there in front of the mirror in the washroom.

"I knew it," he said. "I knew it! You are finding it difficult to give Brenda her ring." He patted my back. "You can do it." When we returned to the table, I did not immediately justify my friend's confidence in my courage. I would take the ring out of my pocket and then quickly put it back before anyone noticed. Finally, when we had finished the main course and cake was being served, I came up with a clever idea. I plucked the ring from my pocket and asked Brenda if she would be willing to cut cake with me in the future.

Well, I guess the idea wasn't all that clever. But it did the trick. Brenda was very happy, as were our friends. It was a delightful evening. We laughed and joked and felt the presence of God with us that night. It is certainly true that God is there during the hard times when you need him the most. But the Lord is also there to share in the joy and merriment.

Encouragement from friends and the prayer times that Brenda and I had together were very important to us. We continued to meet every Friday to pray together until May arrived and several of our friends and family were gathered around us to witness our vows. Our wedding was held in the chapel where I first met Brenda's father and Vince Gallo.

As we knelt to pray I found myself weeping as I recalled all that God had done for me. In a magnificent act of love, He had allowed me to come to Canada and gain a fine education. And, now, there beside me was Brenda, the woman God was giving to me as a wife. There was a representative from Ghana, a student in Ottawa, Sulley Gariba, who spoke on behalf of my family and people. Brenda's dear parents had worked through all of the counsel and had come to feel with us that we were moving in the right direction. They had been so open and honest about the struggle they were going through. That struggle was now behind them and they were rejoicing with us. I felt very loved. My friends at OBC were very kind and did all they could to make it a special day. Our life together had begun.

We rented a little cottage for the summer and I worked at the Paisley's farm to save for school while Brenda continued to work at the bank.

That summer was a joyous time. My relationship with my in-laws deepened in understanding and love. We laughed together day in and day out. We had travelled through some difficult terrain together and, with God's help, had ended up stronger because of the journey. I have often wished that more people could resolve intense emotional disagreements in a similar fashion – with genuine interaction and a constant seeking of God's will. By the end of that summer, I held the Paisleys in the same regard as my family in Ghana.

25

The Annapolis Valley of Nova Scotia

THERE WAS A CHANGE in our original plans. During the winter, I had heard a weather report on the radio that stated that the temperature in Winnipeg was minus forty degrees. MINUS FORTY DEGREES! Now, this African boy had managed to adapt to the Canadian climate but not quite to that extent. I applied to Acadia University in Nova Scotia and was accepted. The weather in Nova Scotia is not as harsh as it is in Manitoba, but it is still a far cry from tropical.

So that joyful summer on the farm was also a hectic one, as Brenda and I prepared to leave for Acadia. We were informed that the student population was at a record high. I had written dozens of letters to places for accommodation, but all the replies were negative. Brenda was trying to get a transfer from her bank to a branch in Acadia, but there were no positions open there. But, ready or not, the day to depart arrived. We packed our things into our little Omni and off we went, not knowing what lay ahead, only knowing that I had been accepted to do my Master of Arts program at the university. It was a pleasant two-day drive to Acadia, Nova Scotia. We went directly to the university and located the dean of Acadia Divinity College. He warmly welcomed us. He also informed us of how difficult it was to get accommodation that year and told us of an inexpensive motel where we could spend the night, and return to see the person in charge of accommodation the following day. He then prayed for us.

Later that evening we received a phone call at the motel. It was the dean. When he had mentioned our case to his wife she told him of a couple that was going to Florida, who usually rented their house to divinity college students, but had not rented it so far. The dean contacted the couple on our behalf and set up an appointment for he next morning. We were thrilled that this man, who barely knew us, had shown such concern. We felt at home in the Maritimes already. I knew right away that I would enjoy my schooling there just because my dean was such a fine person.

The next morning we met the Corbetts, a retired school principal and teacher. They were willing for us to stay with them until they left for Florida and, after a brief discussion, gave us the keys to their home. We could move in that afternoon. They were going away for the weekend. Mrs. Corbett said we were free to use anything in the house and we should make ourselves feel at home. Again we realized that the people of Nova Scotia were special; the Corbetts had seen us for only a few minutes and were prepared to leave their house to our care.

We were thankful to God for the way he had answered our prayers through these people. By this time, Brenda was expecting our first child and I was especially glad for her sake that these details were working out so beautifully. One can not go to the Maritimes without seeing a difference in the pace of life, especially from a big city like Toronto. In the Maritimes, people have time to stop and greet one another. I felt like I was closer to Ghana. I certainly did not feel like a foreigner. As I went to school and met some of the students, I was glad to be part of Acadia University.

Marriage created some unique financial problems for the Mensahs. Folks who had been helping me financially with my education no longer saw any need to do so, or maybe they figured that I needed to get used to the idea of having a lot of responsibility. I had applied for immigrant status in Canada but that process is a slow one. I was still on a student visa, and still unable to hold a job.

For the first few weeks in our new home, Brenda was unable to find a job. We were careful with our funds. I joined a car pool in order to save a few dollars. Our situation improved a bit when a bank asked if Brenda could fill in for someone on an extended maternity leave. The bank was at the end of our street, less than a five-minute walk away. My bride enjoyed the job and the people she worked with. She remained at the bank until she had to take her own maternity leave. When she left, the bank manager told her that she could always return on at least a part-time basis.

Our little daughter Elizabeth arrived in February, 1983. It was a happy time, of course, but also a time rife with anxiety. In the initial moments of Elizabeth's life we came close to losing her. The child stopped breathing. She turned blue and when the nurses picked up her arm and let go, the arm just dropped to the table. Several doctors and nurses worked quickly in an intense effort to revive her. While they worked, a frantic father prayed for the recovery of his first child. How grateful I was when a nurse came to tell me that my daughter was out of danger.

But I still couldn't relax. Brenda became very sick and had trouble regaining her strength. Elizabeth's first few days on earth were very tough on all of us. Six weeks later we were on our way back to Ontario, where I worked that summer on the farm. Brenda was still weak and that summer turned out to be a difficult one for us.

That fall we returned to Nova Scotia and to our home with the Corbetts. Brenda worked part time at the bank and our finances were very tight. I remember one Sunday morning when we could not afford to buy the gasoline needed for the drive to church. I walked behind the house with tears rolling down my cheeks. Yes, when faced with a small problem, I once again forgot that God never forgets his children. He is with us always. In a hoarse, choking whisper, I spoke to God from behind the Corbetts' home. "Lord, you have given me a wonderful new daughter and I need to care for her. You have brought me here to go to school, and I need funds to continue. I know you are able to supply these needs, but today I am finding it difficult to understand why I don't have enough funds for fuel to go to church to worship."

God is gracious. He is also practical and present in time of need – a lesson that I was to relearn that Sunday morning. After opening my heart to God, after praying and weeping, I went back into the house. The phone rang. The pastor's son was calling to say he would be passing our way en route to church, and he just wondered if he could give us a lift. I sat there amazed and my tears again began to flow as I chastised myself. *What a shame, David, that anytime there is a problem, you feel that God has neglected you.* For the rest of that Sunday my heart was filled with a special joy. God always hears the prayers of his children, and He is patient with the stubborn ones who need an occasional reminder.

Another unexpected blessing was on the way. About a week later, the university's financial department summoned me to inform me that I had been granted immigrant status and no longer needed to pay what had been a very substantial additional fee over the usual expenses. In fact, my immigrant status was made retroactive and I was being reimbursed in the amount of $1,400. I couldn't wait until classes were over. I dashed home, grabbed Brenda from her chair and began to shout that we were rich. I pulled out my cheque and recounted the whole story to her. That money helped us a great deal. My studies went very well and we enjoyed those days at Acadia University.

Nova Scotia will always have a very special place in our hearts. I am grateful to all of the wonderful people that we met in that province. At the time, I did not always realize the importance of these friendships. There was a wonderful farmer who ran an apple orchard near the university. He took delight in showing me pruning techniques and other aspects of producing good fruit. Much of that knowledge is being put to work in Ghana today.

On one brisk October day in 1983, I checked my post office box at the university and found a letter from Africa that left me devastated. Three people in my family had died of starvation. I was stunned. In that year Nigeria had expelled over one million Ghanaians and sent them back to Ghana. They arrived back at the worst possible time, when Ghana was in the grip of a terrible drought. With the population up and the food supply down, people starved. I stared at the letter in horror.

A colleague approached me and began some good-natured joking about the letter being a secret note from a mistress. In a jocular manner, he pulled the letter from my hands. One look at what I had been reading, changed his mood completely. He took the letter to the administration of the university and strongly suggested that the school respond to this tragedy. It was close to Thanksgiving day in Canada and he recommended that a way to show the true spirit of Thanksgiving would be to help the people of Ghana. He received no arguments whatsoever. A massive movement began. The students rallied together and raised funds. They went back to their individual churches and got the churches involved. It meant much to me to see these students and faculty responding to the needs of Ghana.

These efforts were not limited to Nova Scotia. In Ontario my father-in-law went to a bulk food store in Stouffville to purchase foodstuffs such as sardines, dried beans, rice, etc. He "happened" to run into the president of that chain of stores. When the president realized why Gene was purchasing the food he sold it virtually at cost. When Gene consulted a shipping company about sending the food to Ghana he discovered that the company had been founded years ago by a devout Christian. That man's principles still prevailed at the company.

The food was shipped free of charge. That shipment saved many lives. Without that help, three villages would have been wiped out. When I look back on those events today – how the students organized, how my father-in-law ran into the president of this food chain, and how the company shipped the goods free of charge – I am still amazed.

This response to the tragedy that had devastated Ghana was the beginning of The Mensah Food and Orphanage Fund. The fund originated in Nova Scotia and today it supports our program in Ghana. The story of how the organization was formed is a story of how God moves through "ordinary" people and events. Even after the initial shipment of food was sent to Ghana, people asked how they could continue to help.

Rev. Porter, the pastor of the Baptist church that Brenda and I were attending in Coldbrook, Nova Scotia, had become deeply involved in the efforts to help Ghana. With the enthusiastic backing of the congregation, Rev. Porter said that his church would be willing to do all of the organizational work required to maintain a permanent organization for helping the people of Ghana. Funds began to pour in.

During that time, I was asked to speak at the Women's World Day of Prayer service in Coldbrook. Many other churches joined with us for that meeting. I spoke about prayer and how we should be concerned for each other internationally; I also talked about how important it is to care for one another. I explained that my mother had to walk eight miles every day to get a pail of water and that her situation was hardly unique. A newspaper reporter was present at the meeting, and the resulting press report created more interest in helping those whose lives were threatened by the drought.

At this point The Mensah Food and Orphanage Fund was officially established, not only as a response to an emergency situation but as a permanent organization dedicated to helping the orphans, widows and the impoverished of Ghana. It has since changed its name to Ghana Rural Integrated Development, feeling that its new title more adequately conveys its mandate.

26

A New School and a New Home

OUR HOME IN NOVA SCOTIA BECAME known as the African Embassy. Foreign students visited us often. One Christmas we invited all the African students at the university over for an evening. It was a special time of sharing together and listening to music from Ghana, Nigeria and Kenya. Graduation came all too quickly and we were sad to say goodbye to Nova Scotia and the many wonderful friends we had made.

Long before graduation, I had applied to the University of Toronto and to McGill University in Montreal to pursue a doctoral program. I was disappointed when I received a letter from McGill stating that I could not be admitted because my first degree had been obtained from a Bible college. Then I received a similar letter from the University of Toronto. But the U of T was willing to make some special provisions. If I was prepared to do an additional year of study at the U of T, and if I achieved an A average in that year, they would allow me to pursue a doctoral program. I was delighted with this option. It would be very demanding, but I was convinced that the God who had led me thus far was capable of helping me to attain the A average that I needed. We packed our Omni once more and headed toward Toronto.

Although it was difficult for us to say goodbye to Nova Scotia and to the many friends we had come to cherish, we were happy for the many good memories. We knew we would never forget the people or the place. God had taken us there for a purpose and had taught us many important lessons. We had been exposed to very caring people and an organization had been established to help the people of Ghana.

En route our well-packed Omni gave us a few problems but we managed to make the trip back to Stouffville. We were excited to see Brenda's parents again. I did not work on the farm that summer. Because of the desperate situation in Ghana, I felt I needed to go and help. The Mensah Food and Orphanage Fund provided the money for my trip and purchased a van for me to take to the people of my tribe.

Brenda and Elizabeth stayed at the farm and off I went. I knew life had become difficult in Ghana since I left, but I could not have imagined just how difficult. Before I landed in Ghana I filled a small flask with water and it lasted me for about two weeks. Water was so scarce that I would sometimes just touch the flask to my lips. During that blistering hot summer my thirst was never quenched. When I saw my mother I didn't recognize her because she had become so lean. There was no food to buy and the drought seemed unrelenting. People would boil leaves to make some sort of soup. That was their meal for the day.

The van became like an ambulance during the two months I was there and I became the ambulance driver. I was constantly called on to transport people to the hospital. The trips were usually long as there are long distances between villages and the areas that offer any kind of medical assistance. There are hundreds of villages without a single vehicle. My whole tribe depended on that vehicle and many would have died without its services that year and in the years that followed. I was glad to have been able to help that summer. But the best help arrived just a few weeks before I left – when rain once again began to fall.

The work I did that summer reaffirmed my desire to work with rural people in their suffering, and thus it was with renewed interest that I prepared for my studies at the University of Toronto.

After the homey atmosphere of Acadia, I felt very lost in the U of T's massive buildings. Here I encountered a professor who had not been in favour of my acceptance. His manner of speech and the way he treated me that day indicated clearly that there were problems ahead. He told me categorically that I had a bad degree from a Bible college and, therefore, he had advised the university that they shouldn't accept me into the PhD program. But my MA work at Acadia had been excellent. On that basis, the school had bypassed his advice and decided to give me a chance. But only an A average at the end of the year would be acceptable. I told him I would work hard toward that goal.

Shortly after this meeting, I learned that the professor who was scheduled to teach a history class I had registered for was unable to teach the course that year. You've probably figured out the rest. Yes, the course was taught by the professor who had recommended that the school not accept me.

There was also no lack of challenges outside of school. The little church we had been attending in Stouffville before we were married suddenly found itself without a pastor. With increasing frequency, the church asked me to preach on Sunday morning. One day I received a phone call from the chair of the elders board, asking if I would consider becoming their pastor. The offer didn't surprise me too much. I had been praying for the church to find a pastor. But the more I prayed, the more I had a feeling that God was asking me exactly what I thought all my training was for. Within a few weeks of receiving that phone call, the church formally called me to be their pastor. It was a new experience to be sure, for I had not pastored a church in North America.

I knew that the challenge would be a demanding one. I had seen that people in North American churches were often introspective and self-centred. People frequently majored on minor issues, such as how people dressed and whether the pastor shook their hand or not. Global issues often received little attention. I trusted I could make a difference in this congregation and I appreciated that they had accepted me as their pastor. At that time, I was the only black in the church, and, for that matter, in the community. There were serious and devout Christians in that church who genuinely wanted to grow.

Before I had left for Ghana the previous summer, Brenda and I discussed our need for accommodation. I had hoped we would be able to buy a small home rather than rent. But all we had was money we had been given as wedding gifts and had, somehow, managed to hold onto. Our "nest egg" wouldn't buy much of a nest. Nevertheless, we decided that while I was away, Brenda would look into accommodation, and if she saw any property we could afford and if she could arrange financing, she would proceed.

The time of my return was drawing near, and nothing had turned up. Then Brenda read a verse in Proverbs: "Prepare your work without, make ready the field and build the house." It was a verse that she couldn't remember having read before. But for some reason it spoke to her, although she was not sure of its meaning. The next day her mother told Brenda that God had given her a verse to share with her daughter. It was the same verse! Still, neither mother or daughter was sure of how the verse applied to Brenda's situation.

Later that day Gene remarked that he wished we could move a house onto the farm. Brenda told him about an empty house she had just seen. She planned to enquire about renting it. It was situated on a golf course. In a phone call the next day the owner told Brenda he wasn't really interested in renting the house. He wanted the house moved off of the property but had no place to move it. Later that day Brenda toured the house and, somehow, felt sure it would be ours. The owner didn't share her certainty. But there were other signs of encouragement. When Brenda returned from looking at the house, she received a call from the bank where she had worked before our marriage, offering her a job. Our financial situation was now a bit more stable.

Brenda's enthusiasm about the house was contagious and I caught it the day I returned from Ghana. We agreed that the house would fit in just fine on the Paisley's farm. But the owner couldn't decide how much to ask for it. We prayed over the matter. Then, after a two-month wait, the owner let us have the house for nothing. We were overjoyed, to say the least. Gene Paisley set aside a half acre lot on the farm for the house. Our wedding savings were finally unleashed to pay part of the house-mover's fees.

The house would be moved about seven miles and all the bricks had to be removed for the trip. Everyone pitched in; church members, family – even our niece and nephew who were only twelve and seven years old. One by one, the bricks were chiselled off of the house, put on a truck, and carried to the farm. The excess mortar was scraped off and the bricks were piled on skids where they awaited springtime to be reunited with the house. By the time the project was finished, those bricks had been handled too many times to count. The house's journey from golf course to farm took place smoothly on a day when Brenda was at work and I was in school.

The location of the house was very interesting. It was in the middle of a field that fronted the farm. Passing farmers frequently mentioned that the house should have been placed in a far corner of the field. The overall appearance would have been much better. True enough, but God's hand was in the choosing of the site. In His time He would reveal His plan to us.

Of course, after the house was transferred to the farm, there was still plenty of work to do. Our congregation was an enormous help in getting these tasks completed. On the night before we moved in, the members of the church joined us in the house for a time of prayer as we dedicated that house to God's service. Throughout our stay there, Brenda and I continued to thank God for this wonderful gift. It was a three bedroom bungalow, but to us it always seemed like a mansion.

That fall was special to me for another reason. Sayibu arrived from Ghana to study at Ontario Bible College. Our home became his on vacation times and weekends.

Our first year in the house found me learning a variety of new trades. I even tried to install aluminum siding on a large area of the house where the wood was becoming worn. I was doing quite well until I got to the last corner, which had several angles. I used what geometry I could remember and managed only to spoil two pieces of siding. Brenda passed by and offered a suggestion. I felt the need to figure it out myself and encouraged her to take Elizabeth for a walk. She took the hint and left me to my calculations. After several more frustrating failures, I tried what Brenda had suggested. Her plan worked perfectly. The aluminum siding fit like a glove but my pride was bent totally out of shape. When Brenda returned and saw that the project was completed, she asked how I had been able to finish the job. I brushed the question off. Brenda understood completely and broke out in laughter. That didn't help my wounded pride much.

We bought a small, very used, tractor that had a snowblower, rototiller, lawn mower and trailer. I soon knew that tractor inside and out and was often to be found underneath it, fixing one thing or another. That tractor taught me a lot of practical lessons about farm machinery. A member of our congregation gave me some sound advice. If something breaks, try to fix it yourself first. If you fail, you can always call a repair man. But in the long run you will save money by trying to do it yourself. I took his advice. My wife often wondered if the equipment in need of repair would ever work again, but my successes soon outnumbered my failures.

As predicted, my year at the University of Toronto was difficult but I achieved the necessary A average and was accepted as a PhD candidate. The professor who had been so unenthusiastic about my presence at the school left at the end of the school year for a position at a different university. From what I was told, he had been wanting that post, so his departure was good news for both of us.

In August of that summer we joyfully welcomed a new daughter, Deborah, into the world and into our family. Elizabeth was pleased to have a baby in the house and enjoyed her new sister immensely. So did her parents. The new addition meant that Brenda would not be working, and we wondered how we could pay all my school fees and our bills. We were thankful to find that, because my marks were high, I was granted bursaries to cover all my fees. A Christian foundation gave me a scholarship and, with that plus my salary at the church, all our expenses were met.

For me, it was all just amazing. Here I was, this confused person who had arrived from Africa with ten dollars in his pocket, and now had a wife, two precious daughters, and a home in this foreign land. Night after night, I would lay on my bed and ponder these things. I remembered where I had come from, and often songs would well up in my heart as I considered the goodness of God. Some nights I would wander behind the house and gaze up at the stars, which were so clear in rural Ontario – just as they were in Africa. Each star seemed to remind me of God's love for His children.

There were still hurdles to jump in my work at school. I had come to the university to study under the guidance of Dr. Gregory Baum. I had met him and talked to him about my desire to study issues related to the Third World and he encouraged me to come and study under him. Within a year of my arrival, he left U of T for a position at another university. A committee was set up to supervise my work. It included a professor from India. I was delighted that there was a Third World person on the committee. Little did I know that this man was going to be a "thorn in my flesh" until my program was complete.

Dr. Hutchinson, my advisor and the chair of the committee, was kind and helpful. He gave good advice to help me achieve my goals. My heart's desire was to focus my studies in relation to the work that I planned to do in Africa. However, many others in the school were pushing me to pursue studies in liberation theology. Dr. Hutchinson encouraged me to look at ethics, relating to my own religious background and to the program in Ghana.

I wrote my dissertation on "Land Use and Environmental Ethics." The paper examined the whole range of modern practices of land use and focussed on how land has been constantly abused. It dealt with the ethics of corporate organizations and the mindset regarding agriculture that prevails in the West. The work was meaningful to me and was met favourably by most members of the committee. However, the Indian professor continued to be a challenge. When the committee recommended that I prepare a ten-page paper to clarify a point, he would insist that I do thirty pages. He seemed to be working in opposition to me. I often wondered if he were trying to see whether I would give up. He often was the cause of lengthy delays which, in the end, added another year to my program. Finally my thesis proposal was approved and the research and writing could begin in earnest.

At this time Brenda's parents decided to sell the farm and retire. My brother-in-law, Gary, was taking over the business and looking for a smaller farm that he could handle on his own. In the meantime, he planned to rent the farm from the new owners for a year. We were happy to see Brenda's parents able to retire after so many years of hard work, but a little sad too, over the change.

On a beautiful, sunny, summer day, Gary and Elenor went into town to clarify some legal matters with their lawyer. I was cutting the lawn when I saw thick smoke moving in my direction. Flames suddenly shot up from the barn. I ran toward the fire. On the way, I met the farm bull running loose. By the time I got to the barn, flames and smoke filled the building. Gene, my young niece and another girl were trying to get the animals out. They could not see how fast the fire was moving toward them. I screamed for them to get out. Less than a minute after they fled from the barn, there was a huge explosion and black smoke engulfed the area where they had been frantically working to save the animals.

An electrical fault had ignited a fire in the dry hay that filled much of the barn. Fire engines and other emergency vehicles arrived but there was no hope for the barn. The crew worked hard so that none of the other buildings or houses caught fire. We concentrated on trying to get equipment away from the burning barn. One of the firefighters called me to help him get a tractor to safety. As I jumped onto the tractor I remembered that I had been working in bare feet. That tractor felt like a giant, hot ember. I managed to get it away from the barn just before one of its tires blew. My back felt as if my clothes were on fire. Somehow, I managed to run back to the barn and rescue a small calf that was too terrified to move. In the midst of this devastation, one of the cows was standing off at a safe distance, giving birth to a calf. After the fire was brought under control it continued to burn and smoulder for three days. The fire chief dropped by frequently during that time.

It was a sad time for all of us as a family. Brenda's parents had worked the farm for more than forty years without any such incident. Gary and Elenor had seen smoke in the sky when they left the lawyer's office and did not like the direction it was coming from. Driving home, they became increasingly uneasy; then they realized that their worst fears were true. However, as difficult as this time was, we could not help but be thankful that no human life had been lost.

Eventually the ashes became cool enough for us to begin the clean up. It was a disturbing task, for more than thirty cattle had died. It was at a time like this that one appreciated the farm community and the care they had for one another. After the confusion had faded, after the news media had stopped calling, the "real people" arrived from all over to help with the job at hand. Some offered to keep and milk the cows until things were sorted out.

On one Saturday, neighbours held a huge work bee. People came with their shovels and tractors. One man came with a backhoe to dig the burial site for the cattle. They worked systematically from morning to evening. Their wives provided lunch for the crew. It was quite a sight to see this farming community – the kinship, the relationships that had been built with one another over the years – in action.

The farm sale closed regardless of the fire because the buyers were investors wanting the land, not the farming enterprise. Gary was able to locate another farm where he could carry on the family business. The entire family was going through great change.

Some of those changes were very happy ones. About two months after the fire, our third adorable daughter, Carole, arrived. Even though I was pastoring the church and working on my dissertation, I still was able to find time to enjoy our growing girls.

It is hard to say what their favourite playtime event was. Perhaps it was when they turned me into "Cherry" the horse and rode me around the living room. They would ride until "Cherry" was worn out, and often rewarded me with a carrot. Perhaps it was when they would climb on my knee and I would tell them the wonderful stories that I grew up with. Perhaps it was when we played "jungle." I would sit on the floor with my knees up, and they would crawl underneath. I don't know what their favourite was, but those playtimes certainly provided their dad with wonderful memories.

The dissertation was coming along better than I had imagined. I was surprised when my advisor told me it was going so well that we should call for the defense. That gave me three months in which to complete the work. Of course, my Indian friend had lots of suggestions – each suggestion creating a lot more work. I gave it my best shot and with Brenda helping me on the computer, we made the deadline with one day to spare.

The date was set for the defense. I happened to be in the university office one day and heard that the Indian professor had gone to western Canada and would remain there for several months. I was so obviously overjoyed that a secretary asked me why I was so happy. I explained my pleasure that this particular professor would not be around for my defense. The secretary cleared her throat and told me that the gentleman would be there. He had specifically requested an airline ticket to make sure that he was on hand for the big event. At this point, I was convinced that this professor was out to get me. When I left the university that day I was concerned – to say the least. I kept wondering what was in the man's mind and what he might do that could sabotage years of hard work. Knowing he would be present, made me prepare all the harder.

The day finally came for the defense, I was given fifteen minutes to present my thesis, and each professor was then given fifteen minutes to question me for the first round. The Indian professor was first and took about forty-five minutes, which slightly annoyed the other professors. They tried to give him a hint by the occasional cough and even squeaking their chairs a bit. It didn't work. Once the other professors got their chance, their questions were well thought out and a delight to answer. When the second round of questioning came, the Indian professor commenced again. I firmly advised him that I knew the parameters of the paper and that I would appreciate his questioning to be on the work that I had done, to which he responded, "If you are prepared to write a PhD thesis you should know everything, you should know what is in the daily papers today."

After the questioning was complete, I was asked to leave the room while the panel deliberated over the work and defense. When the door was opened, my chairman shook my hand and called me Dr. Mensah. In my joy I squeezed his hand so hard that it's a wonder I didn't damage it. The Indian professor came to me and said, "You shouldn't take my questions personally. You proved to everyone here and the committee that you knew your work." I found out later that he had voted in my favour, which gave me a unanimous vote. At the moment I thought, *I wish you hadn't made me prove it to that extent!* Later I learned that I had disagreed with the theology of the man that he had done his dissertation on.

Within a few weeks, I was standing in an auditorium to receive my degree. My wife, daughters, mother-in-law and father-in-law were there to share my joy. As I looked around, I saw only one of my fellow classmates graduating with me. While moving forward with the other graduates, I couldn't help but think of Yaara and Teselima and this boy who had been a candidate to become a trained village assassin, who should have been dead long ago. Here I was in one of the best universities, actually standing in line to receive my degree. It was a moving time for me. It was a light of encouragement, as I thought about people all over the world who were in circumstances similar to those I had endured. If I could do this, others could too; but, like me, they could never do it alone. They had to know God and trust him to direct the course of their lives.

About this time the church increased my salary, and we were not struggling as hard to make ends meet. I received another cheque for about $1,200 from the Christian foundation. With my studies now complete and with my increased salary, I wondered about the ethics of still receiving funds from this foundation. I wrote the Christian Foundation a letter, thanking them for their years of kindness to me and my wife. I informed them that I had completed my education and that the church had increased my salary. I enclosed their cheque and recommended that the funds be given to a needy student. In reply, the spokesperson for the foundation, informed me that I was the first person to have ever returned funds to them, and they appreciated my ethical decision. The committee had met and, because of my action, they wanted me to keep the money and use it toward purchasing something we could use when we returned to Africa.

When my schoolwork was finished, my days of pastoring a church in North America were also coming to a close. I could look back on the experience with a good feeling. Before I arrived, the church had gone through many difficulties. There were often serious disputes. They had not known a smooth transition from one pastor to another. I was determined that with God's help my time with them would be a time of joy, a time of training, a time when we learned together how to turn our problems over to God and to genuinely trust Him. Nothing less could break the chain of quarreling that had troubled that church for decades.

My journey with that church had some bumps. One elder was very antagonistic. He was a very quiet, giving man, but he had an almost obsessive need to control the church. As long as the pastor paid total allegiance to him, everything was fine, but I didn't want to pay allegiance to anyone except God. Of course, I couldn't overlook the legitimate concerns of people in the church – in many cases I made compromises between my wishes and those of others in the congregation. But biblical principles could not be compromised. I prayed a lot over my ministry in that small church. I asked God to help me to show His love to others, but at the same time to provide the congregation with firm leadership in the direction He would want us to go.

As it became obvious that I would not do his bidding, this difficult elder became openly hostile. One day he bluntly told me that he hired and fired the church's pastors whenever he wished. The church always did what he said. Period.

I disagreed and told him, "Not this time. This time you are looking down the barrel of a gun and my hand is on the trigger because I am working for the Lord Jesus Christ, and you are working to serve yourself." He laughed at me. We were obviously heading for a major crisis.

I didn't want the situation to get any uglier. That night I discussed the matter with another elder in the church. This man genuinely loved the Lord and wanted to serve Him. We set up a meeting with the difficult elder. At the meeting, I told this hostile man that he should resign from the office of elder. I suggested that we could then have Bible studies together in which we would focus on the qualities that are required of an elder. He refused to take the suggestion seriously. I informed him that if he didn't resign, I would announce the next Sunday that he had been removed from the elders board. He became incensed. "You do that and the church will collapse overnight. Almost everyone will leave and the few that stay will not be following Christ but following you!"

At that point, I'm sure this elder believed he had once again triumphed by bullying his way through a problem. Surely no one would support the pastor if it came down to a matter of the church losing him. He was stunned when the other elder agreed with me, saying that he felt that the Lord had brought me to that church for a purpose and that the congregation should follow my leadership. The meeting ended with the troublesome elder resigning. His words proved not to be prophetic. Not one person left over the matter. In fact, our numbers grew. The spirit of antagonism vanished and the church moved ahead.

While working on my dissertation, I also searched for ways of getting funding to help our team in Ghana launch the program we had planned so many years before. I heard of a group in Ottawa known as Partnership Africa Canada (PAC), a branch of CIDA that makes monies available to indigenous initiatives in the Third World. This group allowed flexibility to the indigenous groups to make decisions, plan, implement and evaluate their projects. They were not a group imposing programs on Third World countries, but facilitators to programs designed in the Third World. We met all the criteria to be able to apply for funding through The Mensah Food and

Orphanage Fund in Nova Scotia. We sent a proposal and it was approved. The funds were given on a 4-1 matching basis; that is, for every dollar the Canadian group raised, PAC gave three dollars. PAC agreed to give us $166,000 over a two-year period. How joyful we were at this new door that God had opened – and right at the time we were ready to implement the program.

Brenda and I decided it was time for us and our children to visit Ghana. Brenda had not yet met my family or the team we would be working with. We also wanted to look for a house and get a better idea of what we needed to take with us when we made the permanent move. I felt it would be good for Brenda to see the country before we actually went to work there. We set off for six weeks. It was eye-opener for both of us.

For me, I was at long last returning with my Canadian wife and children. I was excited to see how my mother would react to her new daughter-in-law and grandchildren. It was as I had expected; she opened her arms wide to welcome. I spoke to her in our language. "These are your granddaughters." Her eyes filled with tears of joy as she responded, "They are all mine?" She wanted to hug them all, but they were a little reserved at meeting their African grandmother. Within a short time they had relaxed enough to sit on my mother's knee – to her utter delight.

Meanwhile, it seemed as though the whole village of Jugboi rallied together and followed us everywhere we went. My mother dispatched us to greet everyone in the town, which is our custom when you have been away for some time. Someone led us through the village, as I introduced Brenda and the children.

That day brought back many memories and also brought deep gratitude to God for all that He had done for me. It was to this little village I came when I first escaped from Yaara; it was in this land that my grandmother did everything she could to make it possible for me to go to school. Despite her poverty, she sold what few animals she had to pay for books, school fees and my school uniform. It was from here I walked six miles each day to school. Here at Jugboi, most of the people had seen how poor I was.

If someone had told me in those difficult days that someday I would return to Jugboi and my presence would create excitement and draw crowds, I would have said that person was mad. I could bet that a lot of people who watched me through my struggling years were as amazed as I was at how my life had changed.

Even the village chief, who was almost blind, asked some of the children what was going on in town. In response to their answers, he sent people to greet me while we were yet making our way to his house. I remembered a day when the "sanitary inspector" was in town. Grandmother and I had worked hard to make sure our house was in order. When this man arrived, he checked the bowl my grandmother had used to whitewash our little room. He fined her because she had not washed out the bowl. When my grandmother went to the chief to plead her case, telling him that she had just finished whitewashing our house to make it look nice, he did not accept her plea and she was forced to sell a sheep in order to pay the fine. I had often thought about the unfairness of that situation, but that day, when greeting the chief, I could only feel sorry for him in his difficult situation, and glad that we were able to give him a small gift to help him with his needs.

After visiting around the village, we returned to my mother to ask permission to leave to go on to Teselima and greet my uncle. The Jugboi people were not prepared to let us leave town without demonstrating to us that I was their son, even though I had been neglected by them in my youth. After receiving permission, the elders of the village called us to meet under a kapok tree. Two sheep were tied to a tree. My cousins in the village presented a sheep to my wife and the children as a sign that they had accepted them wholeheartedly.

Then, surprisingly, my mother pointed to the second sheep, saying that out of her joy and gratitude she was presenting a sheep to Brenda and the children on behalf of herself and the rest of my brothers and half-sisters (my father had had two daughters with his first wife, before my mother). By this, she too was saying that she accepted them into our family. The village could not have been more warm. Some of their kind gestures and gifts made us want to weep. Eggs, chickens, sheep and the fruit of the land came from poor hands and rich hearts.

To me, the implications of these gifts were far reaching. The people were not only recognizing me; they were recognizing what God had done. I hoped and prayed on that day, that the Jugboi people would look around at the children of the village and gain a new determination to help those children make better lives for themselves.

The next village on the road was Carpenter, my village of birth and the home of my sister. The reunion with my sister was very emotional. She broke down and wept. She spoke of our father and how she wished he was there. She called us into her little room so that together we could thank God for His goodness. Here too, we took the necessary time to greet the entire village, with a crowd of at least fifty children escorting us.

We then moved on to Teselima, where we would be based for the next two weeks. They had been informed of our coming and had made preparations, fixing up rooms in one of the nicest houses in the village. A special pit latrine had been dug for our use. When I saw it, I could tell how much work had gone into digging it with their only tools being hoes and machetes. I was very thankful for these brothers and sisters that were showing great care for us, and I could tell that they were more joyful even than I was. I realized that in every village we went to the people had a sense of pride that it was me, their son David Mensah, who had brought them wealth, for they considered my wife and children as wealth to their tribe. By this, I mean that the villagers believed that my family linked them to another tribe. They hoped that, by my guidance, they would be able to stay in partnership and cooperation with this new tribe. I was amazed that my marriage to Brenda was bringing such delight and joy to the entire Deg tribe.

It was getting late when we arrived at Teselima but there was still time to greet the family and those who came by the house to say hello. As the sun vanished, we prepared our room, bathed and fed the children, and went to bed very tired after a day of travelling and visiting. We slept in a bit the next morning, so we hadn't been up long when we were summoned to a meeting. As we left the house, we saw that the village and family elders had gathered in the courtyard. Two special chairs had been strategically placed for Brenda and I to sit on. One by one the elders gave welcoming speeches. Again, we were the recipients of many wonderful gifts. It was difficult to find the words to adequately convey our appreciation for all they were doing. After this meeting we were led through the streets of Teselima to greet everyone. A large gathering of children followed us every step of the way.

After a delightful week of visiting with family and friends, and receiving many kind gifts, something very special happened. The uncle who had taken me in after my escape from Yaara held a brief ceremony for us. He walked with us until we came to a young bull tied to a tree. He said t was a delight for him to have Brenda and the girls in his house, and to show his joy he was offering the bull. There was pride and joy in his face; he spoke with authority and dignity. His gestures expressed the seriousness of the occasion and the depth of his feelings. We were told we could do whatever we wanted with the bull. Brenda and I decided it would be best to have the bull killed at the village, knowing that rarely do the people of Teselima get to eat good meat. We should make the occasion a genuine celebration. That's what we did. That day the entire village feasted on delicious beef.

While staying in Teselima we took a day trip to Yaara to see my two brothers and my father's brothers. Yaara is about thirty miles away, but it took most of the morning to get there. Though I was driving a sturdy truck, the terrain was difficult. We came to a bridge that had broken. Planks were laid on the broken part so that vehicles could cross. I had my doubts as to the safety of this arrangement but a little woman shouted out from her farm nearby, "It's alright, other trucks have passed on it!" I told Brenda and the girls to walk across, then I drove the truck over those rickety boards. It was a short but nervous drive. Once I was safely across, the family jumped back into the truck and we proceeded on a very narrow path. Then, we turned left at a landmark tree and there was no path at all. You have to say this about Yaara – the place has not allowed itself to be overwhelmed by technological advancement.

Eventually we arrived in Yaara, where even the sight of a vehicle is a big event. My two brothers and I had a joyous reunion. One brother insisted that we stay at a house he had just completed for his own family, and the other provided a sheep for a wonderful dinner.

We greeted the elders and visited with everyone in the village. My father's brothers, who had once been so cruel, seemed like different people. They too were warm and welcoming.

When it was time for us to ask permission to leave, they were not happy. They wanted us to stay in the village, at least overnight, and questioned me as to whether I was not staying because of the things they had done in the past. They wondered whether I had truly forgiven them. After convincing them that I had forgiven them, but that all our things were in Teselima, they gave us permission to go. Convincing them took so long that by the time we were finally on our way, the sun was beginning to set. It was very late by the time we finally made it back across that treacherous bridge and returned to Teselima.

Back at Teselima, we enjoyed a Mensah family reunion. My mother and all my brothers joined with my "Canadian family" for some wonderful days together. But those days passed quickly, and soon Brenda, the children, and I had to leave for Tamale. There were important plans to make.

At Tamale, Brenda and I met with the team and discussed the proposal for which Partnership Africa Canada had approved funding. At our final meeting, we agreed on the need for a base in Tamale. I was going to try and buy a large house in Tamale that could serve as a headquarters for our mission as well as providing a place for my family to live. I remember someone laughing, and questioning my sanity.

"Where do think you are going to buy a house in Tamale, Tamale is not like Canada you know. You don't just buy a house. Besides, there are no decent houses around. You need a good house that will last through any weather."

Discouraging words, to say the least. But we decided to look over some homes with the hope of finding a good house plan. Perhaps we could have someone build a place for us. We visited a subdivision where Ghanaians and Canadians who were involved in development work were living. We walked through an empty house that workmen were repairing and, as we left it, we noticed a similar building across the road. It looked perfect for our needs.

I mentioned to Brenda that I knew a contractor in town who had been a "fan" of mine back in my days as a runner. I thought we could discuss with him the possibility of building a house similar to the one that we had just admired. When we located the contractor at his office, he was more helpful than we ever could have imagined.

"Before we think about building any house," he said, "just this afternoon information came to my office that there is a house for sale in Tamale. You know that you rarely hear of this in Tamale. This is a very good house. You may have even seen it. It is the white house just across the road from the place that the Ghanaian and Canadian development workers live."

The very house we had just been looking at! Brenda and I exchanged glances. How could it be possible that it came up for sale that very day? We made arrangements to see the house. It could not have been better. It had everything that was needed for a great family home and mission headquarters.

We felt sure it was for us, until we heard the price; then we felt very disappointed. We couldn't pay what they were asking, but we put in an offer for what we felt we could afford (by putting a mortgage on our house in Canada). It was less than half the asking price was. The people in charge of the matter were not encouraging. On that rather sour note, the time had come for us to leave Ghana.

A month after our return to Canada, we received a phone call from Ghana. Our offer had been accepted! We were overjoyed. We quickly made arrangements for the loan and sent the funds to Ghana. My colleagues were as surprised as we were. It was also reassuring to Brenda's family to know that we had a house to go to. We were thrilled at how God had orchestrated the whole episode. We sensed, yet again, His guiding hand in our lives.

We hoped that when we went to Ghana, rent from our Canadian house would cover the loan payments on the Ghana house. A little risky to be sure. However, we were convinced that if God had so moved to find us this house in Ghana, He would help us to find a way to pay for it. Indeed, He did.

The Paisley farm was resold to a company that planned to develop the property into an industrial park. We wondered how we would fare being the only residence right in the middle of the development. I contacted the mayor of Uxbridge to express my concern. The mayor was opposed to our staying there. She could not be sure what types of industry would eventually move into the park, and advised us to make a deal with the developers. We felt sure that we would end up with the short end of the stick as we thought of dealing with professionals in this area. We kept committing the situation to prayer, bringing our difficulties to God, in whom we had trusted. Some friends gave us good counsel and a Christian real estate officer valued our property.

For a long time nothing seemed to be happening. Then one day the developers arrived at our door. The mayor had informed them that she did not want us to be stuck in the middle of the development, so in order for them to proceed with their plans they would have to buy us out. They gave us different options: they would move our house to the back corner of the farm, or they would buy another house for us. It was an exploratory meeting. I called the mayor to discuss the options with her. She was not happy with the idea of moving the house because, eventually, the whole property was to be developed and we could face the same problem again.

Then the situation changed quickly. We were informed that a hearing had been scheduled to deal with the proposed industrial park. If the proposal passed at that hearing, the developers would be under no obligation to do anything for us. If we wished to lodge a formal complaint, we would have to do so before the hearing.

I made a quick call to the developers and said I didn't know if we could settle the matter before the hearing or whether I needed to lodge a complaint. Another meeting was arranged and they arrived at our home early one Saturday morning. One of the partners had been working all night and was very tired. I told them we were not interested in having the house moved. One partner told us to look around for a place, and they would buy it for us. I objected and said it was not just a matter of buying a house. A new house would require funds to set it up and its running costs might be different. Then the partner who had not slept decided to cut to the quick. He said it was obvious I had given the matter a great deal of thought. How much money would it take to close the deal? I quoted an amount the Christian real estate agent had told us would be needed to buy a similar home in the area. They agreed with no argument.

At that point Brenda and I understood why God had directed Gene Paisley to put that house in the middle of the field. Had the house been placed in a corner of the field, the developers would not have needed it for some time and would have been under no pressure to reach a settlement with us. Once again we thanked God for what He had done. The funds we received from the sale of the house allowed us to buy a house in a small town nearby, pay for our home in Ghana and buy a vehicle and supplies for our ministry.

That night Brenda and I were still in awe as we reflected on how God had been working in our lives. Brenda quoted the words of David just before he fought Goliath: "The Lord does not deliver by sword or by spear." I reflected on the words from Zechariah: " Not by might nor by power, but by My Spirit, says the Lord of hosts." God's ways are not man's ways. For that reason, we do not always understand or appreciate the fact that God cares for us and is always there. When events bring us into an overwhelming sense of God's presence, it is important that we pause, give thanks and experience our closeness with the Lord. Brenda and I did not speak too much that evening. We didn't have to. It was a time of quiet before the Lord.

27

Hope in a Hopeless World

I BRING THIS BOOK TO A CLOSE WITH a prayer that readers will not misinterpret much of what I have written. I have tried to express my gratitude to God and my sense of amazement at all that God has done in my life. But I am afraid that readers will find my story to be so unusual as to have no application to their own lives. Do the experiences of David Mensah have any relevance to a business person in North America who, on the surface, is leading a comfortable life but is plagued by horrible depression? What about the young person who has joined an inner-city gang that makes the Landary Boys look tame in comparison? For that matter, what does my life have to say to others living in the Third World who are overwhelmed by seemingly impossible circumstances?

Frequently when I talk to non-believers about God, I can see by the expression in their eyes that they are thinking that Christians believe only because they want insurance of heaven when they die. Well, Yesu does offer the gift of eternal life, and certainly that is very important. But there is so much more to the Christian life. It is a life of hope. Not only can you rid your own life of hopelessness, you can help others to do the same. With God's help, you can break the chain of despair that now runs throughout the world. I suffered child abuse, hunger, poverty, and demeaning treatment from my own relatives. My heart responded with a ferocious anger and resentment. Yesu wiped that hatred away and replaced it with love and hope. Hope not only for myself but for the world.

Every day I see hard evidence of God's loving hand in action. The project that my colleagues and I established in Africa has grown in such proportions that not only are Ghanaians benefitting from it but western development workers come to gain insight from our developmental approach. Youth from Canada, the Netherlands and the United Kingdom have visited our project and the impact on their lives has been overwhelmingly meaningful.

Even as I write this, I have on my desk an agreement that we are signing with Augustana University College in Camrose, Alberta. The university has seen the calibre of our development work and has set up a development studies program in the university whereby students will work and learn for one semester at our project site in Ghana. They will witness genuine development work. They will live in the midst of people who have no electricity, running water or any of the amenities that people in the west take for granted. They will discover what happens when a community of 70,000 people has no medical doctor. But they will also find a community of people who refuse to allow their poverty to dictate their state of mind. People who have not surrendered to despair.

The goal of our ministry is to serve people in a holistic manner. We help people spiritually by leading them to their Saviour. We are upgrading medical services to meet the health needs of the population. Our team works alongside communities to dig wells and provide fresh water for the poor to drink. We are helping people to develop new farming techniques that will help them to survive and even prosper. This I call hope. It is this kind of hope that is needed today.

And it is needed everywhere. I remember a meeting I had several years ago with a group of young Canadian Natives at Slave Lake, Alberta. Many of these young people had hearts that were filled with anger. They felt trapped in poverty. I praise God that He used me that night to bring hope into that situation of despair. Those Indians realized that God could do for them what He had done for David Mensah. For some who had given up, it was like a new flower budding. They were prepared to face difficult life situations and look for new ways of counteracting poverty and neglect.

Not only the poor need God's love. How sad it is to see people who have succeeded in the world of business, science and academics, who cannot understand why their lives seem so empty. They have an abundance of material goods and yet their personal lives are rubble. Many of these people have good intentions and try to placate their own misery by performing good deeds or getting involved in worthy causes. But nothing really seems to work for them. It never will as long as God is kept out of the picture.

I am constantly amazed by what God can do. My uncle, the one who abused and hated me when I was a small boy in Yaara, has now become one of my closest friends. He came to me one day and asked "Will you forgive me?" I was startled by the directness and simplicity of the question. Before I could reply, he went through a long list of the injustices and cruel acts he had inflicted on me after my father's death. When he had finished, he looked at me with a sober face, asking again, "Will you forgive me?" I looked at him and replied, "Why not? God has forgiven me for the horrible things that I have done. Why not? Of course I forgive you."

But my uncle was saving his most remarkable statements for last. "I want to tell you something else. The God that you have been serving, that Jesus Christ, I have found Him to be the only way to life. The changes that have taken place in you have shown me that there is no other path to follow. I have gone through witchcraft, and other ways, but after studying you, one day I prayed to that Yesu that you so cherish and I have given my life to Him." I could not believe what I was hearing.He then asked, "If you have forgiven me, do you think you can baptize me as a Christian?"

It was three days before Christmas. My wife and a few believers went to a stream where I baptized my uncle and five members of his household who had also decided to follow Christ. What a privilege. He has now taken the name "Abraham." Now when I am at Yaara, the place where I always felt the demons lived, light is beginning to shine. This uncle who was full of treachery is now becoming a source of light to the people in that village. He is beginning to show love to the children. Many are beginning to see him as the father Abraham of the Scriptures. His genuine compassion can be seen in his eyes and his actions. He is determined, even in his old age, to correct the wrongs he has done in the past. The same Jesus who touched my life and transformed me has touched him. God is able to do more than we can ever fathom.

God also worked in the heart of Sarakpo, my mother's brother who took me in after my escape from Yaara. This uncle turned to God and away from the powers of Satan.

I will never forget being in his house at Christmas time when he brought out a chicken and made his final break with Satan and his ways. He took the chicken, and spoke to the ancestors and the demonic world, telling them how sorry he was for serving them so long, how much havoc he had caused in the tribe through spiritual means. He held the chicken up and told the ancestors that from that day he was breaking all the ties with them. He told them that the God of his nephew, Kwabena David Mensah, was the God he wanted to serve – a God who had compassion and forgiveness. He was giving them this last chicken in front of everyone who was gathered. He now had a new master. He had commissioned himself to following Yesu and had recanted and asked for forgiveness for all the demonic things he had carried out in his lifetime in the Deg tribe.

What a sobering sight that was. It was unthinkable, not only in our house but in the entire Deg tribe. No one could believe it was happening. That man had been known as a powerful fetish priest and spiritual leader. People came to him for medicine. People came to him to throw curses. He was known to possess powers that normal human beings did not have. And now, here he was, saying that he would do these things no more.

That evening after supper, more than forty members of the Deg tribe gathered with my uncle. Every person in the room was now a disciple of Yesu. My uncle, the former fetish priest, asked us to thank God for the transformation that had occurred in that house. He asked if we could sing a song in Deg to thank God. We sang, "Thank you, thank you, Lord God our Rock of Ages, we thank you." Many eyes were filled with tears as we witnessed our uncle turning his back on the demonic spiritual powers that had caused him to do such terrible things in the society. He was starting a new life, not to kill but to love.

He had moved to the point of even discarding the use of the local herbs that could be used for healing. He didn't even want to touch them until I was able to convince him that the trees, plants, grass, animals and birds were all created by Yesu and that he needn't fear to use God's plants to heal in the name of Yesu, but not in the name of Satan. Yesu gives life, but Satan uses those things to camouflage and to kill, to cause barrenness in the wombs of women. I told my uncle that he was being called to use his knowledge to serve others.

As I sat in the darkness that night, gazing at the stars and thinking over all that was happening both in Yaara and Teselima, my heart was full of gratitude. The Lord always kept His hand on me, even when I didn't give Him a thought. God was with me during those days of starvation when I cursed the day that I was born. He knew what was inside my heart when I was acting like a vicious hoodlum, injuring innocent people. He wouldn't let me give up when I failed my exams and was refused a passport. The Lord provided caring people to help me in Canada.

And – most wonderful of all – the Lord has used me to bring others to Him. My uncles, my brothers and sisters and my mother have all become Christians because they have seen the light of Yesu flickering in me. That is why I love to share my story with others. When people find out what has happened to David Mensah, they know that there is no life that is insignificant in God's sight. Out of poverty, and through an outcast, He has made something beautiful. He has been able to raise a bud that has grown into a tree with leaves that birds can sit under for cover.

Becoming a Christian has not made my life comfortable. It has given my life purpose. Jesus Christ can do the same for you. As I accepted Yesu as my Saviour in the presence of that seventy-two-year-old man who spoke about Yesu and His compassionate love and transforming powers, you too may do the same. You too may lift up your head and ask Him to accept you. Perhaps you too are prepared and committed to look for Him, to walk with Him and let Him direct your life.

From my life experience I can tell you that you will never regret that step. My life now is full of joy. I have become so happy within. Many nights I wake up singing inside. The kind of joy God gives is not the kind of joy that money gives, or winning a scholarship gives. It is very deep inside the soul. My life now is also characterized by peace, the kind that the Scriptures call *shalom.* This type of peace does not come from buying new cars or a good job. It is the kind that gives meaning to life.

While in Teselima for a visit, my adopted father Sarakpo called me for a prayer. After a long prayer he concluded with these words, "Yesu, it is a misery to live not knowing you." I couldn't help but say Amen! He then put his hat on and leaned back on his chair. He lay there and I knew that his tears were about to flow but that he didn't want me to see. He had gone deep down in his soul's history to come up with those words about Yesu. Even though he had spoken to his own soul about Yesu, I felt that he had spoken to the rest of the world.

"Yesu, it is a misery to live not knowing you!"

David's brother Yaw Joseph (left) and David (right).

David's brother Peter.

David and his mother.

David and Brenda.

David and Brenda's three daughters (left to right):
Deborah Fulamuso, Carole Onunwii, Elizabeth Afua Laura.

Laura and Eugene Paisley, my wonderful in-laws, who continue to be a constant support to our family and our work in Ghana.

Map of Ghana

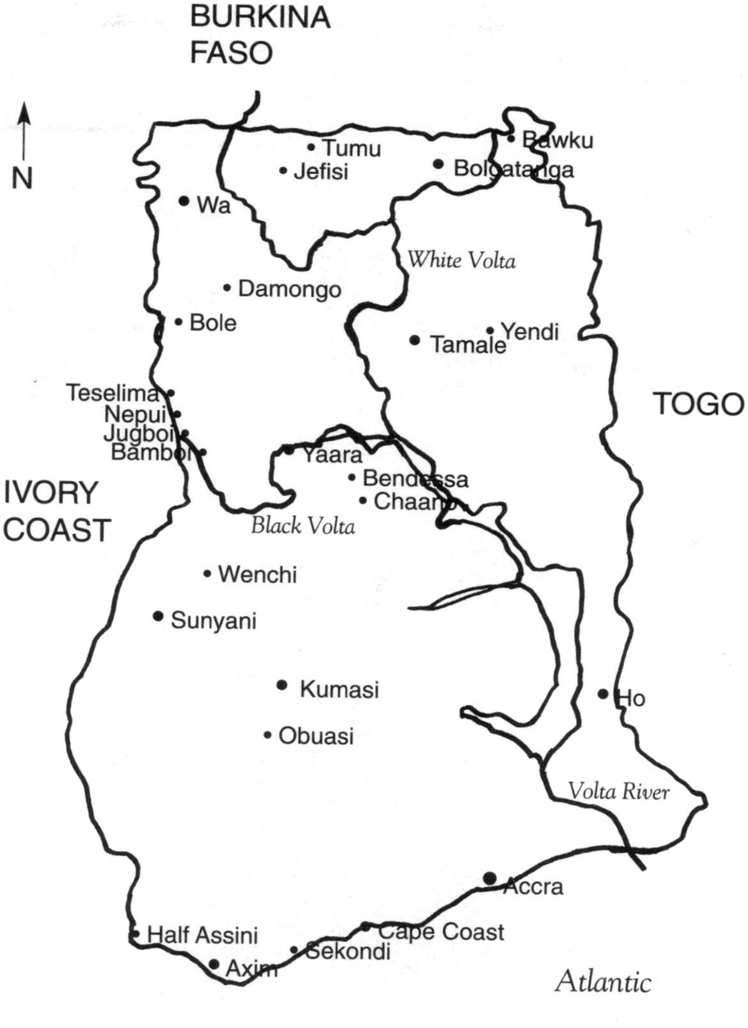

BURKINA
FASO
N
Tumu
Jefisi
Bawku
Bolgatanga
Wa
White Volta
Damongo
Bole
Yendi
Tamale
Teselima
Nepui
Jugboi
Bamboi
TOGO
Yaara
Bendessa
Chaano
IVORY
COAST
Black Volta
Wenchi
Sunyani
Kumasi
Obuasi
Ho
Volta River
Accra
Half Assini
Cape Coast
Sekondi
Axim
Atlantic

For more information about the author and/or his ministry in Africa, please contact:

Ghana Rural Integrated Development
Box 185
Bridgewater, NS
B4V 2W8